INTRODUCTION TO FAMILY THEORY AND THERAPY

Exploring an Evolving Field

These symbols refer to Figure 5.3 / Sample Genogram on pages 82 and 83.

Symbols used in a Genogram (From Kerr & Bowen, 1988)

◯ = female   ▢ = male   ✕ = deceased

△ = abortion, spontaneous or induced   ═══ = appropriate affiliation

〰〰〰 or ⇉ = conflict   ≡ = enmeshed, over involved

↑ = over functioning   ↓ = under functioning

= divorce

= family projection process

From *Family Evaluation: An Approach Based on Bowen Theory,* by Michael E. Kerr & Murray Bowen, Copyright ©1988 by Michael E. Kerr and Murray Bowen. Used by permission of W.W. Norton & Company, Inc.

INTRODUCTION TO FAMILY THEORY AND THERAPY

Exploring an Evolving Field

JUNE BLUMENTHAL GREEN, Ph.D.

THOMSON
™
BROOKS/COLE

Australia • Canada • Mexico • Singapore • Spain
United Kingdom • United States

THOMSON

™

BROOKS/COLE

Sponsoring Editor: *Julie Martinez*
Marketing Manager: *Caroline Concilla*
Marketing Assistant: *Mary Ho*
Assistant Editor: *Shelley Gesicki*
Editorial Assistants: *Amy Lam, Mike Taylor*
Project Editor: *Kim Svetich-Will*
Production: *Buuji, Inc.*

Manuscript Editor: *Cheryl Hauser*
Permissions Editor: *Mary Kay Polsemen*
Cover Design: *Laurie Albrecht*
Cover Photo: *Ian Cartwright/Getty Images*
Print Buyer: *Vena Dyer*
Compositor: *Buuji, Inc.*
Printing and Binding: *Transcontinental Printing, Inc.*

For more information about our products,
contact us at:
Thomson Learning Academic Resource Center
1-800-423-0563
For permission to use material from this text,
contact us by:
Phone: 1-800-730-2214   Fax: 1-800-730-2215
Web: http://www.thomsonrights.com

Library of Congress Cataloging-in-Publication Data
Green, June Blumenthal.
Introduction to family theory and therapy: exploring
an evolving field / June Blumenthal Green
p. cm.
Includes bibliographical references and index.
ISBN 0-534-59328-3
1. Family.   2. Family psychotherapy.   I. Title.

HQ503 .G77 2003
306.85—dc21   2002021527

Brooks/Cole–Thomson Learning
511 Forest Lodge Road
Pacific Grove, CA 93950
USA

Asia
Thomson Learning
5 Shenton Way #01-01
UIC Building
Singapore 068808

Australia
Nelson Thomson Learning
102 Dodds Street
South Melbourne, Victoria 3205
Australia

Canada
Nelson Thomson Learning
1120 Birchmount Road
Toronto, Ontario M1K 5G4
Canada

Europe/Middle East/Africa
Thomson Learning
High Holborn House
50/51 Bedford Row
London WC1R 4LR
United Kingdom

Latin America
Thomson Learning
Seneca, 53
Colonia Polanco
11560 Mexico D.F.
Mexico

Spain
Paraninfo Thomson Learning
Calle/Magallanes, 25
28015 Madrid, Spain

With appreciation
to my family

BRIEF CONTENTS

CONTENTS

PART III | SYSTEMIC BRANCHES   6 5

PREFACE

Marriage and family theorists offer a different way to understand mental health and mental illness. In general, the philosophy supporting family therapy demotes the emphases on individual pathology and the labeling of people as diseased. It utilizes family and societal contexts to help individuals and families seeking relief from symptoms of emotional distress.

Family theorists often create new terminology to describe their ideas. They think of people in relationships as mutually influential parts of an interactive system. In this book we will discuss how all systems are continuously challenged to maintain the status quo or to adapt to changing circumstances. Family theories seek to explain how interactive systems are subject to changing environments. They continue to develop new branches, even as they remain rooted in the understanding that relationships influence mental health. Although family theorists see family relationships as primary to a person's development, societal influences are included as part of the larger system of influence in everyday life.

This book covers the birth of and development in the field, and discusses theorists and their theories in a practical, demystifying way.

There is no single answer to what constitutes a family, healthy or disturbed, or what helps them reorganize into a more satisfying life-enhancing environment for each family member. That theories differ, and often seem to conflict with one another, does not suggest any are misguided or any are the best. Any one theory may be partly correct or all of them may be partly correct, and the final answer may involve the combination of part-truths into yet another theory.* Family theory is continually evolving.

This book is organized into five sections. Section 1, "Sowing the Seeds," includes Chapter 1, which covers issues of cultural, religious, ethnic, racial, gender, age, disabilities, and other societal differences that challenge the therapist's biases. Chapter 2 explores professional and ethical issues a therapist needs to consider and looks at how a therapist's preference towards different theories and his or her personal history may bring up some ethical concerns.

Section 2, "Founding Roots," begins with Chapter 3, which offers a history of major systemic family therapy concepts from the inception of the ideas that gave birth to systemic family theory to current theories. It includes a review of multidisciplinary studies of systems, cybernetics, and group theory. Chapter 4 offers an overview of the process of change that is particularly relevant for the theories discussed in Section 3.

In Section 3, "Systemic Branches," Chapters 5 through 9 describe five systemic theories in which the therapists are seen as experts whose roles are to redirect family transactions to more functional interactions.

Section 4, "Language as Reality," follows the adaptation of postmodern thinking and social constructionism by family theorists and therapists. Chapter 10 introduces the reader to the more recent postmodern ideas that use mutual conversations to re-story individual and family misconceptions. The therapist is no longer seen as an expert on the family, but only as an expert on what questions to ask and stories to tell. They collaborate with families in a way that awakens participants to the possibility of more successful stories and actions. Chapter 11 discusses solution focused therapy, which is seen as evolving from the strategic therapies and moving into the language-ordered collaborative therapies. Chapter 12 describes collaborative and narrative theory and therapies.

Section 5, "Research Perspectives," contains Chapter 13, which takes a critical look at the effectiveness of family therapy and Chapter 14, an epilogue.

Each chapter is followed by a series of experiential activities. These activities are designed to assist the instructor in offering ways for students to practice some of the ideas described in the chapter and to facilitate discussions on theoretical concepts. An effort has been made to address issues raised by diverse social contexts.

Instructors can help expand students understanding of each theory and style of therapy by using videos in the classroom. Videos such as training tapes offering demonstrations by various theorists are available from the various professional associations such as the American Association for Marriage and Family Therapy and the National Association of Social Workers.

---

*From Schultz, D. (1986). Theories of personality (3rd ed.). Pacific Grove, CA: Brooks/Cole.

It may be useful for instructors to assign segments of contemporary movies depicting family dilemmas and have students design interventions using various theories to help those fictional families. In addition, instructors and students can find a vast amount of information on the Internet, referenced either by theorist's name, by theory, or from the Web pages of the various organizations linked to family systems concepts.

Students interested in marriage and family therapy as a profession are encouraged to pursue in greater depth, the ideas that best fit with their own personalities. The synergistic match of a therapist's personality with a theory and therapy style in which he or she feels at home conveys confidence to clients and offers the therapist a greater opportunity to successfully help troubled families find solutions for their difficulties.

Acknowledgments

This project may never have been started without the encouragement of my niece and mentor, Sydney Ellen Olman Schultz. Sydney listened to my ideas, guided me through the preparation of the book proposal, and offered information and editing assistance along the way. I am also indebted to her for presenting the proposal to Brooks/Cole–Thomson Learning.

I thank Julie Martinez, sponsoring editor at Brooks/Cole, who saw the merits of the proposal and encouraged me to continue working on it. Brooks/Cole provided a liason, Cat Broz, who kept our dialogue going until the assistant editor, Shelley Gesecki, came on board. Shelley offered support, information, and direction. I am grateful to Brooks/Cole for the personal interest and know-how they brought to the development of this project.

I am also grateful to Cheryl Hauser, the copy editor; Laurie Albrecht, the cover designer; Kim Svetich-Will, the project editor at Brooks/Cole, and the staff at Buuji, Inc., who worked to produce the final text. Special appreciation goes to the reviewers for their constructive criticism and feedback that improved the manuscript in process: Gary Bailey, Elon College; Alice Chornesky, New Mexico State University; Donald Daughtry, University of North Dakota; Diane R. Gehart, California State University, Fresno; Aaron P. Jackson, Brigham Young University; Jean-Louis Marchand, Chesapeake College, Wye Mills Campus; and David J. Westhuis, University of Southern Indiana.

As the writing progressed, my husband Al proofread every chapter, served as my sounding board, and helped me to achieve the clarity and understanding I wanted to bring to the text for the students and instructors who will be working with it.

Anne Rambo and Pat Cole gave freely of their time and offered ideas and resources to make this text more comprehensive, and through personal interviews I benefited from the work of Christopher Burnett and Barry Duncan. They are all connected with my alma mater, Nova Southeastern University. Barbara Buzzi, Ph.D., a former student and currently a professor in the graduate program at St. Thomas University, also shared her time and many good ideas with me.

These were the key players in this project, but there were many others who also played a role in it. Although they go unnamed, I hope they know who they are and that their help has been warmly appreciated.

Of course, this project would not have been possible without the inspirational and innovative thinking and writing of many theorists, clinicians, and researchers. These are the people who continue to challenge us as they struggle to describe the intricacies of human systems and search for better ways to resolve human dilemmas.

June Blumenthal Green

SOWING THE SEEDS

PROFESSIONAL ISSUES AND ETHICS

INTRODUCTION

Ethical behavior is acting in accordance with the rules and standards of right and wrong. Professional groups promote a set of ethical standards of behavior for their members. They also provide procedures for disciplining members who are found to be engaging in unethical behaviors. Professional codes of ethics for therapists are prescribed and monitored by most professional associations including, but not exclusively, the American Association for Marriage and Family Therapy (AAMFT), the Association for Marriage and Family Counseling (AMFC), American Association for Sex Education, Counseling, and Therapy (AASECT), American Family Therapy Association (AFTA), and the National Association of Social Workers (NASW). The codes of these associations are designed to protect the public by establishing standards and regulating the behaviors of the association members, teachers in the field, students, and interns.

Ethical behavior begins with the individual therapist. Throughout this textbook we advocate respect and empathy for the client. We stress the importance of the therapist "knowing" the ways certain client populations resonate with his or her biases and of taking personal responsibility to work through biases or prejudices with colleagues and in supervision. We suggest the therapist model, within the therapy session, many of the behaviors he or she hopes to engender within clients and their families—behaviors such as open communication and clear and specific expressions of wants, feelings, and needs and respectful listening. The ethical and trustworthy interaction between the therapist and the client creates a context for the understanding and trust that moves the client toward discovering and implementing solutions. Meanings are cocreated through dynamic communication exchanges called psychotherapy (Duncan, Soloney, & Rusk, 1992, p. 23). It is a new experience, for most clients, to be heard without judgment, and to be helped to listen to other family members and the therapist.

For family therapists, the responsibility is profound. An ethical and honorable intent is essential and has the potential to help clients break out of the attitudes of despair or discouragement that brought them to therapy. "Conscious deceit, therefore, is not only objectionable on a basic, moral level, but it also may undermine the core of the therapeutic relationship and interfere with, if not preclude, success outcome" (Duncan et al., 1992, p. 215).

Some forms of therapy, such as strategic therapy and its use of paradox as being unclear and deceptive, have raised concerns regarding its ethical use. Haley (1987) asserts it is not only naïve to believe that one can lie without being caught, but also that lying is patronizing and ultimately teaches the client that the therapist is untrustworthy. Strategically designed interventions fall in the realm of helping clients with respect to their presenting problem. When clients pick up on inconsistent messages, it not only undermines the effectiveness of the intervention, but also undermines their trust in the therapist.

Basic ethical behaviors include knowing the ethical standards of the profession and knowing when to ask for help and supervision with problems or conflicts that may impair the therapist's performance or judgment. It means staying up-to-date with new developments in the field. Basic to all helping professions is the prohibition of sexual or other potentially exploitative activities with clients or their families. Therapists must not act in any way that is demeaning to clients. Therapists must be aware of the client's perceptions of her or his influence, and use special care with professional recommendations and public remarks. And the therapist must respect the confidentiality entrusted to them by their clients.

MAINTAINING CONFIDENTIALITY

Confidentiality is explicit in all the helping professions. The therapist must not reveal details of the therapeutic relationship without the client's permission. For family therapists who are often seeing more than one person in a session, any release of information must be agreed to by all parties. The stated exception is when the therapist fears the client will do harm to him or herself, or to another person.

In the current arena of managed care, maintaining confidentiality may sometimes be problematic. The managed care companies often require specific information before they will approve further sessions. The therapist needs to discuss this issue with the clients and inform them of what they are required to share with third-party payers. It is good practice to discuss the diagnosis being given and the expected treatment, such as number of sessions and type of approach, with the client and to ask them to sign an understanding of that information. This process, of informed consent, allows the client to decide whether and how they are willing to proceed, and protects the therapist who may otherwise be questioned as to their protection of the client's confidentiality.

The AAMFT Code of Ethics, for example, addresses all of the above as well as financial, research, advertising, and other business and professional concerns that protect the legitimacy of the therapeutic profession and shows consideration for clients. It is the responsibility of therapists to know and to adhere to the code of ethics of the professional organization with which they affiliate. It is their responsibility to know about and utilize social services and other resources that could be helpful to client families. When therapists make referrals, they need to make sure clients understand and agree that referral will be helpful for them.

States that license family therapists also provide a code of ethics, as well as laws and procedures to monitor and discipline licensees. Although specific details may vary between states, the overall message remains the same: Therapists are to act responsibly, be nonexploitative, protect client confidentiality, and in general be respectful and do no harm.

RESPONDING TO LIFE-THREATENING BEHAVIORS

There are times, when the client is endangering him or herself or others, that a therapist must intervene to protect both the client and the potential victim. The decision to react to those situations is always difficult, usually as painful to the therapist as to the clients. A therapist should utilize his or her professional support system, supervisors, and colleagues to help implement these actions and for support after having taken the necessary action. In general, calling on supportive professionals helps to reduce stress and burnout.

CONSIDERING CLIENT EXPECTATIONS

In addition to consideration of culture, race, religious, gender, disabilities, social and economic class, educational level of clients, therapists need also be aware of the client's perceptions of the therapist. A therapist should consider the following questions: How does the client respond to a person of your age, your religion, of your gender, of your sexual orientation, whether you are married, or are a parent, and what they know of your background? Will the client have the courage to ask you about the things that concern them about you?

SUPERVISION AND CONTINUING EDUCATION

It is not ethical to allow biases to interfere with providing appropriate services to clients, but how open should one be? These issues should be addressed in supervision. When the therapist becomes aware of being uncomfortable with clients around bias issues or any others, he or she should process those concerns with a supervisor, or colleague. It is in the therapist's as well as the client's best interest for the therapist to participate in a supervision group, or at least have a colleague available for support and consultation. This is true as long as a therapist is in practice. If the therapist finds him or herself unable to overcome those feelings of discomfort regarding particular clients, he or she must find a positive way to refer them to someone who will be able to work more successfully with them. Each association, and most states, have specific requirements for supervision, as well as for continuing education. Continuing education includes attending conferences offered by professional associations, workshops, seminars; reading professional books and journals; and holding case conferences with colleagues.

A COMMON THREAD

Which theory and therapy is best? Is there one way that is best for all clients? Many therapists discover they need to reassess their assumptions about their chosen theoretical orientation after disappointing experiences shatter the illusion that "one size fits all." The therapist may have an attachment to a specific theory, perhaps developed during his or her training period or that is connected to a favorite instructor or supervisor. But therapists may be confronted with cases that do not fit their chosen model. Clients, who should get better according to the selected therapy model being used, do not.

If it becomes apparent that the selected model has limitations for the client's situation, clinging to one model of therapy fails to consider the inherent complexity of clinical practice and the uniqueness of clients and their situations. Therapists must learn to be open to the diversity of available theories and techniques. Clients provide therapists with opportunities to reassess their work and serve as powerful influences on them to search for more effective practices (Duncan et al., 1992, pp. viii–x). Listen to them, observe their nonverbal behaviors. They are the best teachers.

When reviewing the theorists discussed in this textbook, look for the common factors among their therapies. There are many. Outcome literature suggests that positive outcome is in large part, related to "common factors such as empathy, warmth, acceptance, encouragement, and trust in the relationship, rather than to specific techniques" (Lambert, 1986, & Patterson, 1984). Those factors are essential to all therapeutic relationships.

Although each theory provides a long list of "Terms to Know," there is a great deal of overlap in meaning. Those terms represent the theorist's attempts to describe the uniqueness of their thinking. The underlying rationale of each theory and therapy may approach the meaning and treatment of family dilemmas from various therapeutic points of view, but all have the goal of helping family members interact in ways that are empowering and more fulfilling for all family members. Although some purists may insist on a "one size fits all" therapy style, most systemic family therapists recognize the value of *client-focused* approaches that best meet their client's needs. Experienced family therapists recognize also, that when one approach is not working, they can add, integrate, introduce, and adjust what they are doing onto a more effective path. It is unethical to stay with one approach when it becomes obvious that the therapist is not connecting with or helping the client reach his or her goals.

LET THE CLIENTS BE THE GUIDE

Not all theorists describe "goals" in the same way. Neither do all clients. There must be agreement between all participants, therapists and clients alike, as to what can be expected from the therapeutic experience. A cross-pollination of ideas can evolve into flexible and effective client-centered approaches.

All interventions depend on the client's resources, strengths, and ability to grow. Through it all, the therapist–client relationship is the most important factor, regardless of the theoretical approach. The therapist's selection of content influences the direction of the dialogue. Interventions based on the client's meaning set an expectation for change. That expectancy is enhanced as the therapist's manner conveys hope that change can occur.

Accept the meaning clients give to their problems as the guiding theory from which to begin. Then draw from the multiple models to generate new meanings that permit the clients to make the desired choices (Duncan et al., 1992, p. 242).

SYSTEMIC FAMILY THERAPY: AN EVOLVING PROCESS

Running through this book is the concept that systemic family therapy is an evolving process. Utilize the flexibility that evolutionary process offers and become a part of that process. The activities of experienced family therapists are often very similar even though they may conceptualize their ideas through different theoretical lenses.

RESOURCES

Anyone entering the field of family therapy owes it to themselves and to their clients to seek resources from both academic and community sources. Workshops, seminars, and supervision meetings are ongoing and essential for therapists in taking care of their own needs, expanding their worldview, and enhancing their professional skills. Workshops and seminars help to confirm ideas and practices, as well as introduce new possibilities.

There are vast resources available, both on the Internet and through professional organizations and conferences, for video and audiotapes demonstrating specific therapeutic practices. Movies, theater performances, novels, and short stories can broaden the therapist's understanding of the context in which clients live. Instructors may have suggestions for resources, or students use the Internet and look up family therapy resources, and various association's Web pages. Affiliating with a professional organization keeps therapists and students up-to-date on the latest thinking in the field.

THE PROFESSION OF FAMILY THERAPY

Family therapy is an exciting, challenging, and rewarding profession. The many branches of family therapy continue to evolve. Mutations, as well as exciting new ideas, emerge. How the therapist thinks about what he or she is doing with clients and why, the therapist's ability to be flexible, and his or her ethical stance all interact with the meaning systems of clients. No one theory is exclusively useful for all people or situations. It is appropriate for the therapist to work from a framework most suitable for him or her, *and* remain open and responsive to the client's needs and behaviors, offering new perspectives that more effectively meet those needs.

All theories may be stories. They reflect the context of the theorist's worldview. These stories provide therapists with useful ways of thinking that, when integrated into the therapist's worldview, helps focus on the *process* going on between therapist and client, and between clients and their *context*. Family therapists need to be well-grounded in systemic thinking and have an understanding of the theories underlying the process of therapy. They need to have respect for the families they serve, and for their perceived place in society. They need to be flexible enough to adapt to the variety of people and situations placed in their care. And they need to care—for themselves, as well as for their clients. They need to be able to care about their clients—and then to let go. A professional family therapist has the opportunity to grow from every therapeutic encounter with a client.

EXPERIENTIAL ACTIVITIES

1. Research and discuss the code of ethics of a professional association.
2. In class, discuss how the concept of confidentiality affects clients.
3. Research and report on how local state laws on supervision and continuing education.

REFERENCES

AAMFT Code of Ethics (1991). Washington, DC: American Association for Marriage and Family Therapy.

Duncan, B. L., Solovey, A. D., & Rusk, G. S. (1992). *Changing the rules: A client-directed approach to therapy.* New York: Guilford.

Lambert, M. (1986). Implications of psychotherapy outcome research for eclectic psychotherapy. In *Handbook of Eclectic Psychotherapy* (pp. 436–462). New York: Brunner/Mazel.

Patterson, C. H. (1984). Empathy, warmth and genuineness in psychotherapy: A review of reviews. *Psychotherapy, 21,* 431–438.

2

DIVERSITY:
WHERE DO YOU STAND?

CULTURAL AND RACIAL DIVERSITY: A NATION OF IMMIGRANTS

Social, cultural, and familial environments are the experiences that influence the development of individual and family worldviews. People adapt their biases and beliefs about their own possibilities and their opinions and expectations of other people from the everyday repetitive messages of their surroundings. Those worldviews direct people's perceptions and the way they address difficulties in their lives and relationships.

It is therefore important that therapists are aware of the conditions that may be influencing their client's thinking. Therapists must also be alert to their own biases developed as a result of their own life experiences. It is in that framework that this chapter is presented before any of the theories. Therapists are urged to approach each client with appreciation of the differences and similarities fostered by diverse cultural, ethnic, religious, racial, age, and gender issues.

THE THERAPIST AND PERSONAL BIAS

Before therapists work with clients whose cultural or racial origins differ from theirs, they should examine their values and biases. The following questions are good ones to get the therapist thinking about personal bias:

What is my level of acceptance when clients from ethnic backgrounds with values that clash with mine, or racial backgrounds that evoke prejudice or fear in me?

Will I be comfortable enough working with people whose differences trigger emotions in me, to provide caring and professional help to them? (For example, a therapist of Jewish background who lost family members in the Holocaust may have great difficulty working with first generation German Americans whose family may have been perpetrators of Nazi horrors.)

Has my racial or ethnic group of origin had negative or traumatic experiences at the hands of the client's group? (For example, an Irish American facing an Anglo American of a different religion who has had relatives killed in the conflict in Northern Ireland may not be able to be unbiased.)

It may be an advantage or disadvantage to be of the same ethnic, racial, or religious group as the client. The therapist's own background may reflect back to him or her from the client family, intensifying personal value conflicts. Being openheartedly curious and having a willingness to learn mutually with the clients is a good approach. Therapists need to know their own limitations. And if they believe their issues may get in the way, refer the client to another therapist.

Have you ever thought about what it would be like to be a stranger in a new country? What would it be like if you had no choice about going there? What would it be like if you had to leave your family and friends back in the

"Old Country"? What would it be like if you had made a conscious choice to come to a new country to better yourself economically and then were confronted with ethnic or racial barriers that kept you from doing the kinds of things you had hoped to do? Could any of those situations happen to you and your family? Have you considered what all that might mean for someone coming in for help with individual or family problems? What would that mean for someone wanting to be a family therapist if he or she had an ethnic or racial family history different from most of the clients that came in for help?

In the United States, everyone was an immigrant at one time or another. All immigrants have a story. Native Americans, who were here centuries before the European explorers arrived, were driven from their lands by white explorers and settlers, and have suffered the trials of forced immigration and the loss of the lands of their ancestors.

Some groups were forced to immigrate, such as Africans who were brought here by force to be sold as slaves, enduring tremendous hardships and abuse, and separation from family members. Other immigrant groups left their homelands with hopes for a better life in America. Some were fleeing poverty; some were refugees escaping persecution; some sought religious and economic freedom.

Each era brings new immigrants from many countries and for myriad reasons. Within the different cultural, ethnic, and racial groups, the reasons for immigration change according to what is happening in the country of origin at the time they left, and what the immigration laws of the United States allows. Each group has its own way of interpreting the immigration experience relative to its traditions around family, religion, and community support. Each generation within immigrant families faces intergenerational conflicts over loyalty to their cultural past and a desire to fit into the mainstream of the dominant American culture.

THE 2000 CENSUS

The first official release of Census 2000 reported that hundreds of thousands of people took advantage of the opportunity to identify themselves as members of more than one race. Census 2000 was the first that allowed people to mark "one or more races." This increasing mix of races as well as ethnic groups within a family challenges its members to adapt to each other's traditions. The data also confirmed the explosive growth of Asian and Hispanic populations. "We're on our way to becoming a country literally made up of every other nation in the world," said social scientist Kenneth Prewitt, former head of the Census Bureau. The figures documented trends long predicted, depicting an increasingly diverse society as the new century dawned (Armas, 2001, p. 11A).

Population changes affect everyone. State legislators will use the long-awaited census data to reshape congressional, state, and local legislative district boundaries. The figures will also be used to redistribute more than $185 billion a year in federal money among states and communities (Armas, 2001). A debate has formed within the United States: Should government allocations use race as a basis for redistricting and for allocation of federal money? Should the allocations be based on economic need without knowledge of race? Is it appropriate today to even ask about race in census questionnaires? And, who defines race? Is race defined by the person who feels an identity as a member of a particular race, or as one who others identify as part of a particular race or ethnic group because of how others see him or her? And what of the increasing numbers of multiracial individuals and families? How will their needs be addressed?

A Reality Check About Diversity

As an example of the attention now being given to diversity in American communities, note a publication prepared by the *Sun-Sentinel*, a newspaper in Fort Lauderdale, Florida. The newspaper produced a multicultural directory. Using data from Broward, Palm Beach, and Miami-Dade counties in Florida, this 40-page directory listed organizations geared to a variety of national, religious, ethnic, gender, and racial entities. They included 63 business and professional groups, representing 52 different cultural identities; 16 political groups, representing 11 cultural identities; 93 cultural groups, representing 78 different cultural identities; 44 festivals, representing 35 different cultural identities; and so on. It includes 56 social/health services, 23 radio/TV shows, 49 newspapers, and 69 consulates (Gremillion & Hunt, 2001).

IMMIGRATION: ACCULTURATION AND ASSIMILATION

A goal for most immigrants who want to stay in the United States is *acculturation*. Acculturation is a process, over time, that affords the individual, or family, the ability to maintain identity with their culture of origin while adapting to the host culture. Another form of adaptation is *assimilation*. This form of adaptation denotes a total adoption of the dominant culture's norm (i.e., U.S. lifestyles and values) to the exclusion of one's historical cultural identity. Assimilation may result in being cut off from one's family and isolation from the kinship group; it may separate grandparents and parents from their "Americanized" children. Therapists may need to explore the immigration history of clients, to help them clarify how they see themselves within the American culture.

"The concept of peoplehood is based on a combination of race, religion, and cultural history and is retained whether or not members realize their commonalities with one another. The consciousness of ethnic identity varies *within* groups and from one group to another"(McGoldrick & Giordano, 1996, pp. 1–2). Families that are not of the dominant culture generally feel they are under pressure to give up their values and conform to the norms of the more powerful group. These pressures may be in conflict with pressure from their kinship network, or religious groups, who want them to adhere to old customs and beliefs. Intrafamily conflicts over the level of accommodation often arise as individual family members absorb more behaviors from the dominant culture than others, letting their own cultural traditions lapse, breaking from traditions espoused by the family network.

JOINING WITH A CLIENT'S BACKGROUND

Ethnicity interacts with race, economics, class, religion, politics, geography, family expectations, gender, expected roles, the length of time in this country, pre-immigration history of the specific group, particular family traditions, and its individual members. The availability of community support with roots in, or acceptance of, their homeland traditions also affects identity as part of an ethnic group. How people are able to express themselves; whether the particular ethnic group tends to be open or repressed, affects their ability to share their problems, or even consider coming to a therapist for help. In joining with clients, it helps to speak with them about their immigration experience and help them understand the historic influences of their identity. It is helpful to learn how much and to what degree they want to adapt to a multicultural society like the United States.

CLASS: A TROUBLESOME DISTINCTION

Class intersects powerfully with ethnicity, race, and gender, and must always be considered when a therapist is trying to understand a family's problems. For example, India's traditional caste system, a social hierarchy with Brahmans at the top and the so-called untouchables at the bottom, has been illegal in India for decades. Discriminating against someone on the basis of caste in employment and housing may mean winding up in court. Unofficially, however, the social order in the rural areas remains strong, determining how most people live, whom they marry, and with whom they socialize. In a killer earthquake in February 2001, authorities set up six distinct tent camps for the earthquake homeless, all separated by caste or religion. When relief groups arrived, town leaders presented them with six lists of residents. Relief groups found themselves wrestling with the country's ingrained social hierarchy. Those at the top of the pecking order used their connections and prestige to get the pick of the goods (Coleman, 2001). As humans, we live in a global community, and events that occur outside U.S. borders impact attitudes and behaviors within the United States. This is an example of class discrimination, and while the situation in India may seem extreme, therapists don't have to go outside U.S. borders to observe the effects of economic class on the lives of clients.

For example, in many racial groups, skin color is frequently seen as an indicator of class, with lighter complexioned people within the group seen as of a higher class than the darker complexioned of the same group. This bias plays out in family issues related to marital decisions. Therapists may be confronted with issues of unequal power among clients identified as from the same race, but with the darker partner, for instance, being seen as having a lower standing than his or her lighter tone partner.

An important part of any family therapist's training should include doing his or her own genogram. A genogram is a diagram representing three generations within a family. Genograms are discussed in greater detail in Chapter 5. Genograms help therapists (and clients) explore their ethnicity, race, and religion, and learn how those factors affected their parents and grandparents. Asking questions about one's ethnicity and race can help understand bias: How does that history affect you today? Ask family members about their immigration and acculturation experiences. Is yours a culture that is well accepted in this country? Have you and your family of origin adapted to the dominant norm? How much of past traditions and beliefs are a part of your present? Which characteristics of your own group do you like best? Are there any you feel some embarrassment or shame about? Would your family voluntarily seek help from a family therapist? How do you think they would react to being referred by some social agency?

ACCEPTING DIFFERENT FAMILY NORMS

Therapists need to be able to be open to values different from their own. It is useful for therapists to question their stance in relation to some of the beliefs and practices adhered to by their clients. Some cultures may have behaviors that in the dominant American culture are not seen as ethical, such as the physical discipline of children, or the oppression of women, or the repression of feelings. Except for those situations where there is legally defined abuse, the therapist must initially accept that these differences may be norms for the clients' culture. Work toward educating parents about parenting and marital expectations in this country, while showing respect for the family values they bring with them.

If the family's functioning is not being adversely affected by traditional behaviors, and the individuals within the family are comfortable with those ways, it may be to their advantage to work within those traditions, and, in some cases, even reinforce them. Understandably, many people have difficulty accepting traditions that relegate women to subservient roles. Yet, it may be more therapeutic to work within those roles, at least until the consequences of confronting them are carefully explored.

Family Secrets

Many groups, not just recent immigrant families, have a tradition of keeping secrets within the family. There is a long-standing tradition in the majority American culture of keeping family problems within the family. Family members may not be comfortable sharing certain thoughts with a therapist, with everyone else present. If there is a possibility of abuse in the family, it is especially important that the therapist be sensitive to the fear of speaking about it in front of the abuser. In the exploratory stage of therapy, it may be a good idea to meet with subsets of the family—the parents, siblings, wife, or husband—alone or together. If a therapist is planning to work with subsets, he or she should discuss that fully, early in the session, and explain his or her reasons for working that way. That will help reduce concerns of family members that they have somehow brought those separate sessions on themselves or that that process is somehow punitive or undermining of their place in the family.

Generate Trust

Many immigrants are suspicious of authority and often perceive the therapist as a person of authority that they need to be wary of. The first order of business for a therapist is help develop trust with the client. For clients whose background differs greatly from the therapist's, this task may be an even bigger task.

The therapist can generate trust by showing acceptance of and respect for the clients' traditional ways of presenting their stories. Listening, not just to their words, but observing their nonverbal nuances, may offer clues to how they relate to others. Inviting them to share their stories in a narrative fashion can be helpful. Asking questions that invite more details and shows the therapist's interest in their story is another good approach. Look to Virginia Satir's style of joining with the client's language as a way of helping them feel understood and accepted. Satir's work is covered in Chapter 6.

Learning the Family's History

After the therapist establishes an atmosphere of mutual trust with the client, it may be appropriate and helpful, in a friendly, conversational way, to ask more specific questions, such as these, about the history of his or her immigration experience:

Did you come here alone, or with family?

Who did you leave behind?

Do you plan to stay permanently in the United States or do you hope to return to the country you came from?

The therapist may ask about their pre-immigration experiences:

What was going on in your country when you left?

Did you choose to leave or did you feel forced to leave?

In this country, do you have accessible kin or community support you can relate to and depend on?

The therapist should ask how much the individual and family members identify with their group and with its religious beliefs and traditions:

Validate and strengthen ethnic, racial, or religious identity and help clients connect with their cultural heritage.

Help the family identify and resolve conflicts between family loyalty expectations and individual aspirations (McGoldrick & Giordano, 1996).

Therapists should be aware that some clients may use ethnic, racial, or religious identity as a defense against change or as a justification for half-hearted involvement in therapy (i.e., "People in my country are never on time."). Explore their goals. If they indicate that they want to "get ahead," and succeed as a productive citizen of this country, gently educate them about taking personal responsibility for meeting some of the expected norms of American culture. This strategy can be especially helpful when job security and school compliance are presented as issues.

Therapists should always explain in advance why they are asking these questions and explain that the answers can help the therapist work with them better and to find solutions that will resonate with their cultural beliefs. Clients who come from totalitarian countries, or who are in this country illegally, or have had bad experiences with authorities and bureaucracies in this country, need assurance that the therapist is asking these questions to help them and not to hurt them.

RESPECTING DIFFERENCES

Realize that families from different cultures frequently live with different values and expectations for their families. Styles of communication may differ from group to group. Having said that, it is important not to get caught up in generalities that may short circuit the therapist's ability to develop a therapeutic connection. He or she may have some preconceptions based on familiar stereotypes proffered in the media and literature about different groups. Therapists need to remain open to the uniqueness of each individual and family and join with them as they present themselves. Therapists need to be aware that generalities are just that, and each family interprets itself and expresses itself in its own unique way.

When people from different groups intermarry, those different ways of communicating may be what leads them to a therapist's office.

CULTURE AND INTERGENERATIONAL ISSUES

Americans currently speak more than 150 languages in U.S. public schools. Women, minorities, and new immigrants constitute a major part of the U.S. workforce. In the United States, mental health professionals are challenged to develop flexible treatment models responsive to a variety of ethnic, racial, and religious groups. Migration can be so disruptive it seems to add an entire extra stage to the life cycle (McGoldrick & Giordano, 1996). Adjusting to a new culture is an ongoing developmental process that affects individual and family life-cycle adjustments and may feed intergenerational conflict over many generations. In general, young adults seem to have an easier time adjusting to new cultures. Parents may acculturate more slowly than their children, upsetting the traditional hierarchies of their previous environment and creating parental children with responsibilities beyond their developmental tolerance. In adolescence, peer pressure from schoolmates presents challenges to the expectations of parents and community that often distress intergenerational relationships.

THERAPEUTIC ISSUES

The concerns and issues presented here will be addressed in more depth in the chapters that describe specific theories and the form of practice they promote. Approaching mental health symptoms as a function of the family and of social issues impacts the way therapists think about and respond to various mental health diagnoses. Some of the terms used, such as "postmodern" and "family systems" may be unfamiliar. However, they are used to point out some differences and concerns addressed when mental health symptoms are seen as relational rather than individual.

Various immigrant groups may be puzzled when a medical diagnosis such as substance abuse, anorexia, bulimia, or family violence is imposed on them by social agencies and health professionals. This confusion, along with these troubling labels, are often presented by clients to family therapists. Originally, systemic thinkers criticized family therapists who saw the symptom as the issue, rather than the interactive systems within families. At this time, the systemic purists have been largely outvoted and many workshops and requirements have been added to the family therapist's repertoire, teaching them how to address specific, recurring symptomatic behaviors. For instance, the American Association for Marriage and Family Therapy (AAMFT) now requires courses in substance abuse for accreditation. Many states require continuing education on domestic violence.

Systemic therapists still understand those problems from the perspective of family interactions. Even as they object to labeling the identified patient as having a "disease," many family therapists will address the specific symptom and refer clients and their families to specific treatment modalities, such as drug treatment centers. Utilizing community resources can be a helpful adjunct to family treatment.

POSTMODERN ISSUES WITH MEDICAL LABELS

Postmodern thinkers see labeling a problem as an illness or disease (e.g., DSMIV "clinical depression," "alcoholic," "bulimic") as an imposition of an identity on a person by an authority figure that may give the message that the person is flawed and powerless over the problem. In North America, there exists a tendency to medicalize certain social problems. Addressing the identity of substance misuse as a disease, Sanders states: "As long as the general public believes that dependency, or addiction is an individual problem, the necessity of addressing social issues related to the problem will continue unabated" (Sanders, 1998, pp. 144–145).

In addition, Peele (1991) wrote:

> To intervene in the economic and social policy area is the most powerful way of addressing these problems. But we're afraid to redirect resources into the inner city, whether public or private. . . . There's a deeper problem, and that is a lack of a sense of community in this country. . . . Black versus white, inner city versus suburban or rural. And going along with this loss of sense of community is the fact that we tackle problems individualistically rather than socially. . . . Addiction is a very real, social-psychological and cultural phenomenon influenced by a host of social considerations. (pp. 26–27)

Sanders (1998) wrote that therapy is not about helping persons adjust to the status quo. It is about directing therapeutic conversation toward the eradication and elimination of oppressive restraints. "In a word, therapy can be viewed as a form of liberation" (pp. 154–155). Guided by the thinking of Anderson and Goolishian (1990) and White and Epston (1990), Sanders offered some questions he uses in working with people presenting as substance *misusers* (his term). The therapist presents these, and most questions they pursue, in a respectful, conversational, nonconfrontational style

How has cocaine/pot/valium/alcohol, etc., been affecting your life?

Has use of those substances created a wedge between you and the person who cares for you?

Describe how activities you used to enjoy have been affected by substance misuse.

Would you say that a substance-misusing lifestyle is working for you or against you?

Are there specific situations or contexts in your life that drugs are more likely to take advantage of?

Describe some of the plans or dreams you had that drugs interfere with.

Are there times when drugs seem to be your jailer? (p. 157)

Postmodern therapists question the idea that substance *misuse* lies within the person's biochemistry, or that it is a disease needing treatment, in medical terminology.

Sanders (1998), and other postmodern thinkers, believe that as long as substance misuse is seen as a medical problem, the social issues related to it will not be addressed. One concern with the use of diagnostic labeling of one as an addict (or any other disease label) is that one begins to think of self as one-dimensional—"an addict."

CHALLENGING TRADITIONAL ROLES

There is a concern, especially when working within the framework of the postmodern therapies (see Chapters 10–12) that the absolute neutrality they profess allows oppressive situations to remain unchallenged. For example, the life experience of women, children, and minorities need to be carefully considered in systemic theory and therapy. Power, or lack of it, within the family or culture, might best be explored as a search for the availability of options and resources. Some theories, based on traditional family structure, have been remiss in confronting the traditional roles that limit both men's and women's options. Feminist family therapy will be discussed in Chapter 5, as an example of an activist theory that addresses the inequality of power of women in a patriarchal society. The thinking and processes described for feminist family therapy can serve as a model for social justice for other groups such as ethnic minorities, people with disabilities, and the aged.

If we agree that people are defined, and define themselves, through the dominant stories of their culture, as the postmodern therapists suggest, we understand that those stories affect our relationships with ourselves and with others. What we come to recognize, as male or female, is mediated by relationship to others through language practices. In this sense, language not only shapes and forms our interactions with others, but with our bodies as well (Elliott, 1998, p. 41).

GENDER BIAS AND PSYCHOTHERAPY

Many family theories and therapies have been criticized for gender insensitivity (MRI, Bowen, strategic, and structural, in particular). Because they are seen as largely behavioristic, they omit women's ways of connecting and learning through relationships. They are also seen as reinforcing the status quo of gender oppression (Hare-Mustin, 1987). Despite a therapist's more open way of thinking, he or she may inadvertently introduce gender bias into the session, simply by not questioning gender beliefs and roles within a specific family.

Conventional meanings ascribed to gender have tended to focus on *differences*. Such a focus is inherently biased and limited. Hare-Mustin and Maracek (1990) named two biases in gender theory that may help people to understand the complexities that emerge in clinical practice. They describe "Alpha bias" as a tendency to exaggerate differences between men and women. They explained that Alpha bias permits recognition of women's unique capacity for relationship and her inner experiences. It counters the cultural devaluation of women by encouraging greater self-acceptance. Alpha bias has been criticized, however, as inadvertently supporting stereotypes that support the status quo by denying that change is needed in the *structure* of work and family (Gilder, 1987). Alpha bias has also been criticized for minimizing the differences or variability *among* women. Viewing women as a set of so-called feminine traits ignores the complexity and diversity of an individual woman's experience. Men are usually viewed as individuals, while women are too often seen as a largely homogeneous group (Park & Rothbart, 1982).

"Beta bias" is described as the *minimization* of differences and is seen as both helping and hindering gender sensitivity. On the positive side, minimizing differences and gaining equal treatment under law enables women to gain access to educational and occupational opportunities previously denied them. The negative consequence is that it draws attention *away* from women's special needs and the difference in power and resources between men and women (Hare-Mustin & Maracek, 1990). When differences are ignored, and norms of behavior based on the male experience are accepted, that often ignores how women, who still have less power and fewer choices, are affected. For example, in no-fault divorces, settlements have usually been found to raise men's standard of living by 42% and lower women and children's standard of living by 73% (Weitzman, 1985).

Gender theory requires discriminant application, just as all the other theories related to human interactions, behaviors, and emotions do. Gender bias can be avoided by the therapist's adoption of a cautious and respectful stance regarding perceived differences that emerge in the therapeutic conversation. When gender difference seems relevant to the dialogue with the client, the therapist should describe it as such. This naming of the concerns related to gender bias begins the cocreation of new meanings. Like with any other new meanings offered to clients, it is unethical to introduce ideas about gender differences and insist those are the only right ideas. The client must be the ultimate judge of what fits for him or her regarding gender, as with any other suggestions or issues.

Gender sensitivity is critical to the therapeutic process. However, placing gender theory above the client's meaning system regarding the presenting problem demotes the therapeutic attitude of empathy and respect. Therapists must appreciate the uniqueness of each individual, male or female, and recognize the larger contexts, the education, the society they live in, and their status in their community. When advocating for change, a therapist must recognize the consequences that may occur if they change or leave their current situation (Duncan, Solovey, & Rusk, 1992). Consider if the woman in an abusive situation has a workable plan. Will she be able to support herself? Are there adequate community resources to assist her? Will she be in a position to learn new skills so she can improve her situation? What about child care? Is it available? And will she be safe? If there has been violence, what is the danger of her abuser's retaliation?

In her plenary address at the AAMFT annual conference in New Orleans (1988), Monica McGoldrick suggested family therapists consider the following "Rules of Thumb."

1. Pay attention to the income and work potential of husband and wife and the implications for the balance of power in their relationship.
2. Pay attention to the relative physical strength of the men and women in the family and to the impact of any intimidation or incident of physical abuse, however long ago, as a regulator of the balance of power between them.
3. Help the couple clarify the rules by which male and female roles are chosen and rewarded in their families and on their jobs. (Who makes decisions? Who handles finances? Who buys and wraps birthday present? Who cleans the toilet? At the meta-level, who makes the rules?)
4. Place the couple's attitudes toward male and female roles in context, clarifying the broader political, social, and economic issues, such as divorce, aging, and childbearing, and encourage them to educate themselves about these matters.
5. Validate the wife's focus on relationships and at the same time empower her in areas of work, money, and participating in the job market. (We need to validate her ways of being in the world, not just accept the male value system.)
6. Help her find more effective ways of dealing with her anger than blaming herself.
7. Be sensitive to the price husbands have to pay in job advancement and in being invalidated by other men if they change their success orientation to give higher priority to relationships, caretaking, and emotional expressiveness.
8. Urge family members to nurture their friendship systems. (For women, close female relationships have been reported as second only to good health in importance for life satisfaction and men often have no close friends, yet friendship is an extremely important resource for everyone throughout life.)
9. Recognize the importance of sibling and other family relationships as part of the emotional network of marriage. (It makes no sense to limit the focus to the couple alone, just because that's the way the problem is presented.)
10. Encourage attention to spiritual values. (We need to help couples to ask themselves questions about what really matters to them in the long run and in the very long run.)

Patriarchal Residue

Most cultures developed from a patriarchal stance and maintain that stance. In many parts of the world, even today, women are seen as chattel, they are at the mercy of their husbands, and hopefully, of a benevolent mother-in-law. When people come to the United States, it may be their first experience with egalitarian ideas of family roles.

Many women who come from repressive cultures find themselves discontent living as they had before they immigrated. Many of these women exhibit symptoms of depression. The bolder among them find themselves in angry conflict with their spouses. The spouses are confused. This sometimes leads to violence and abuse. They cannot address these issues within their community. Sometimes the police or other social agencies step in and refer the couple for therapy. Both husband and wife may fail to understand what they are being accused of and why the authorities intervened. The therapist's initial job is to help clients understand why they were referred and to explore with them how they think they might benefit from therapy.

CHANGE IS IN PROCESS

We don't have to look only to those overtly patriarchal groups for repression or limitations in women's lives. While changes have occurred, and are occurring in U.S. society, they have not been eliminated. It's important for the therapist to realize the repression or abuse of women is not the exclusive domain of new immigrant families, or particular racial, religious, or economic groups. There are women at every level of society who have been, and are being, subjected to these pressures. It may be easy to miss abusive relationships in those clients who seem to come from privileged homes. Therapists know, too, that medical profession tends to deny or minimize evidence of domestic abuse in general. Many women are too ashamed or frightened to speak out. It is the job of the therapist to ask probing questions, respectfully, to help them express their fears. This is another situation where separating out individual family members, or subsets of family members, to explore some of these issues can be helpful. Go slowly. Be tolerant of a woman's reluctance to make a move away from a marriage that is overtly abusive. She may fear that as more complicated and frightening than enduring what is known.

SEXUAL ORIENTATION ISSUES

People present with many different ways to love and relate to one another. Same sex couples do come in for therapy. Though they often offer presenting problems that are the same as heterosexual couples, for example, jealousy, money management, or role disagreements, it is important to recognize the additional pressures they are under from society. As with all clients, the initial challenge is to build trust and to help them feel accepted. When that trust is established, it's important to look into their support systems, family attitudes, and job issues, all of the concerns that any minority group finds itself dealing with.

Work to understand how societal messages impact lesbians and gay men who are clients and the families of these clients. If the therapist feels bias, he or she needs to explore his or her personal issues and work through them, in order to be able to be comfortable and authentic with the clients. When individuals and couples and their families gain personal understanding of their strengths, the impact of prejudicial messages is weakened.

PEOPLE WITH DISABILITIES

How do people feel when they encounter a person with a visible disability? The majority (92%) say they often or occasionally feel admiration, 74% feel pity, 58% feel awkward or embarrassed, 16% experience anger because persons with disabilities cause inconvenience, and 9% feel resentment because persons with disabilities get special privileges (Yuker, 1994). A number of clients with disabilities have told this author they feel people are often afraid to get involved with them. Some of the reasons for that fear, they explained, might be a fear of "catching" the disability, of being seen negatively by others for their association with the person with the disability, or of becoming burdened or taken advantage of. Just as with myths about race, religion, ethnicity, gender, sexual orientation, or any group that differs from the dominant group, myths and stigmas about disabilities abound and self-perpetuate. People who have little contact with persons with disabilities have little opportunity for corrective experiences or increased information. Attitudes of the public toward persons with disabilities are strongly influenced by the friendliness and social skills of one person they encounter with a disability. This is an extra burden placed on persons with disabilities; attitudes toward "their people" can be negatively influenced by a grumpy mood on a bad day (Olkin, 1999).

Too often a therapist's thinking about disabilities does not consider other contextual factors. Therapists need to incorporate all the factors that may impact or be impacted by the disability, including race, religion, ethnicity, gender, age, life-cycle stage, family dynamics and ability to help, or economic situation (Olkin, 1999). Work toward understanding the whole person in context. Stay watchful of the laws available or needed, to assist persons with disabilities.

Olkin advocated for the disabled. He described them as the largest minority group in the United States. He asserted it was the responsibility of the psychotherapists to encourage research and training directed toward better understanding of the needs and potentials of disabled persons (Olkin, 1999).

OUR AGING POPULATION

At the beginning of the 20th century, life expectancy was around 45 years. At the turn into the 21st century, the fastest growing population is of people 85 years and older. Between 2010 and 2030, the over 65 population will rise over 70%. A child born in 2000 could expect to live 76.9 years, about 29 years longer than a child born in 1900. Over 2.0 million persons celebrated their 65th birthday in 2000. There were 50,545 persons aged 100 or more in 2000. The percentage of Americans over 65 has more than tripled. The older population itself is getting older (from Internet releases of the U.S. Bureau of the Census and National Health Statistics, 2001). Therapists may see three, four, even five generations of families represented in their offices. Social expectations have been changing. Women are working outside the home in a variety of nongender designated fields. Older parents often move away from the family's hometown. Children, as they complete college or take jobs or marry, often move far from their hometown. People sometimes feel disconnected. Issues are left unresolved. And then, as the parents age even more and begin to feel the physical and mental impact of age-related changes, families need to create new ways to relate and help one another. Many families are ill prepared for these changes. More and more older people are coming to family therapy offices, and involving all the generations of their family in the process when they can. Dependency issues related to the parent's growing need for attention and who is caring for whom challenge family understanding. Parents usually want to maintain their independence and decision-making abilities. Adult children become anxious and worried and think their parents need to give them more authority over their lives. Sibling resentments may arise when one is perceived as not sharing enough of the responsibility for their parent's needs.

It is again an area that the therapist needs to explore with clients: What are your feelings about aging? What do you know about the issues of loss that aging parents evoke in the other family members and that they experience about their own abilities? These are sensitive issues, and new territory for many therapists.

OTHER SOCIAL CONCERNS

A look at a directory of social service agencies will show dozens of other populations in U.S. society that evoke prejudicial or biased responses. This chapter cannot go into all of them. All of these people are people, deserving of caring. Although the discussion in this chapter has focused on differences, in many ways each person, each group, is more alike than different. Each group warrants the respect and caring. So, as a potential therapist, asking some of the self-searching questions provided in this chapter, it could be helpful to interchange the word, "race" or "religion" for instance, with a word describing one of the other groups mentioned in this chapter. As a student experiencing or researching specific differences, respect the fact that named differences are generalities, and not absolutes defining the individuals and families who come for help.

No one can be completely free of biases, but each person can become more aware and sensitive toward the people they work with. Cultural sensitivity should be woven throughout curriculum designed to train psychotherapists. Students need to develop their thinking about differences, and work within the various theories and therapies, with an awareness of human diversity and the issues it raises for them.

BEWARE OF GENERALIZATIONS!

Generalizations represent only partial truths. Stereotyping serves as a shorthand to understanding. Don't lean on it too heavily. Ask about variations within the client family that may differ from the popular conceptions about their group of origin and its individual members. Therapists need to be aware of their clients' personal origins, their experiences with inter-ethnic, interracial, interfaith relationships, sexual orientation, perceptions of male-female roles within various cultures and economic levels, and of the individual uniqueness of all the members of the client families they meet with. A tall order, yet, seeing one family at a time, and taking care to understand oneself in relation to that family, can lead to mutually rewarding therapy outcomes.

HOW TO HELP

Which of the therapies will work best with which clients? No specific in-depth research validates prescribing any one therapy for any one group. However, in general, it seems that a structural approach is most accepted by those groups that have rigid family roles and structures and want the therapist to be an expert authority. The paradoxical interventions used in strategic approaches may be most problematic for people from groups who bear the least trust for the therapy process. (Paradoxical interventions are covered in Chapter 8.) But don't rule them out. Strategic therapies are an effective method of working with some cultural groups. Bowen's coaching methods, to reconnect family members through direct member-to-member discussions, is often useful. The genogram is an essential tool for eliciting family history and bringing emotional conflicts into the open, where they can be worked through (Chapter 5). Boszormenyi-Nagy's therapy, dealing with loyalty and ledgers, certainly has a place for those families having difficulty with inter-generational issues raised by the process of acculturation or assimilation. For some, these multigenerational therapies may be more than the client wants or needs (Chapter 5). Satir's methods, of joining with the language style of the family, as well as her warmth and acceptance of every family member can enhance trust with most any family (Chapter 6). Narrative therapy offers a way to join, to enter the family, collaborate for change, and yet it may be too "friendly" for people from cultures that expect more directive roles from professionals (Chapter 12).

As stated many times in this chapter, joining and building trust are essential for any therapy to be effective. The therapist's comfort with the form of therapy used is also essential for successful treatment. Getting to know a client by learning about the history of their family of origin should help guide a therapist find the style of therapy that will be most helpful. It may be "parts of many"—a more eclectic model—that adapts to the process experience between therapist and clients. A therapist needs to be adaptable to meet the client's needs.

LEARN, LEARN, LEARN

Students of family therapy should learn more about the works of those particular theorists that they feel drawn to, and find books, workshops and videos to help them learn more about those theories. Sensitivity training may be useful to help student's experience what it may be like to be from a particular culture, race, or lifestyle. Novels, movies, or personal stories written about specific life challenges can add to a student's understanding. Pursuing higher education that focuses on specific theorists may be useful. Students should get supervision and an internship that supports their direction. When therapists feel secure in the theoretical direction they have pursued, they can expand their repertoire to be flexible and integrate a variety of approaches in response to the client needs. When a therapist has done that, he or she will be able to better accommodate to and meet the needs of the diversity of clients who enter the therapy room.

EXPERIENTIAL ACTIVITIES

1. Instructor's may suggest students keep a journal, noting their reactions to seeing or being with persons of different roots from theirs, different lifestyles, different genders, as well as of persons with disabilities. Students may then write a theme paper describing what they learned about themselves through their journal.
2. Instructors may assign groups of three or four students to interview people, or families from a variety of racial and ethnic backgrounds or lifestyles. Set up small group presentations in class to process what they have learned. Encourage larger group to participate with questions and comments.
3. Instructors may assign a research paper to examine how state and federal laws affect specific groups. Provide a list of the different groups, including gender and sexual orientation, economic class, as well as racial, religious, ethnic, and people with disabilities. Allow students to select which groups they will research. Students are then invited to give an oral report on their findings.

REFERENCES

Anderson, H. D., & Goolishian, H. A. (1990). Beyond cybernetics: Comments on Atkinson and Heath's "Further thoughts on second-order family therapy." *Family Process, 29,* 157–163.

Armas, G. C. (2001, March 9). Census figures show a more diverse America. *Ft. Lauderdale Sun Sentinel,* p. 11a.

Coleman, J. (2001, February 8). Old caste attitudes impede quake aid. *Ft. Lauderdale Sun Sentinel,* p. 20a.

Duncan, B. L., Solovey, A. D., & Rusk, G. S.(1992). *Changing the rules.* New York: Guilford.

Elliott, H. (1998). Postmodernism, feminism, and narrative therapy. In S. Madigan and I. Law (Eds.), *Praxis: Situating discourse, feminism and politics in narrative therapies* (p. 41). Vancouver, BC: Cardigan.

Gilder, G. (1987). *Men and marriage.* Los Angeles: Pelican.

Gremillion, B., & Hunt, S. (2001, February 4). Multicultural directory. *Ft. Lauderdale Sun Sentinel.*

Hare-Mustin, R. T. (1987). The problem of gender in family therapy theory. *Family Process, 26,* 15–27.

Hare-Mustin, R. T., & Maracek, J. (1990). *Making a difference: Psychology and construction of gender.* New Haven, CT: Yale University Press.

McGoldrick, M., & Giordano, J. (1996). Overview: Ethnicity and family therapy. In *Ethnicity and family therapy* (2nd ed.) (pp. 23–24). New York: Guilford.

Olkin, R. (1999). *What psychotherapists should know about disability.* New York: Guilford.

Park, B., & Rothbart, M. (1982). Perception of out-group homogeneity and levels of social categorization: Memory for the subordinate attributes of in-group and out-group members. *Journal of Personality and Social Psychology, 42,* 1051–1068.

Peele, S. (1991). Interview with Don Powell "Addiction is a Myth and . . ." In *Practice: The Magazine of Psychology and Political Economy,* 26–27. Reprinted by permission.

Sanders, J. (1998). A postmodern inquiry: Substance misuse. In S. Madigan & I. Law (Eds.) *Praxis: Situating discourse, feminism and politics in narrative therapies.* Vancouver, BC: Cardigan. Reprinted by permission.

U.S. Bureau of the Census and National Health Statistics (2001) Internet release, www.census.gov

Weitzman, L. J. (1985). *The divorce resolution: The unexpected social and economic consequences for women and children in America.* New York: Free Press.

White, M., & Epston, D. (1990). *Narrative means to therapeutic ends.* New York: Norton.

Yuker, H. E. (1994). Variables that influence attitudes toward persons with disabilities: Conclusions from the data. *Psychosocial Perspectives on Disability: A Special Issue of the Journal of Social Behavior and Personality, 9,* 3–22.

FOUNDING ROOTS
OF SYSTEMIC THEORY

A NEW SYSTEMIC PERSPECTIVE ABOUT MENTAL HEALTH

CHAPTER 3

KEY THEORISTS

Murray Bowen—a psychiatrist, evolution-based natural family systems

Ludwig von Bertalanffy—a biologist, founder of general systems theory

Mary Richmond—social work

Norbert Wiener—a mathematician, cybernetic roots

Gregory Bateson—an anthropologist

Paul Watzlawick—a Jungian psychiatrist

Don Jackson—a psychiatrist

John Weakland—a chemical engineer

Virginia Satir—a social worker

Milton Erickson—a psychiatrist and hypnotist

Kurt Lewin—a social scientist, group dynamics

Theodore Lidz—a psychiatrist, role theory

Alfred Adler—a psychiatrist, child guidance

Nathan Ackerman—a psychiatrist, child guidance

Lyman Wynne—a psychiatrist, combined psychoanalytic concepts and systems theory

TERMS TO KNOW

systemic

family as a system of interacting parts mutually influencing one another

identified patient

context

general systems theory

family of origin

structural and functional patterns

rule-governed system

mutual reinforcement of behaviors

circular recursive events

mutually influential interpersonal context

homeostasis

intrapsychic

interpsychic

reciprocal relationships

"The sum is greater than its parts."

reframe

here-and-now

complementarity

epistemology

worldview

pathology of epistemology

family system

family cohesion

cybernetic systems

feedback loop

negative feedback

positive feedback	embedded
family rules	redundancies
double bind	complementary relationships
family life cycle	symmetrical relationships
second-order change	brief therapy
first-order change	utilization
cybernetics	indirect suggestion
circular causality	role reciprocity
circular feedback loop	mutual patterns of interaction
interactional effects of communi-cation	natural and rational consequences of behavior
process	coalitions
content	reorganize the structure
metacommunication	family subsystems
paradox	pseudomutuality
semantics = content/report	rubber fence
pragmatics = process/command	pseudohostility
recursive patterns of interaction	alignments and splits
conjoint family sessions	communication deviance

Note: These terms may look overwhelming at first. They will begin to make sense in the context of the text. They serve as a guide for what to look for as you study the text.

AN OVERVIEW OF THE DEVELOPMENT OF SYSTEMIC THINKING

The shift from an individual to a **systemic** perspective was revolutionary. It provided a profoundly powerful tool for understanding and helping people resolve human problems. It offered a whole new philosophy on the origin and maintenance of mental health and mental illness. Those readers whose training has focused on individual psychopathology will need to keep an open mind. Individual psychology and family theory each offer various approaches to treatment. Knowledge of both individual psychology and family systems ideas provides the clinician with a *both/and* opportunity that expands his or her potential to be an effective helper.

Considering the **family as a system of interacting parts mutually influencing one another** suggests that emotional distress and mental illness are largely a by-product of *how* individuals function within the family and society, rather than from the result of the internal pathology of the individual. If the way the family system functions is related to both individual and familial distress, then that distress may be best treated by changing the way family members, and other significant persons, interact. To accomplish that, all the significant people in an **identified patient's** life need to be included, or at least considered in therapy, as part of the current **context.**

Early Influences on Systems Theory

In his book, *Cosmos,* Carl Sagan (1980) reported that humans used a fairly sophisticated level of systems ideas in construction work, as early as 500 B.C. Systems ideas eventually helped move the world into the Renaissance in about the 15th century. Darwin was among those who introduced systems thinking and the evolution of life forms in the mid-19th century. Einstein's theories developed in the early 20th century dealt with nonhuman factors. It was not until the mid-20th century that systems ideas became incorporated into studies and treatment of human behavior (Kerr & Bowen, 1988).

In the 1940s there were at least two kinds of systems theory already in existence. One, **general systems theory,** developed by Ludwig von Bertalanffy, was based on mathematical concepts; the other was developed from technology by Norbert Wiener. According to Murray Bowen, an intergenerational psychiatrist covered in Chapter 5, those existing systems theories did not fit well with his ideas about the human as an evolutionary being. Bowen fashioned a natural systems theory that placed the human as a more evolved life form, part of the evolutionary life chain (Kerr & Bowen, 1988).

Understanding Human Behavior in Context

Family therapy is not just a new set of techniques; it is a whole new approach to understanding human behavior as fundamentally shaped by its social context. The initial and primary connection is with the family into which a person is born, a **family of origin. Structural and functional patterns** make the family a **rule-governed system,** a system of interconnected lives governed by strict, often unspoken rules. Therapy based on this thinking is directed toward changing the way the family is organized—*how* family members interact and **mutually reinforce each other's behavior.** When this *how* is changed, the life of each family member is transformed. Since family therapy exerts change on the entire family system, improvement tends to be long lasting. Changing interactions between family members mutually reinforces those changes.

Family theorists propose that psychological symptoms are best explained in terms of **circular recursive events** that focus on the **mutually influential interpersonal context** in which they develop. Psychological symptoms are maintained within the social context of the family, rather than the sole result of intrapsychic pathology. Those symptoms often serve to maintain the stability of that family (**homeostasis**). Looking at psychological symptoms within this contextual perspective moves the responsibility for change *away* from the internal world of individual patients (**intrapsychic**) to the transactional context of the entire family and other significant relationships (**interpsychic**). New terminology was, and is still, being created to describe systemic ideas.

The foundation of this shift to a systemic perspective includes group dynamics, the child guidance movement, social work practices, research on family dynamics and family roles, studies of the etiology of schizophrenia, and the practice of marriage counseling (which had begun earlier, outside the constraints of the medical model).

Families as Natural Social Systems

A family is a natural social system (Goldenberg & Goldenberg, 1980). The structure of families is always changing. In the not too distant past, a nuclear family, consisting of a mother, father, their offspring, and grandparents, was the norm. The roles and expectations for each family member were relatively constant. The picture today is ever more complex. There is more mobility, not only of where people live, but with whom they live, where they work, what their roles are within the family, and who is considered a member of a family. Many couples have dual careers—some by choice, some by necessity. Divorce and remarriage have spawned diverse arrangements of parents and stepchildren, raising issues around parental rights and the rights of grandparents. Single parents, male and female, and same sex parents, add additional challenges to the definition of family, and what is involved in its stability and growth. Since life expectancy has increased, it is not unusual to find three, four, and even five generation families. Grandparent's roles are changing. The young-old are active seniors, often living far from their offspring. The old-old may require special care, adding to the responsibility and burdens of the middle generation while it is working to meet its expected roles of supporting and rearing children. In studying the evolution of family theory, consider the parallel evolution of how the shape of families is changing. Consider also, that although the family is the optimal unit for therapeutic intervention, family therapists embrace the societal and cultural influences in which the family lives. Marriage and family therapists must consider all those influences—the full context in which the family lives—when framing interventions.

Family therapy emphasizes relationships—the interconnectedness essential for mental health in the human community. It blends well, also, with the increasing interest in spirituality. Family therapy is a philosophical orientation—a way of thinking about the creation, maintenance, and solutions of individual and family problems. Lasting change is often accomplished in fewer sessions than in most traditional individual psychotherapies.

Most people acknowledge, praise, or complain about the influence of family members, past and present, especially in relation to obligations, encouragements, and constraints. But most people are not aware of how much they have influenced, and continue to influence others in their own families, and how circular those influences are. It is sometimes difficult for an individual to see his or her thoughts and feelings and actions as being part of a network of **reciprocal relationships.** To understand the original thinking of family theorists, it is important to appreciate the foundation of their thinking: We are part of something larger than ourselves. **The sum** [of all the people in our family] **is greater than its parts** [each individual]" (Bertalanffy, 1968).

Even though many marriage and family therapists treat people individually as well as in family groups, the presenting problem is always **reframed** into relational terms. No matter who is in the treatment room, one, two, or more people, the family therapist formulates a diagnosis based on the family and its larger context, rather than on the psychological problem as symptomized by the identified patient. Although early family theorists tended to deny the existence of intrapsychic pathology, the current thinking in the field tends to recognize the existence of medical and chemical disorders and incorporates those medically diagnosed conditions into treatment. They see the medical or chemical conditions as mediated, maintained, or alleviated by family transactions.

Systemic Thinking Is Inclusive

Family therapists do not ask why something happened. They ask *what* is going on, in what *context*. For most systemic therapists, the focus is present centered, and examines and focuses treatment on **here-and-now** interactions. They acknowledge the **complementarity** of the many sides to a dilemma. Systemic thinking is inclusive. It sees the world and the people in it as intricately connected and giving meaning to each other.

There is a term, **epistemology,** often used by family theorists, as a synonym for one's personal framework or interpretive system. It refers to one's **worldview**—the belief system through which each person operates in every aspect of life. Although people are rarely aware of it, everyone has an internalized set of theories that enable them to feel they have some order and predictability in their lives. That worldview was learned in the family of origin, in schools, and from meaningful experiences. An individual's worldview provides him or her with basic assumptions of how he or she believes the world is, should, or will be.

Bateson wrote that it was extremely important to be conscious of the frameworks used for personal theories, the assumptions on which they are based, and the possibility of logical inconsistency. When people are not conscious of their epistemology, Bateson (1972) said, they have "**pathologies of epistemology.**"

Students of family systems need to challenge and examine their own personal epistemology and worldview—assumptions and biases about reality. Therapists need to check out the beliefs and biases through which they perceive their world and how those biases and beliefs influence their relationships with their clients. Family therapists must challenge the interpretive systems of clients, helping them expand their beliefs about reality in such a way that new behaviors become possible. For students, therapists, and clients, overcoming "pathologies of epistemology" is a shared goal (Becvar & Becvar, 1982).

FROM INDIVIDUAL TO FAMILY: MULTIDISCIPLINARY CHANGES

How, when, and why did this new way of thinking about psychological symptoms germinate?

Leading individual-oriented therapists such as Freud and Rogers believed that while early family life does shape one's personality, the most influential and dominant forces controlling human behavior were internal, subjective beliefs, myths that patients had created about their families. Psychoanalytic and phenomenological therapists were trained to segregate patients from their families for therapy and to focus on their patient's intrapsychic and behavioral symptoms away from the influences of their troubling family. Family therapy may have evolved out of the frustration of some psychiatrists with the ineffectiveness of the reigning paradigms of psychoanalysis and the medical psychiatric model. It began as recognition of social and theoretical changes in the field of psychiatry. It was nurtured by many other changes fostered by other disciplines.

Bertalanffy and General Systems Theory

The seeds of systemic ideas as applicable to families may have begun with a presentation on general systems theory by Bertalanffy in 1945. Ludwig von Bertalanffy was a prominent German biologist who wondered if the laws that applied to biological organisms (plants, animals) might also apply to the human mind or even the global ecosphere. Although he had published widely, he did not initially have personal contact with the pioneers of family therapy.

Bertalanffy emphasized that systems are open to, and interact with, their environments, and that they can acquire qualitatively new properties through emergence, resulting in continual evolution. Rather than reducing an entity to the properties of its parts or elements, systems theory focuses on the arrangement of, and relations between the parts, which connect them into a whole. Bertalanffy suggested that the same concepts and principles of organization underlie all the different disciplines (such as physics, biology, technology, or sociology). He said general systems theory provided a basis for understanding all the sciences. According to Davidson (1983):

> A Bertalanffian system can be physical, like a television set, biological, like a cocker spaniel, psychological like a personality, sociological like a labor union, or symbolic like a set of laws. . . . A system can be composed of smaller systems and can also be part of a larger system, just as a state or province is composed of smaller jurisdictions and also is part of a nation. Consequently, the same organized entity can be regarded as either a system or a subsystem, depending on the observer's focus of interest. (p. 26)

Bertalanffy said a **family system** should be seen as more than just a collection of individuals, but rather as a group of interacting participants in an ongoing pattern of reciprocal relationships.

When early family theorists adopted a systemic perspective for working with families, they at first focused solely on the family as a system and neglected to consider the larger systems of influence in which the family was embedded. It soon became apparent that families did not stand in isolation. Societal influences play their part in the reciprocal interactions that stabilize and destabilize families and communities, and need to be considered in the therapy process.

Homeostasis   Early family therapy researchers explained the concept of homeostasis as the tendency of systems to regulate themselves to maintain the status quo in response to changes in the environment. They suggested that when events or behaviors occurred that stressed the ability of the system to maintain its status quo, one or more family member would develop symptoms that tended to pull the system back into itself.

The term *homeostasis* was coined by French physiologist Claude Bernard in the 19th century to describe the regulation of such conditions as body temperature or blood sugar levels, suggesting it was a natural tendency for systems to regulate themselves to maintain the status quo, but Bertalanffy believed that an overemphasis on this conservative aspect of the organism reduced family systems to the level of a machine. He wrote, "If this principle of homeostatic maintenance is taken as a rule of behavior, the so called well-adjusted individual will be defined as a well-oiled robot"(in Davidson, 1983, p. 104). However, the homeostatic tendency to maintain the status quo seems apparent in many families unwilling or unable to adapt to changing circumstances.

Richmond and Social Work

The profession of social work began with concerns for the family, both as a critical social unit and as the focus for intervention (Ackerman, Beatman, & Sherman, 1961). Family caseworkers visited families in their homes and interviewed both parents at the same time to get an accurate picture of a family's problems. They worked with the parents and their social and economic context. In her classic text, *Social Diagnosis*, Mary Richmond, an early social worker and researcher, wrote that the whole family was the correct locus of treatment (Richmond, 1917). Her concept of **family cohesion** preceded later work on role theories, group dynamics, and structural family theory. According to Richmond, the degree of emotional bonding between family members was critical to their ability to survive and flourish.

Wiener and Cybernetics

The study of cybernetics was developed and named by Norbert Wiener, a mathematician at MIT. During World War II, Wiener was asked to work on a problem of how to get guns to hit moving targets. From that work, he expanded his ideas about **cybernetic systems**—that is, systems that are self-correcting.

At the core of cybernetics is the concept of **feedback loop**—the process by which a system gets the information necessary to self-correct in its effort to maintain a steady state or move toward a preprogrammed goal. This feedback includes information about the system's performance relative to its external environment, as well as the relationships among the systems parts. **Negative feedback** limits change or deviation (maintains homeostasis); **positive feedback** amplifies change, and can result in a runaway, destructive breakdown of a system *or* be a catalyst for constructive adaptation to change (Wiener, 1948). An example of feedback that is often used is a thermostat. As long as the temperature stays within the set point, the thermostat is receiving negative feedback and is able to maintain that set point. When a change in temperature occurs, this perturbs—stimulates—the thermostat to initiate an action toward bringing the temperature back to the set point (homeostasis). If the change in temperature is beyond the ability of the thermostatic system to maintain its set point (positive feedback) something different has to happen. The system may have to be adjusted, changed, or it could break down.

Applying Cybernetic Concepts to Families   Families are most open to change at time of crisis. Recognition that positive feedback can lead to appropriate change was the conceptual foundation for some of the crisis-inducing forms of family therapy put forth by Haley and Madanes (covered in Chapter 8). Haley (1971) wrote, "If a treatment program subdues and stabilizes the family, change is more difficult. To change a stabilized, miserable situation and create space for individual growth of family members, the therapists must induce a crisis which creates instability" (p. 8). Positive feedback can promote a crisis that may help the family system adjust to changed circumstances (Haley, 1971; Satir, 1972).

Therapists can carefully choreograph a crisis within the client family to push them beyond the reciprocal patterns of their usual coping behaviors. In crisis, people tend to seek different ways to relate with one another. Those different ways of interacting can be the precursors of more healthful relationships, reducing or eliminating the symptoms.

In relation to families, cybernetics focuses attention on the following:

- **family rules,** that *govern the range of behaviors* a family system can tolerate (its homeostatic range)
- **negative feedback,** mechanisms that families use to enforce those rules (e.g., guilt and other controlling behaviors)
- **double bind** messages, confusing sequences of family interaction around a problem
- **positive feedback,** what happens when a system's accustomed negative feedback is ineffective, and positive feedback loops are triggered

Example: A 17-year-old daughter yells loudly at her parents over curfew rules. Mother cries. Father is outraged and comes to mother's defense. He grounds the daughter for a month (negative feedback—it does not yet go beyond any of their usual patterns of tolerance or response). But then the daughter becomes angrier and goes beyond her usual behaviors. She stays out even later than she had before. When scolded by mother, daughter speaks back nastily, challenges her mother's authority. Mother cries and fires back some guilt-making barbs. Father again yells, grounds, and threatens. The cycle escalates further. The daughter runs away. This moves the system past the limits of previous interactions (positive feedback). Social services become involved. If family therapy is prescribed, the family meets with a therapist and is encouraged to examine the rules and behaviors that are no longer working for them. They may be educated about age-appropriate expectations and coached to change the ways in which they interact with one another as a means of solving the problem.

Negative and Positive Feedback   Negative feedback is "more of the same," maintaining usual patterns or limits of behavior. It maintains homeostasis and stabilizes transactional patterns within the family. Negative feedback patterns become problematic when family members ignore the **family life cycle** developments of its members and maintain interactions less appropriate for the current status, age, or health of its members. (Chapter 5 introduces family life cycle concepts.) Positive feedback occurs when a crisis pushes the system to change and breaks through the stabilizing patterns. In the earlier example, recognizing the daughter's age-appropriate need to assert herself challenged the way the parents responded to her actions. When family therapists encourage families to stretch beyond their usual limitations and rules and reexamine and change those rules, cybernetically oriented family therapists say they have accomplished **second-order change.** When family members make behavioral changes, but are still governed by the same unchanged rules and beliefs, family therapists call that change **first-order change** (Watzlawick, Weakland, & Fisch, 1974).

Around the same time these ideas were being formulated in the 1950s, psychiatrists treating hospitalized patients diagnosed as schizophrenic had begun to pay attention to what happened when patients were discharged. After a short time back home with their families, many patients had to be readmitted to the hospital, often with increased symptoms. Psychiatrists also noticed that when the hospitalized patient did well and was able to maintain his or her stability, someone else in the family often developed symptoms. Those psychiatrists began to include families in their treatment milieu and to pay more attention to the influence of family members on one another.

Bateson, the Palo Alto Project, and Communication Theory

Cybernetics was introduced to family therapy by Gregory Bateson. Bateson was born in England, the son of a biologist. He studied physical anthropology at Cambridge, but made his career in the United States. While married to anthropologist Margaret Mead, he worked with her on the study of the culture and personality of the Balinese and Samoans. His interest in cybernetics was important to his work with communication and learning patterns among aquatic animals, as well as with people with schizophrenic behaviors and their families. Bateson became interested in the feedback processes of systems and pioneered a conceptual shift that moved family systems thinking toward the ideas of **circular causality.** He helped change the way people think about psychopathology, from something that is caused by events in the past (and has been internalized into the personality) to something that is part of ongoing, **circular feedback loops.** Bateson rejected the idea of linear causality that he said was useful for nonliving objects but not for living things, because it did not account for the **interactional effects of communication** in relationships.

The Nature of Communications   The Palo Alto project began in the fall of 1952, when Bateson received a grant from the Rockefeller Foundation to study the nature of communication in terms of levels of influence on behavior. In 1953, Bateson was joined by Jay Haley and John Weakland. In 1954, the group received a two-year Macy Foundation grant to study schizophrenic communications and was joined by Don Jackson (Nichols & Schwartz, 1998).

Bateson set out to study communications in humans and other animals. His working hypothesis was that there were different levels of organization of communicative messages. He observed that otters employed the same gestures in both fight and play, but while in fights they would bite each other to shreds, and in play they only tickled each other. He saw that as good evidence of the existence of a communicative level (**process**) different from that of the messages (**content**) that guided behavior toward fight or play. He said that was a higher level of communication and named it **metacommunication.** Among humans this phenomenon revealed itself more clearly. Each communicative action was attached to a higher level. For instance, in learning how to knit, a person also learns *how to learn* how to knit.

He spoke of two types of communicative units that revealed conflicts between levels: **paradoxes** and **double binds.** If I were to command you, "Don't read this message," you disobey that instruction by the very act of reading it. In this paradoxical command, there is a conflict between the meaning of the message (**semantics = content/report**), and the act of issuing the message and obeying it (**pragmatics = process/command**).

Double Bind Theory   Bateson offered a typical example of a double bind from his observation of an interaction between a mother and her son, who had been diagnosed as having schizophrenic symptoms. The young man was hospitalized, and during a visit, he greeted his mother effusively, putting his arms around her shoulders. She immediately stiffened and he pulled his arms back. Then she asked him if he did not love her anymore, and noticing his embarrassment, she said, "Dear you must not be so easily embarrassed and afraid of your feelings" (Bateson, Jackson, Haley, & Weakland, 1956). It was a situation in which the patient would be damned if he did express affection toward her, and damned if he did not. At one level, the mother wanted her son to love her and so to express himself, but at another level she was uneasy with the intimate situation. Double bind messages were regarded as missiles fired by the speaker, missiles against which the person being spoken with had no defense.

There are six basic elements of a double bind:

1. Two or more persons in a significant relationship, such as parent(s) and child.
2. Repeated experiences.
3. A primary negative injunction, such as, "Don't do X or I will punish you."
4. A second injunction, at a more abstract level, conflicting with the first, enforced by a punishment or perceived threat: "Do X."
5. A third negative injunction prohibiting escape and demanding a response. Without this restriction, the recipient would not feel bound. "You'll be punished if you don't do the first X."
6. Over time the complete set of ingredients is no longer necessary, once the recipient is conditioned to perceive the world in terms of double binds; any part of the sequence becomes sufficient to trigger confusion, panic, or rage (Bateson et al., 1956).

Bateson and the Palo Alto group's 1956 paper on the double bind proved to be one of the most influential and controversial in the history of family therapy. It challenged the orthodox assumption that schizophrenia was a biological disease. The observation that schizophrenic behavior seemed to develop in some families didn't mean that families cause schizophrenia (Bateson et al., 1956). Rather it pointed out the effects of **recursive patterns of interaction** over time on family members. These ideas launched the use of **conjoint family sessions** with hospitalized patients and their families. This process meant that families were included *with* the identified patient in therapy sessions.

The Bateson group recognized and stressed the centrality of communication to the organization of families.

People Cannot *Not* Communicate   Communication theorists assert that people are always communicating. All behavior is a form of communication. People cannot not behave, nor can they not communicate. Everything one does, whether outgoing or retiring, sends a message (Watzlawick, Beavin, & Jackson, 1967). All messages have two functions: report (content) and command (process) (Bateson, 1951). The report (content) of a message conveys information. This is what the words say. The command (process) is a statement about the relationship. Command (process) refers to how the words are said, the context, the tone and body language, and how the message is received. The how of sending and receiving reflects the relationship between speaker and receiver.

Watzlawick and Communication and Context

Paul Watzlawick was born in Vienna, Austria. He earned a Ph.D. in philosophy and modern languages from the University of Venice, Italy, in 1949. He studied at the Jung Institute in Zurich, Switzerland, for 10 years, and trained analysts in Zurich. He later became a professor of psychotherapy at the University of El Salvador and a research associate at Temple University Medical Center, in Philadelphia, Pennsylvania. Growing dissatisfied with the results of psychotherapy, he joined the Mental Research Institute at Palo Alto in 1960 and became involved in Bateson's research.

Watzlawick's theory of communications is that a phenomenon cannot be understood completely without the examination of the context in which it occurs and in which it is **embedded.** Thus relationships, as created and developed through communication, were seen as the appropriate focus of study (Watzlawick et al., 1967). He was primarily concerned with pragmatics—the behavioral effects of communication. Watzlawick defined the goal of therapy as problem resolution. Problems were viewed as situational, arising from difficulties in interaction. Resolving problems involved altering the client's perception of reality by changing the language employed to communicate about the problem. The language of change was described as the function of the right hemisphere of the brain (emotions). Watzlawick suggested it was the therapist's task to gain access to the right hemisphere through the use of homonyms, synonyms, ambiguities, and puns, which block the brain's logical left hemisphere. (The process is similar to the confusion technique of hypnotherapist Milton Erickson, who is covered later in this chapter. There was an active intermingling of ideas between members of the Palo Alto group and Erickson.)

Watzlawick described the *type* of relationship between participants as a primary factor affecting how people respond to the command part of communication. For example, a therapist may respond sympathetically to a wife crying about a child's behavior, whereas her husband, having heard it all before, may respond with irritation at what he sees as self-pity. The therapist and the husband heard the same content/report—the wife's sadness about the child's behaviors. Yet each had a different reaction because each experienced a different relationship with her. Those relationships generated different perceptions and responses to the metacommunication (the implied command).

Jackson and Family Rules

Don Jackson was one of the earliest researchers in the area of communication theory. He joined Bateson's research team in 1954 as a psychiatric consultant. In 1956, he was coauthor, with Bateson, Jackson, Haley, and Weakland, of the landmark article "Toward a Theory of Schizophrenia." In 1959, he founded the Mental Research Institute (MRI) and invited Virginia Satir to join the group. (Chapter 6 covers her work.)

Jackson's major contributions in the field dealt with the organization of human interactions. He wrote that in families, command messages are patterned as rules of interaction that can be observed over time, as the **redundancies** of the interactions. Jackson used the term *family rules* as a description of the regularity of patterned interactions (Jackson, 1965). Most rules are unspoken and family members are often unaware of them. These rules, or regular patterns, serve to maintain an acceptable behavioral balance within the family. He described them as homeostatic mechanisms serving to resist change or disruption in the family unit. He said homeostasis described the conservative aspect of family systems and was similar to the general systems theory concept of negative feedback, or maintaining the status quo.

Complementary and Symmetrical Relationships   Relationships between people were also described as being either complementary or symmetrical. **Complementary relationships** are built on differences that fit together. Think of couples where one is more submissive and the other more assertive. These roles mutually reinforce and sustain one another. One does not cause the other. Each role supports the complementary relationship. As long as both parties in a complementary relationship are comfortable with their arrangement, they mutually behave in ways that reinforce the maintenance of their complementary pattern (negative feedback) and maintain the status quo.

Symmetrical relationships are based on equality of roles. The behavior of one mirrors that of the other. An example of a symmetrical relationship between husband and wife is one in which both are free to pursue individual careers and share equally in housekeeping and child rearing. There is no reason to assume that such a relationship would be more or less stable than a complementary one. As long as both parties are comfortable with their recursive symmetrical interactive patterns, they mutually reinforce those patterns (negative feedback) and maintain the status quo.

In either type of relationship, complementary or symmetrical, if one party changes his or her usual pattern, and the interactions between them are unable to draw them back into their expected roles, changes escalate. That escalation perturbs the system (positive feedback) and new patterns emerge, redefining their relationship. The perturbation, or deviation from the usual pattern, could occur as a result of new information, life-cycle transitions, health changes, and societal and job demands. Pattern changes could evolve into a more satisfying, healthier relationship, or could be a catalyst for dissolution of the relationship. Changes in roles and patterns can be reinforcing or destructive of the existing relationships.

For example, Mom and Dad for many years have maintained the family balance by supporting each other's parenting. Dad was hardly ever home and deferred to Mom most of the time. However, when Dad loses his job, he stays home. He begins to notice what the children are doing and unilaterally adds additional restriction to daughter's curfew. Mother now sides with daughter. She feels Dad is stepping on her turf and doesn't like how he's doing it. She is also feeling anxious that her husband is out of work and is upset with and for him. The daughter rebels at Dad's new input and restrictions. Her behavior, and Dad's situation, pushes the parents into a crisis (positive feedback). They blame each other for what is happening. Threats of separation add to their stress. They could end up dissolving the family or they could learn to change their patterns of interaction and work together to reestablish some family stability. They need to work on reinterpreting their roles and their relationship as a couple and as parents, and mutually define age-appropriate rules for the family.

The behaviors that communication theorists observe are the patterns of communication linked together in sequential chains. When the response to one family member's problematic behavior pushes the limits of the usual interactional pattern (positive feedback), it disrupts the status quo. The therapist's task is to focus on the repetitive patterned interactions (negative feedback loops) that perpetuate the problem. By altering those patterned interactions, the therapist can help the client family change the way they relate with one another, and establish more satisfying relationships (Jackson, 1965).

Weakland and Brief Family Therapy

When John Weakland came to Palo Alto in 1953, he had degrees in chemistry and chemical engineering. He began his career as an industrial researcher and plant designer. He was interested in sociology, anthropology, Chinese culture, family personality, and political behavior. Bateson had been Weakland's professor of anthropology during his graduate studies at the New School for Social Research in New York.

As a member of Bateson's group, Weakland studied hypnosis and therapeutic practice with Milton Erickson. He worked with Don Jackson to study psychotic behavior and family therapy. He was codirector of the schizophrenic research project and used that learning in his part-time private practice in brief family therapy. Weakland taught at several universities. At the time of this writing, he was working as a clinical anthropologist and family therapist at MRI, as an associate director of the Brief Therapy Center, and as advisory editor for the journals *Family Process* and *Family System Medicine* (Nichols & Schwartz, 1998).

Along with the Bateson group, Weakland initially focused on communication among family members where one family member was exhibiting schizophrenic behaviors. Families were seen as a particular culture and Weakland's goal was to describe both the normal and abnormal behavior patterns within this culture. Even though therapy with these families had not been part of the original plan, an interest in helping to alleviate pain and solve problems gradually developed among his research team members. The outcome was the concept of **brief therapy.**

In the brief therapy model, *only* the issues defined as problems by the family are the focus for change. Problems had to be specified in clear behavioral terms, along with the desired outcomes of therapy. A maximum of 10 sessions were allocated for the therapy, and family progress was evaluated during a follow-up session several months after termination (Weakland, Fisch, Watzlawick, & Bodin, 1974).

Satir and Rule-Governed Systems

The only woman in the original Bateson group was Virginia Satir. She was also the only social worker. When Don Jackson invited her to join MRI, Satir had been doing family therapy for several years and had taught family dynamics in Chicago. She had also met with Murray Bowen in Washington, DC.

Satir presented the results of her work to the Bateson group at the Veterans Administration Hospital in Palo Alto. She began what was probably the first training program in family therapy shortly after MRI opened its doors. Her fundamental strength was her unique ability to really get to know the families of both her students and clients. In 1964, she published *Conjoint Family Therapy* (1967), one of the first major books in the field. The same year, she became director of the residential program at Esalen Growth Center in Big Sur, California. This experience led her to a more holistic approach to therapy. Her model, though based in communications, was also experiential in nature and incorporated many holistic ideas she learned at Esalen.

Satir's model for therapy was that "the therapist and family join forces to promote wellness" (Satir, 1972, p. 12). She believed that families are rule-governed systems, which through the basic components of communication and self-esteem provide the context for growth and development. (Since the purpose of this chapter is to introduce the diverse origins of family therapy, specific therapeutic processes espoused and practiced by Satir will be saved for Chapter 6, on experiential family theory and therapy.)

Erickson and Hypnosis

The writings of Milton Erickson offer the authoritative word on techniques of inducing trance, experimental work exploring the possibilities and limits of the hypnotic experience, and investigations of the nature of the relationship between hypnotist and subject (Haley, 1967). Erickson developed a major innovation in therapeutic technique that may or may not involve the *formal* induction of trance.

Erickson was the founding president of the American Society for Clinical Hypnosis, as well as the founder and editor of that society's professional journal. His interest in hypnosis began when he was an undergraduate student in psychology at the University of Wisconsin. After receiving his medical degree at the Colorado General Hospital, he trained at the Colorado Psychopathic Hospital and then accepted a position of junior psychiatrist at Rhode Island State Hospital. He subsequently served as psychiatrist, researcher, and instructor at a number of academic facilities.

When training psychiatrists as well as medical students, Erickson put great emphasis on developing skills of patient observation. His own extraordinary powers of observation are legendary. He has said that his physical limitations improved his powers of observation. He had a polio attack when he was 17 years old and reported he could not even tell the position of his arms or legs. He spent hours trying to locate his hand or foot and became acutely aware of whatever small movements there were. In medical school, he learned the nature of muscles, and used that knowledge to develop an adequate use of the muscles polio had left him and learned to limp with the least possible strain.

Erickson's struggle with polio made him extremely aware of physical movements. He was able to apply his experiences to his work with clients. He observed that much of our communication is in our bodily movements, not in our speech (Haley, 1967).

He described therapy as a way of helping patients extend their limits, a process he had done in his own life.

In the mid-1950s, Erickson settled in Phoenix, mainly for health reasons, and set up a private office in his home. His living room was the waiting room. Patients were exposed over the years to his family life and his eight children. His office was small and simply furnished, its sparseness relieved by family mementos scattered about the room. The office walls and most of his clothing were purple, the only color he could visualize through his color-blind eyes.

Along with Clark Hull, an American behaviorist, Erickson developed a pioneering experimental approach of hypnosis and suggestibility. Instead of using progressive relaxation and direct suggestion, which was the way hypnosis had been done for at least the prior 100 years, Erickson demonstrated a style which eventually came to be known as **utilization** and **indirect suggestion**. He began studying the effects of communication and hypnosis as a child and taught his approach throughout his graduate school years. His work was subject to professional criticism because he had not automatically incorporated the psychiatric beliefs of his time—insight and noninvolvement of the therapist. He supported and promoted brief therapy, family therapy, use of hypnosis with amnesia, use of active and paradoxical interventions by the therapist, encouragement rather than confrontation, and analyzing resistance from the client (Erickson & Rossi, 1981, p. 74).

Erickson offered no theory of personality, but rather a theory of intervention. There are several features that typify an Ericksonian approach:

1. indirection—the use of indirect suggestion, binds, metaphors, and resource retrieval
2. conscious/unconscious dissociation—multiple level communication, interspersal, double binds, multiple embedded metaphors
3. utilization of the client's behavior—paradox, behavioral matching, naturalistic induction, symptom prescription, and strategic use of trance phenomena. "Whatever the patient presents to you in the office, you really ought to use" (Erickson in Erickson & Rossi, 1981, p.16).

Erickson kept in his mind the idea that individuals know more than they think they know. Change is a matter of initiating new and creative responses to their environment. He was willing to be flexible with people so they could find their personal and unique adjustments to their situations (Lankton & Lankton, 1983, p. 10).

Lankton and Lankton (1983) outlined 11 treatment principles focused on establishing an attitude toward the client and the process of change using the types of treatment interventions typical of an Ericksonian approach:

1. People operate out of their internal maps and not out of sensory experience.
2. People make the best choice for themselves at any given moment.
3. The explanation, theory, or metaphor used to relate facts about a person is not the person.
4. Respect all messages from the client.
5. Teach choice; never attempt to take choice away.
6. The resources the client needs lie within his or her own personal history.
7. Meet the client at his or her model of the world.
8. The person with the most flexibility or choice will be the controlling element in the system.
9. A person can't not communicate.
10. If it's hard work, reduce it down.
11. Outcomes are determined at the psychological level. (p. 12)

Each of these principles deserves a chapter of its own. However, in the context of this textbook, they are offered in an outline for interested students who choose to study Milton Erickson's work in more detail. Since Erickson has written over 150 published works, and many others have written about him and his work, it will not be difficult to find resources to fulfill the most ardent disciple's curiosity.

Another important facet of psychological level communications is related to understanding how metaphor and indirect suggestion facilitate therapeutic changes in the client's experience. This use of metaphor and indirect suggestion is accomplished without the client's being consciously able to explain the problem in the therapist's terms or to say exactly what happened. Erickson said that hypnosis per se doesn't affect a cure, but that cure is accomplished by a re-association of the client's experiential life (Erickson & Rossi, 1981, p. 38).

The Ericksonian approach uses metaphor and indirect suggestion to gain rapport, retrieve resources, and link those resources to previous stress signals or typical stimuli in the client's environment. When the client encounters a situation that had previously been difficult, "something" clicks; a new idea, feeling or behavior comes to mind, rendering the situation less threatening or even enjoyable. The conscious mind is then free to examine and concentrate on more enjoyable, adaptive, and appropriate experiences (Lankton & Lankton, 1983, pp. 26, 27).

Erickson's intention was consistently geared toward helping individuals locate and use the various psychological experiences within themselves to live in the world successfully, creatively, and enjoyably. He saw the professional's role as that of a catalyst, an informed expert who actively helped point the way to strategic uses of inner resources. His work was about shared growth and a love for humanity. He placed his highest value on the development of the individual and conceived of an individual as someone who was always in relationship to others (Lankton & Lankton, 1983, pp. 351, 352). Erickson enjoyed ongoing interactions with many of the researchers and clinicians in the Palo Alto Group and MRI.

Lewin and Group Dynamics

The principles of group dynamics are highly relevant to family theory. Although there is a major difference between interactions with a group of strangers with no history and the interactions that go on over a lifetime in families, group researcher Kurt Lewin offered some important ideas that could be generalized to families. He saw a group as more than the sum of its parts and noted that group discussions were more effective than lectures in changing behaviors and ideas. He also noted that group members seemed to stabilize maladaptive patterns of behavior (negative feedback, homeostasis) and that changes in group behaviors were brought about only after a disruption of the group's accepted habits and beliefs (positive feedback) (Lewin, 1951). These ideas laid the foundation for treatment approaches for many different forms of family therapy. Group studies were adapted by family theorists who came to understand that it was not *what* the group members said (content/report) but *how* they said it (process/command) in the perceived relationship (context) that both created and alleviated emotional distress. Adapting these ideas to families, therapists were able to disrupt symptom-inducing patterns of interaction between family members and change the way family members related with one another. They observed that when successful, these changes in interaction alleviated the presenting patient's symptoms and made room for each family member to individuate in an age-appropriate way.

Lidz, Role Reciprocity, and Mutual Patterns of Interaction

As early as 1941, while completing his residency at Johns Hopkins, Theodore Lidz, a graduate of Columbia Medical School, focused his work on the roles family members fulfill and the effects of faulty parental models on children. One of his findings that differed from most other researchers who had focused mostly on the mother/child relationship was his attention to paternal influences. Fathers who were ineffectual or uninvolved were frequently as disabling of healthy development in their children as were overbearing mothers (Lidz, Parker, & Cornelison, 1956).

Lidz also looked at the defects in the marital relationships he studied. He suggested the underlying difficulty for these couples was a lack of **role reciprocity**. He concluded that for a successful marriage it was necessary *first* to fill one's own role and then to support the role of the spouse. Lidz emphasized he was not proposing simple and direct causal links between parental pathology and schizophrenic symptoms in children. He asserted, however, that the **mutual patterns of interaction** he observed within families were powerful components in the development of schizophrenic symptoms (Lidz, Cornelison, & Terry, 1957).

Adler, Ackerman, and the Child Guidance Movement

Child guidance clinics were established on the premise that psychological problems began in childhood and early intervention was the best way to prevent the future occurrence of mental illness. It had become apparent that treating the child separately did not make the family's problems go away. Child guidance workers determined that a child's symptoms were usually a function of emotional distress in the family.

Alfred Adler   Alfred Adler was a psychiatrist who began his career as a disciple, then critic, of Freud. He received his medical degree from the University of Vienna Medical School in 1895.

Adler developed a flexible, supportive psychotherapy to direct those emotionally disabled by inferiority feelings toward maturity, common sense, and social usefulness. His strong awareness of social problems was the principal motivation in his work. He stressed consideration of the patient in relation to his total environment.

Adler and a group of followers severed ties with Freud's circle in 1911 and began developing what they called individual psychology. It described the individual in context with social motivations. Adler suggested that the overriding motivation in most people is striving for self-realization, completeness, or perfection. This striving may be frustrated by feelings of inferiority, inadequacy, or incompleteness arising from physical defects, low social status, pampering or neglect during childhood, or other causes encountered in the natural course of life. The individual's lifestyle forms in early childhood and is partly determined by what particular inferiority affected him or her most deeply during those formative years.

Adler contended that the striving for superiority coexists with another innate urge to cooperate and work with other people for the common good. He called this drive social interest. He described mental health as being able to reason and to have social interest and concern for others.

In 1921, Adler established the first child guidance clinic in Vienna and rapidly established 30 more, all under his direction. In 1934, the government in Austria closed his clinics as it began its ouster of Jewish professionals. In the United States, Adler became visiting professor at Columbia University in 1927 and visiting professor of Long Island College of Medicine in New York in 1932 (from the Internet source <http://ourworld.compuserve.com /homepages/hstein/adler.htm>).

Alfred Adler was the first of Freud's followers to pursue the idea that treating the growing child might be the most effective way to prevent adult neuroses. In his child guidance clinics in Vienna, not only children, but also families and teachers were counseled. Adler's approach was to offer encouragement and support in an atmosphere of optimism and confidence. His technique was designed to alleviate children's feelings of inferiority so they could work out a healthy lifestyle, achieving competence and success through social usefulness (Nichols & Schwartz, 1998). The child guidance clinics initially focused on the mother/child relationship. Originally, the process was that the child and his or her mother were seen separately. More often than not, the psychiatrist saw the child, and the mother was seen by a social worker who offered information, psychoeducation about parenting behaviors. Adlerian theory promulgated a therapy based on **natural and rational consequences of behavior.** A number of psychoeducational parenting programs have evolved from his teachings, such as the STEP program (Systematic Training for Effective Parenting), developed by the late Don Dinkmeyer, an Adlerian psychologist and author. Adlerian psychotherapy, as it is practiced today, tends to incorporate behavioral tasks and stay focused on here-and-now issues. Parents are taught how to reward desired behaviors, to explain natural consequences, and to plan rational consequences for inappropriate behaviors in their children.

Nathan Ackerman Nathan Ackerman was a psychoanalytically trained child psychiatrist. After completing his psychiatric residency, Ackerman joined the staff at the Menninger Clinic in Topeka, Kansas. In 1937, he became chief psychiatrist of the Child Guidance Clinic. At first, he followed Adler's child guidance model of having a psychiatrist treat the child and a social worker see the mother. But by the mid 1940s he began to experiment with having the same therapist see both. He later reevaluated the whole concept of psychopathology and began to see the whole family as the basic unit for diagnosis and treatment.

In 1955, Ackerman organized and led the first session on family diagnosis at a meeting of the American Orthopsychiatric Association. There, Jackson, Bowen, Wynne, and Ackerman learned about each other's work and began to share their ideas. Ackerman published a number of books and articles. Some consider his article "Family Diagnosis: An Approach to the Preschool Child" (Ackerman & Sobel, 1950) as the beginning of the family therapy movement (Kaslow, 1980). In 1957, Ackerman opened the Family Mental Health Clinic of Jewish Family Services in New York and began teaching at Columbia University. In 1960, he founded the Family Institute, which was renamed the Ackerman Institute following his death in 1971.

Ackerman said that just as an individual expresses the conflicts of id, ego, and superego as dynamic parts of evolving personalities, family members are dynamic parts of the whole family system, expressing their roles through **coalitions** within the family. These coalitions could be made up of mother and child or father and child across generational boundaries, or of one generation against another. While other family therapists downplayed the psychology of individuals, Ackerman was always concerned with what goes on inside of people as well as between them. Ackerman talked about how families confront some issues while avoiding and denying others, especially those involving sex and aggression. He believed his role as a therapist was to stir things up and to bring family secrets into the open.

In a case he described in the book *Treating the Troubled Family* (1966), Ackerman's playful yet prodding interventions were clearly illustrated:

> A family of four came for treatment after the fighting between the 11-year-old daughter and 16-year-old son exploded beyond acceptable boundaries. The girl had recently threatened her brother with a butcher knife. As he sat down in Ackerman's office, the father sighed. Ackerman asked him why he was sighing and refused to be put off by the father's excuse that he was tired, suggesting that perhaps he had another reason to sigh. The mother broke in to announce she'd been keeping a journal of everyone's misdeeds during the week. Her stridency perfectly complemented her husband's mild-mannered evasiveness. Ackerman's bemused response was, "You come armed with a notebook. Fire away!"
>
> As the mother began to read out her bill of particulars, Ackerman, who sensed this was just business as usual, commented on the father's nonverbal (metacommunication) behavior. "You're picking your fingers." This triggered a discussion about who does what, which the mother gradually took over and turned into an indictment of the father's many nervous habits. At this point the son broke in, and pointing to his mother, said, "She belches!" (protecting Dad). The mother acknowledged this little embarrassment, and tried to change the subject. But Ackerman wasn't about to let her off the hook.
>
> It turned out the mother's belching occurred mostly when she was lying down. The father said he was upset by her belching in his face. They were quickly interrupted by the children, who started bickering. (Notice the patterns of the transactions. The children rescued the parents when Ackerman came too close.) Ackerman said, "Isn't it interesting that this interruption occurs just as you two are about to talk about your love life?" The father then described how he felt when he wanted to kiss his wife and she belched in his face. "You need a gas mask," he said. The daughter tried to interrupt, but Ackerman asked her to move her seat (she had been sitting between them) so that her parents could sit next to one another and talk.
>
> A few minutes later Ackerman asked the children to leave the session. Alone with the parents, he "reopened the door" to the parents' bedroom. At first the couple played out their familiar pattern: She complained. He withdrew. Specifically the wife complained her husband wasn't romantic and she was the one who had to take care of birth control by using a diaphragm. Meanwhile the husband retreated into meek silence. They were a perfectly matched complementary pair: She was up, he was down. Ackerman unbalanced them, playfully teasing the wife and provoking the husband to stand up for himself. It's worth noting that the wife didn't seem to feel criticized or put down by Ackerman. Nor did the husband seem to get the idea that Ackerman was trying to elevate him over his wife. Rather, by the end of the session, this grim, angry couple was beginning to laugh and appreciate one another. They acknowledged they had drifted apart and had allowed the children to distract them. This is a fine example of early efforts to **reorganize the structure** of families. (pp. 48, 49)*

---

*From *Treating the Troubled Family*, by N. W. Ackerman. Copyright © 1966 by Basic Books, Inc. Reprinted by permission of Basic Books, a member of Perseus Books, L.L.C.

Ackerman came to recommend that everyone living under the same roof be present in family interviews. He encouraged open and honest expression of feelings. He pointed out that each person's identity has various aspects: as an individual, a member of various **family subsystems,** and as a member of the family as a whole. He was alert to the coalitions revealed through the way family members interacted in the interviews. He noticed how people arranged themselves when they entered the consulting room, who sat next to whom. Ackerman noted that once family members started talking among themselves, it was easier to see how they were emotionally divided and what problems and prohibitions were present. He also paid close attention to non-verbal cues, because he believed that disguised feeling were conveyed in body language far more eloquently than in words.

In order to promote honest emotional interchanges, Ackerman "tickled the defenses" of family members, his phrase for provoking people to open up and say what was really on their minds. The playfulness of this phrase nicely reflects Ackerman's style. Ackerman did not hesitate to confront, provoke, challenge, or even argue with family members. He believed it was more therapeutic for the therapist to become a target of anger and hostility rather than to allow those emotions to explode onto other family members.

Ackerman said that interpersonal conflicts promote intrapsychic conflict and vice versa (Ackerman, 1961). To reverse symptomatic disturbances, the therapist must bring conflicts into the open within the family so new solutions can be found. As long as conflicts remain locked within the individual, Ackerman believed psychopathology remained fixed and relatively unchangeable. He was describing a *both/and* idea that integrated individual and family therapy (Ackerman, 1961).

Wynne and Family Dynamics

In the mid-1950s, Lyman Wynne, a psychiatrist from Harvard, began to study family dynamics. Wynne looked at the effects of communication and family roles. He visited Tavistock Clinic in London as a traveling fellow. There he developed a group therapy approach to family therapy. Wynne's study of families who had members that exhibited schizophrenic symptoms began in 1954, when he started seeing parents of his hospitalized patients in twice-weekly psychotherapy. He continued that practice over three decades. He addressed their observable chaos from the point of view of psychoanalytic concepts and role theory set in the framework of systems theory. He developed the concepts of **pseudomutuality, rubber fence,** and **pseudohostility.**

Pseudomutuality describes a facade the family develops that gives the impression that members have good relationships. It masks conflicts as well as affectionate and sexual feelings, has little tolerance for differences, and thereby limits any real intimacy.

Rubber fence describes a mechanism used by the family to quell any sign of separateness, either inside or outside the family. A family with a member who has schizophrenic behaviors often lives behind a rubber fence and becomes a complete and isolated society within itself, with a rigid boundary and no openings.

Pseudohostility describes collusion among family members to avoid the acknowledgment of problems with an individual within the family. Wynne believed families could be explained in terms of **alignments and splits.** An example he gave of his understanding of alignment was of an alliance between one parent and the child that resulted in a split between the parents.

Wynne theorized that the mental chaos of schizophrenic symptoms is in part derived from having internalized chaotic family structures. He saw confusing communications as the vehicle for transmitting thought disorder. He explained that **communication deviance** is a more interactional concept than thought disorder, an individual psychology term, and more readily observable than double binds. One of the most important observations, transferable to the diversity of the family theories, was Wynne's observation that communication deviance is not confined solely to families where a members exhibits schizophrenic behaviors, but rather degrees of deviance exist on a continuum—the greater the deviance, the more severe the pathology (Wynne, Ryckoff, Day, & Hirsch, 1958).

FOUNDING PRINCIPLES

The sum is greater than its parts: The human family is composed of individuals living together over time, with a shared history. The family unit has a personality of its own, representing the sum of all its members acting together. Students may want to consider their own family—how even though each of them, their parents, grandparents, siblings, and children are individually unique, collectively they are identified as being part of a family.

A family system consists of family members (who is included as a family member may need to be reexamined) interacting in circular, recursive, and mutually reinforcing patterns of communication. When something changes, such as the loss of a job, a baby being born, a child going off to college, or illness, divorce, or death, family members attempt to maintain stability by acting in familiar ways. People have a natural resistance to changing the ways they behave with one another. If the stress is greater than the resistance, families make changes.

Repetitive, recursive patterns of behavior are maintained by negative feedback. They are altered when perturbed, that is, pushed beyond their usual pattern limits (positive feedback). Positive feedback can lead to healthy change, or it can create chaos.

Communications theorists speak of levels of communications to describe their understanding of metacommunications: The words are the content, which is one level. Body language and context add meaning to the words, which is another level. The relationship of the people communicating is the context. But considering all levels together and paying attention to how people metacommunicate, the therapist gains a more complete picture of the impact of interactions between family members.

Family relationships are reciprocal, mutually reinforcing. Family rules, the accepted behaviors expected by members of the family, evolve, often unspoken, through these reciprocal, mutually reinforcing behaviors. As long as nothing happens to change the way members interact, the status quo (homeostasis) is maintained. When events stress those patterns, or perturb those rules (positive feedback), change occurs in healthy or unhealthy ways.

Some family theorists define families as healthy when all participants are interacting in ways that are flexible, reflect appropriate family life-cycle transitions, and respect the hierarchy within the family. Families are seen as unhealthy when they are rigid and not responsive to life-cycle development, when they blur hierarchal boundaries (cross-generational coalitions), or lock people into roles (perhaps from double bind patterns) that are stress inducing and symptom producing for them.

SUMMARY

The 1950s were a seminal time for systemic ideas. For therapists, systemic thinking opened exciting new possibilities for the treatment and relief of psychological symptoms. Researchers approached these systemic concepts from a vast diversity of disciplines whose studies emerged into a new discipline, family systems theory. This field is constantly evolving through new ideas offered by the latest crop of theorists and therapists.

The way a family functions, establishes roles, and communicates and responds to transitional changes, both internal and external, has implications for the development and well-being of individual family members. In general, the family therapist's task is to help families recognize that what they have been doing, their repetitive behavioral interactions, is not working, and to coach family members to be open to more options, more ways to successfully handle family life-cycle transitions that stress their system.

This chapter was intended to offer the foundations and theories underlying the development of family theory and therapy. In the next chapters, we will cover how these ideas were organized by specific theorists and explore their unique theories and treatment plans. Students should imagine themselves as therapists working with each of the different treatment designs and notice which system feels most comfortable, appropriate, and workable. Each person must first identify the framework he or she is most comfortable working within, in order to convey confidence to the clients, so that the framework can be helpful to them.

EXPERIENTIAL ACTIVITIES

1. In class, instructors will organize small groups to create examples of how terms, such as "mutual reinforcement of behaviors," explain family interactions. One group may discuss and then demonstrate how the interactions within the task group reinforce the behaviors of all of them. Another group may observe those interactions and discuss their observations.

2. One small group could use a sports event to describe the "redundancies" or "circular patterns of interactions" in play. For example, think of a baseball game and the repetitive patterns of interaction that keep the game going.

3. One small group could act out the effect of negative and positive feedback in a family role play. For instance, a family group could be chosen and a particular issue described for the family to deal with. Family members may decide on roles without telling the others what role they are playing in connection with the issue. At some point one member of the family will change his or her interactions enough to put the family off balance, and to provide new behaviors. After this role play goes on for about 10 to 15 minutes, ask the group members to reflect on and discuss the experience.

4. Set up a parent-education discussion group. Make a list of appropriate and inappropriate behaviors for school-age children. Ask participants to demonstrate rewards, and natural and rational consequences for specific child behaviors.

5. Some ideas for class discussion:
   - The diverse backgrounds of the early theorists and how students think they were able to build on each other's ideas.
   - Understanding double binds. Ask class to offer family examples.
   - Why were the early family systems ideas seen as controversial?
   - What do students think of what they have read so far?

REFERENCES

Ackerman, N. W. (1961). A dynamic frame for the clinical approach to family conflict. In N.W. Ackerman, F. L. Beatman, & S. N. Sherman (Eds.), *Exploring the base for family therapy.* New York: Family Services Association of America.

Ackerman, N. W. (1966). *Treating the troubled family.* New York: Basic Books

Ackerman, N. W. & Sobel, R. (1950). Family diagnosis: An approach to the preschool child. *American Journal of Orthopsychiatry, 20,* 744–753

Ackerman, N. W., Beatman, F., & Sherman, S. N. (Eds.), (1961). *Exploring the base for family therapy.* New York: Family Service Assocation of America.

Bateson, G. (1951). Information and codifications: A philosophical approach. In J. Ruesch & G. Bateson (Eds.), *Communication: The social matrix of psychiatry.* New York: Norton.

Bateson, G. (1972). *Steps to ecology of mind.* New York: Ballantine.

Bateson, G., Jackson, D. D., Haley, J., & Weakland, J. (1956). Toward a theory of schizophrenia. *Behavioral Sciences, 1,* 251–264.

Becvar, R. J., & Becvar, D. S. (1982). Systems theory and family therapy: A primer. Washington, DC: University Press of America.

Bertalanffy, L. von (1968). *General system theory: Foundation, applications.* New York: Braziller.

Biographical Sketch of Alfred Adler—Alfred Adler Institute of San Francisco, 2002.

Davidson, M. (1983). *Uncommon sense: The life and thought of Ludwig von Bertalanffy.* Los Angeles: JP Tarcher.

Erickson, M. & Rossi, E. (1981). Experiencing hypnosis: Therapeutic approaches to altered states. (pp. 38, 71–90). New York: Irvington.

Goldenberg, I., & Goldenberg, H. (1980). *Family therapy: An overview* (5th ed.). Pacific Grove, CA: Brooks/Cole.

Haley, J. (1967). Milton H. Erickson, M.D. in *Advanced techniques of hypnosis and therapy: Selected papers of Milton Erickson, M. D.* (pp. 1–6). New York: Grune & Stratton.

Haley, J. (1971). Family therapy: A radical change. In J. Haley (Ed.), *Changing families: A family therapy reader.* New York: Grune & Stratton.

Jackson, D. D. (1965). Family rules: Marital quid pro quo. *Archives of General Psychiatry, 12,* 589–594.

Kaslow, F. W. (1980). History of family therapy in the United States: A kaleidoscopic overview. *Marriage and Family Review, 3,* 77–111.

Kerr, M. E., & Bowen, M. (1988). *Family evaluation: An approach based on Bowen theory.* New York: Norton.

Lankton, S. R., & Lankton, C. H. (1983). *The answer within: A clinical framework of Ericksonian hypnotherapy.* New York: Brunner/Mazel.

Lewin, K. (1951). *Field theory in social science.* New York: Harper.

Lidz, T., Cornelison, A., & Terry, D. (1957). Intrafamilial environment of the schizophrenic patient. II: Marital schism and marital skew. *American Journal of Psychiatry, 114,* 241–248.

Lidz, T., Parker, B., & Cornelison, A. R. (1956). The role of the father in the family environment of the schizophrenic patient. *American Journal of Psychiatry, 113,* 126–132.

Nichols, M. P., & Schwartz, R. C. (1998). *Family therapy: Concepts and methods* (4th ed.). Boston: Allyn & Bacon.

Richmond, M. E. (1917). *Social diagnosis.* New York: Russell Sage.

Sagan, C. (1980). *Cosmos.* New York: Random House.

Satir, V. (1972). *Peoplemaking.* Palo Alto, CA: Science and Behavior Books.

Satir, V. (1967). *Conjoint family therapy.* Palo Alto, CA: Science and Behavior Books.

Watzlawick, P., Weakland, J., & Fisch, R. (1974). *Change: Principles of problem resolution.* New York: Norton.

Watzlawick, P. A., Beavin, J. H., & Jackson, D. D. (1967). *Pragmatics of human communication.* New York: Norton.

Weakland, J. H., Fisch, R., Watzlawick, P., & Bodin, A. M. (1974). Brief therapy: Focused problem resolution. *Family Process, 13,* 141–167.

Wiener, N. (1948). *Cybernetics: Or control and communication in the animal and the machine.* New York: Wiley.

Wynne, L. C., Ryckoff, I., Day, J., & Hirsch, S. I. (1958). Pseudomutuality: In The family relationships of schizophrenics. *Psychiatry, 21,* 205–220.

4 CHAPTER ELEMENTS OF THE PROCESS OF CHANGE

TERMS TO KNOW

survival myth	regression	task assignments
ambivalence	framework for	
bounce theory	freedom	

WHY CHANGE?

This brief chapter offers background information for understanding the process of change. It is applicable for most of the theories that follow. Postmodern theorists (see Chapter 10) may have differences with these ideas since so much of their work is based on the social and linguistic creation of reality.

For the most part, families and individuals seek psychotherapy because they feel stuck. They have probably been dealing with their presenting problem for a long time. Most often people try the same solutions over and over despite the fact that those solutions have not helped. In fact, they have probably only helped to solidify the original problem in a repeated pattern of problem: solution attempt, frustration, then despair. By the time patients seek therapy, they have often lost confidence in themselves and are confused about what they can do, if anything, to make things better.

To make changes means taking risks. It means doing something different and recognizing that change is a process involving small steps, small changes over time, with the inevitable regressions as much a part of the process as goal attainments. The systemic therapist must anticipate, predict, and plan for the stages of learning in order to effectively and efficiently promote positive changes. When people take time to think about it, most people can be in touch with how difficult it is for them to change the way they do things, or to change the meanings they hold onto about things in their own lives. Yet change is something all people live with, and adjust to, every day. Just the usual events involved in growing older, of going from infancy to childhood, to adolescence, to adulthood and work, and choosing to be married and become parents, or choosing to stay single, or adopting a lifestyle different from one's family of origin, are changes and challenges in everyone's lives. Problems often arise when people refuse to adjust and adapt their lives to new life stage circumstances.

The following is an outline and brief discussion of some useful ways to think about change. The ideas are presented as an underpinning for the therapeutic process.

ELEMENTS OF CHANGE

The following ideas identify major segments in action in the process of change:

1. **Survival myth:** Change is often associated with psychological death or disaster. This motivates people to hold on to the status quo at all costs.

2. **Ambivalence:** Change is typically desired and feared simultaneously; even achieving positive change arouses anxiety about being able to maintain it.
3. **Bounce theory:** Change often occurs as an opposite extreme. The bounce is greater initially, and slowly diminishes as change is reinforced and rewarded. (Think of the swing of a pendulum.)
4. **Regression:** Change produces a natural consequence of ambivalence and bounce. This must be expected, and framed positively, not as a failure or disappointment.

Steps of a Therapy Session

Keeping the above ideas about change in mind, consider how they fit into the steps of a therapy session. These steps may differ among family therapists working within different theories, but they do provide an outline of the basic format for most family therapies.

1. Join with all family members. Build acceptance and trust. Connect with the family's style and worldview.
2. Promote a positive climate—warm, honest, supportive. Be inclusive, let the family know you are genuinely interested in them and accept them.
3. Balance structure and flexibility. Create a **framework for freedom**—a plan that is flexible within certain guidelines. Have a plan, but be responsive to the needs of the clients and their style of interaction.
4. Plan for change sequences; predict resistance, regression, and ambivalence, and reframe them as useful, purposeful, acceptable behaviors. This means letting people know that changes they make may often feel like two steps forward and one step back. Lasting change requires repetition and practice.

Integration of old and new behaviors promotes better maintenance of the changes. It's the old "Don't throw out the baby with the bath water" concept. There are often valuable parts of old behaviors, that when altered by some pattern changes or context changes, can help clients stay committed to the changes they make. It allows some familiar and comfortable behaviors to remain in the family even as the family members change the symptom producing/maintaining ways they interact.

Respecting the Client's Pace

Respecting the client's pace, which means not pushing an agenda but allowing the client to move along as he or she is able, and acknowledging those efforts, encourages the client to gain confidence in his or her ability to change without feeling pressured or that he or she is disappointing the therapist or others. Respecting the client's pace also means being nonjudgmental. Clients begin to learn that change is possible without disaster. It reduces disappointment and anger for all participants, and models positivity and hopefulness.

Task Assignments

Task assignments are directives offered by the therapist for something to be done by the clients within and between sessions. Assessment and diagnosis are ongoing, so the way the clients respond to the directives provides important information for the therapist and the family about what needs to be done next. Tasks provide practice and reinforcement of new behaviors initiated within the session. Tasks focus on repatterning new interpersonal behaviors, and they reinforce that learning. Tasks help family members learn to work together to develop new ways for resolving interpersonal conflicts. The reinforcement of practicing the new family tasks at home empowers people to try out new ways of tackling other problems that arise in the future.

The therapist develops tasks as he or she observes family interactions that lead to hypotheses about the interactional changes that need to be made. Before the end of each session, the therapist creates a task assignment with the goal of strengthening new interpersonal experiences.

PROCEDURE

1. Therapist joins with the family. Every effective therapeutic process begins by making good connections with all clients present in the session.
2. Therapist observes spontaneous and directed interactions. Notices who relates to whom, who is excluded by whom, who is respected or feared, and how that is enacted.
3. Therapist assesses transactional patterns. Develops an initial hypothesis from those observations.
4. Therapist makes explicit the unstated patterns governing the family's transactions. Describes observations of relationship patterns observed.
5. Therapist selects one area of conflict and the family members' usual pattern of dealing with it.
6. Therapist points to pain-producing characteristics of this pattern. Reframes problem in relationship terms.
7. Therapist directs the family members to continue dealing with this conflict, but suggests specific new interactions. They include changes like doing the same things they had been doing that were problem maintaining, but at a different time, or in a different place, or for a different length of time. These relatively small changes often prove to be important first steps toward interrupting old problem maintaining.
8. Changes introduced by the therapist need to be acceptable to the worldview of the client family and related to the therapeutic goals as understood by clients and therapist.
9. Therapist points out obstacles that could get in the way of following through on the task, and asks each person what might get in the way of doing this task at home. The discussion continues until all parties understand what is expected of them and how, when, and where they will do it. Therapist clarifies with each family member what each will be doing while the others are doing their tasks.

10. Therapist predicts clients may have difficulties following through, even as he or she describes the task as an opportunity for reducing the difficulties maintained by doing things their old symptom-producing ways.

In the follow-up session, the therapist asks all family members to review their experiences and what they've learned. No judgment is offered that implies good or bad, but rather the therapist emphasizes what has been learned and what the family thinks about what happened. If the family has not complied, the therapist reassesses the family's interactions and designs a different or revised task he or she believes will be more relevant for the family and will increase the probability of compliance. Most family therapists assume responsibility for the process of therapy. The client family is responsible for how they change. When the family does the task as planned, it may be appropriate to encourage continuance of the task, sometimes with some added dimensions. Not all theorists or therapists prescribe tasks in this structured way. However, since change involves recognizing patterns and doing something differently, tasks may be implied by the way the therapist asks questions.

Task assignments are a tool toward change. Therapy generally starts with small tasks that family members need to perform in their relationship patterns in order to reduce or eliminate the symptoms. Tasks are offered with warmth, sensitivity, and, where possible, playfulness by the therapist.

Never underestimate the value of appropriate humor and playfulness to take the edge off the tension felt by the family. Realize family members are there because of some perceived failure for not being able to handle their problems. Clients come in eager to talk about difficulties. Family members need to learn to lighten up and discover ways to enjoy each other, despite their difficulties. Therapists should move quickly to help them become aware of their strengths and, as much as possible, normalize their situation.

Postmodern therapists would probably not use the word "tasks" to describe their interventions. If a postmodern therapist offers an assignment it will be done tentatively, more from a "What if you tried this?" type of suggestion. In general, postmodern therapists do not diagnose problems or give direct assignments. Rather, they serve as conversational managers, asking questions that encourage the client to explore alternative meanings for their dilemmas (see Chapter 12).

Therapeutic Goals

Family therapists are active, directive, and specific in the details of their process of therapy. Some enter the therapy sessions in the role of expert, not only for the process of therapy but also for guiding the family to accept goals suggested by the therapist. Postmodern therapists make the distinction that the therapist is the expert on the *process* of therapy only. They emphasize that the client is the expert on his or her own life.

Regardless of the theoretical underpinnings, the underlying goal for therapy is to empower family members to become effective problem solvers, and to generalize what they learn in therapy, so they are able to manage their lives without the guidance of a therapist in as short a time as possible.

THE CERTAINTY OF CHANGE

If there is anything certain in family theory, it is the certainty of change, not only through new theories, but also from adaptations and mutations within existing theories. Family therapy as a discipline lives by the rules it proposes: A healthy system is one that is flexible and responsive to change.

EXPERIENTIAL ACTIVITIES

1. Instructors may want to try a simple exercise such as directing the students to cross their arms across their chests. As soon as they do this, ask them to quickly change so that they cross a different arm in front of the other. Process with group how that felt.
2. Students may meet in groups of three. Two students talk for about three to five minutes. The third student observes, then describes the patterns of interaction he or she observed, and suggests to one or both of the students to make a specific change in the way they interact. For example, the observer may suggest that if one is more outgoing, or makes good eye contact, that that person look away and wait for the other to begin the new dialogue. The pair tries the suggested changes for three minutes. Then, each group member describes to the class how they felt during this exercise.

SYSTEMIC BRANCHES

PART III

INTERGENERATIONAL AND PSYCHOANALYTICALLY BASED FAMILY THEORY AND THERAPY

CHAPTER 5

Key Theorists
Terms to Know
The Influence of the Family of Origin
Outline of Family Life-Cycle Stages
Bowen Family Systems Theory and Therapy
Bowenian Theory: Founding Principles
Ivan Boszormenyi-Nagy and Contextual Therapy
Feminist Family Therapy: An Activist Approach
Suggested Genogram Questions
Experiential Activities
References

KEY THEORISTS

Murray Bowen—differentiation of self

Ivan Boszormenyi-Nagy—relational ethics

Hare-Mustin—a pioneer in addressing gender issues

The Women's Project: Walters, Carter, Papp, and Silverstein

TERMS TO KNOW

Bowenian Terms to Know

family of origin

immediate families

family life cycle

family systems theory

Bowen family systems theory

natural systems

emotional systems

feeling systems

intellectual systems

symbiosis

differentiation of self

triangulization

family relationship system

family emotional system

continuum

scale of differentiation

pseudo-independence

triangles

nuclear family emotional system

family projection process

multigenerational transmission process

sibling position

emotional cutoff

societal emotional process

enmeshment

fusion

reactive polarities

emotional relationship system

resiliency

coach

unresolved emotional attachments

anxiety

family diagram

genogram

Contextual Theory Terms to Know

ethical obligations

accountability

trust

loyalty

ledger

entitlement/ indebtedness

relational contexts

invisible loyalties

relational ethics

legacy

revolving slate

merit

split-filial loyalty

multipersonal loyalty

creditors

debtors

intergenerational feedback system

reciprocal obligations

fusion

multidirectional partiality

invisible threads of credits, merits, debts, and loyalties

THE INFLUENCE OF THE FAMILY OF ORIGIN

This chapter highlights two specific psychoanalytically trained theorist-therapists—Murray Bowen and Ivan Boszormenyi-Nagy. Both emphasize the influence of one's **family of origin** on individual family members and both work in the here-and-now, connecting the generations to effect change. Although they both suggest it is important to look at the patterns and histories of three generations in order to understand psychological symptoms, each offers a unique approach to the resolution of those symptoms.

OUTLINE OF FAMILY LIFE-CYCLE STAGES

Before embarking on a study of intergenerational theories, it is important to look at the interactive life-cycle changes in families as members move through their individual life stages.

The structure of families continues to evolve. At one time therapists could pretty much count on predictable family life-cycle stages related to the nuclear family—a married couple with varying numbers of offspring and at least one set of grandparents was the norm. Additional transitional stages need to be mentioned and addressed as the impact of divorce, remarriage, stepchildren, and a variety of unmarried long-term relationships form families. Even the way families are described has changed—nuclear families may now be talked about as **immediate families.** Immediate families are any group of people living under one roof with a history of a relationship over time. When speaking of two people in a relationship, it is now more useful to use the term couple relationship than marital relationship. There are many ways people can form long-term relationships as a couple: a married couple, heterosexual live-ins, and same-sex live-ins.

It is still appropriate to refer to the stages of the **family life cycle.** Each transition in the family life cycle involves a process of change with specific challenges for the individuals making the changes and for their families.

Carter and McGoldrick prepared a convenient way to look at those stages. Their ideas are paraphrased in Table 5.1, with certain additions to accommodate lifestyle changes.

Carter and McGoldrick describe a family as comprised of two or more people who have "a shared history and a shared future, over three, four, or even five generations. The family group is connected by blood, legal, and/or historical ties" (Carter & McGoldrick, 1999). Looking beyond the family, they depict a more inclusive view of the issues at multiple levels of the human system: "The individual, the immediate family household(s), the extended family, the community, the cultural group and the larger society" (Carter & McGoldrick, 1999, p. 1). McGoldrick asserts that therapists without an understanding of how cultural norms and values differ from one ethnic group to the next may impose their own cultural biases on families. They may see certain behaviors and attitudes as dysfunctional, rather than as legitimately different in keeping with specific cultural traditions (McGoldrick,

TABLE 5.1 | FAMILY LIFE-CYCLE STAGES

Emotional Process in Transition	Second Order	Changes in Family Status Required for Developmental Growth
Leaving home: single, young adult	Begin accepting emotional and financial responsibility	Differentiation of self in relation to family of origin. Self-respect at work. Develop intimate peer relationships.
Join families through marriage or other couple arrangement	Commitment to new group	Realignment of relationship with extended families and friends to include spouse/partner.
Families with young children	Make space for children	Adjusting marital/couple relationships to join in child rearing and new responsibilities. Include relationships with extended family and grandparents. Must consider other relationships involved with divorce and stepchildren and be sensitive to family-of-origin issues related to adopted children, especially if from different cultures.
Families with adolescents	Expand flexibility of family boundaries to allow for teen's growing independence and awareness of grandparent's frailties	Shift parent/child relationships to permit adolescent to move into and out of family system. Refocus on midlife issues of parents. Consider concerns of care for older generation.
Launching children	Accepting various exits from and entries into family: new relationships/marriages and death of grandparents	Renegotiate marital/couple dyad. Develop adult/adult relationships with grown children. Include in-laws and dealing with loss— one's own aging process as well as disabilities and death of older generation.
Families in later life	Accept shifting generational roles	Maintain own and/or couple-functioning interests. Explore new living and social arrangements. Make room in the system for the wisdom and experience of the elderly. Help the older generation without over-functioning for them. Learning to deal with loss and awareness of mortality.

Preto, Hines, & Lee, 1990). In their book, *The Expanded Family Life Cycle*, Carter and McGoldrick (1999) describe in detail the variations of family life cycles as they are impacted by poverty, racial, ethnic, and societal influences. For instance, stages in the life cycle of family members are at times shortened and at times lengthened by some societal or cultural circumstances. In some cultures, children are protected longer and stay dependent longer. In others, they are forced to make their way in the larger world sooner. Adult responsibilities and role expectations are also influenced by family economics. The oldest family members may be counted on for familial support more in some cultures than in others. These and other environmental and situational differences in life-stage expectations and realities may become problematic for therapists unfamiliar with the norm for their client's situation. Family life cycles are especially relevant for intergenerational theorists and therapists, who explore the effects of how the client's family is currently organized, as well as how previous generations were organized.

BOWEN FAMILY SYSTEMS THEORY AND THERAPY

Bowen's development of family systems theory was at least as bold a conceptual leap as that made by Freud 60 years earlier (Kerr, 1988, p. 23). **Family systems theory,** later called **Bowen family systems theory,** is based on the assumption that human behavior is significantly regulated by the same natural processes that regulate the behavior of all other living things (Kerr & Bowen, 1988, p. 3). It assumes that Homo sapiens are far more like other life forms than different from them. Bowen family systems theory offers an understanding of human beings in the context of **natural systems.**

Bowen's theory of family systems was not based on concepts described in general systems theory. That had been based on the mathematical expressions described by Bertalanffy (1968). Rather, Bowen assumed the family was a naturally occurring system. The word *natural* refers to something that is formed by nature without human intervention. The principles that govern a natural system are written in nature and not created by the human brain. Examples include the solar system, the tides, or cell formation. He said the human family system sprang from the evolutionary process. Bowen called it an **emotional system,** shaped and molded by evolutionary processes. Although evolutionary effects have increased the complexity of the emotional system, its most fundamental characteristics have probably not changed since life first emerged on earth (Kerr & Bowen, 1988, p. 26).

Family systems theory describes two other systems in addition to the emotional system as important influences on human functioning and behavior: Feeling and intellectual systems are both fairly recent acquisitions by the evolutionary line of animals that led to Homo sapiens. The **feeling system** probably has a greater influence on the social process than the thinking, or intellectual, system. People can be aware of feelings by virtue of experiencing them. The **intellectual system** refers to that part of a human's nervous system most recently acquired in evolution. The thinking system includes the capacity to know, to reason, and to understand. Bowen made an important distinction between thinking that is not influenced by the emotional and feeling processes, and thinking that is influenced by it. It appears that the emotional system is made up of feeling and intellectual systems that mutually influence one another (Kerr & Bowen, 1988, pp. 30–33).

Bowen's interest in families began when he was a psychiatrist at the Menninger Clinic in the late 1940s. Families that had a member who exhibited schizophrenic symptoms became a primary focus of his family studies. Kerr, a long-time family systems researcher who worked with Bowen at Georgetown, suggested that families that contained *any* serious clinical problem could have been an equally profitable focus of study (Kerr & Bowen, 1988). Bowen's study of mother/child **symbiosis** among families with a member with schizophrenic symptoms led to the formation of his concept of **differentiation of self.** One observation about patient and family interactions that particularly intrigued him was that when patients had contact with relatives, and most especially with their mothers, each person had a tremendous emotional impact on the other. Believing that the mother/patient symbiosis was based on deep evolutionary biological pressures, he proposed that what was observed in clinical situations was simply an exaggeration of a natural process (Kerr & Bowen, 1988, p. 5).

Bowen moved to the National Institute of Mental Health (NIMH) in 1954 where he instituted a project of hospitalizing entire families that had a member with schizophrenia. It was there that he expanded the concept of symbiosis to include the role of fathers and siblings. That led to the concept of **triangulization** (diverting conflict between two people by involving a third). The emotional functioning of individual members was so interdependent that the family could be more accurately conceptualized as an emotional unit (Kerr & Bowen, 1988, p. 7). For example, if father and mother were arguing, and she called in their son to take her side against her husband, she triangulated their son, and created a coalition between her son and herself against the father. When these triangulations were intense, the family members became more anxious and/or symptomatic. It was as if each person became an emotional prisoner of the way the other person functioned and neither was able to change his or her functioning enough to stop the process (Kerr & Bowen, 1988, pp. 7, 8). Another phenomenon was the existence of cycles of distance and closeness. "These cycles were orchestrated with such precision and predictability within the various family relationships that any explanation for them based on the psychological makeup of any individual family member alone seemed awkward and inadequate" (Kerr & Bowen, 1988, p. 9).

Bowen made the distinction between the **family relationship system** and the **family emotional system.** The relationship system offered a description of *what happened,* and the emotional system was an explanation of *what drove what happened* (Kerr, 1988, p. 11). Bowen stressed that the way a therapist thinks about what energizes or drives the process he or she observes in a family will govern what is addressed in therapy.

In 1959, Bowen moved to Georgetown Medical School in Washington, DC, where he was a professor of psychiatry and director of his own outpatient research and training program until his death in the fall of 1990 (Nichols & Schwartz, 1998). At Georgetown, it became apparent that the relationship processes that were first observed in seriously dysfunctional inpatient families were present in *all* families. These processes were basically more exaggerated in the seriously dysfunctional families. This observation suggested that family processes exist on a **continuum:** an emotional process as it becomes increasingly intense, family members become increasingly dependent on and reactive to one another, and eventually symptomatic. When individuals are no longer in control of their emotional interactions, the relationships are in control of the emotional aspect. The self is lost in the web of real or perceived family emotional demands. Bowen's observation of a continuum was important for developing his concepts of differentiation of self and the **scale of differentiation,** which can be seen in Figure 5.1.

The lower the level of differentiation, the greater the percent of energy that is tied up in the relationship. The higher the level of differentiation, the greater the percent of energy that is retained to direct one's own functioning (Kerr & Bowen, 1988, p. 68).

Eight Concepts Central to Bowen's Family System Theory

By 1966, Bowen published the first six concepts of his theory: differentiation of self, triangles, nuclear family emotional system, family projection process, multigenerational transmission process, and sibling position. Two additional concepts, emotional cutoff and societal emotional process were added in the 1970s (Bowen, 1976). An explanation of each of the eight concepts follows:

1. **Differentiation of self:** Defined as the degree to which one balances emotional and intellectual functioning, intimacy and autonomy, distance and closeness in interpersonal relationships. More highly differentiated individuals can experience strong emotions *and* can also shift to calm, logical reasoning for decision making and problem solving, as appropriate to the context of the experience. These are the people who are able to have an emotional response to a situation and then let it go. They don't get hooked into disruptive attitudes that keep them in an emotionally dependent state with their family of origin, or lead to rebellious cutoffs from important people in their lives. Differentiated people don't hold a grudge. They don't build resentments. They respect differences in people and ideas, and feel comfortable asserting their own ideas.

    In contrast, undifferentiated people tend to act solely on the basis of feelings. The degree with which people conform to, placate, resist, or rebel defines their level of differentiation. Undifferentiated people tend to act solely from feelings. Conformity is a reactive response of people who have little sense of themselves outside of meeting the needs or

FIGURE 5.1 | DIFFERENTIATION OF SELF SCALE

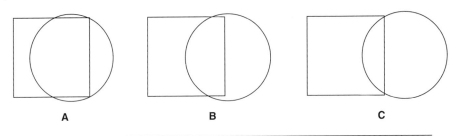

As a person moves from relationship A to relationship C, the amount of life energy that is bound in the relationship decreases. Relationship C is more differentiated, less fused, less stuck together than relationship A. It is a continuum that could show many more subtle changes in the degree of involvement between people.

From *Family Evaluation: An Approach Based on Bowen Theory*, by Michael E. Kerr & Murray Bowen. Copyright © 1988 by Michael E. Kerr and Murray Bowen. Used by permission of W. W. Norton & Company, Inc.

requirements of family members. Rebellion is often a reactive response indicating a person is still tied into proving something to another person influential in his or her life. It is not real independence. Bowen called it **pseudo-independence.** We can see this in the actions of many teenagers as they defy parental limits. Remember, Bowen spoke of finding a balance that satisfies the individual's needs for *both* autonomy and intimacy in relation to their family of origin, other intimates in the present, and their own individuality.

2. **Triangles:** Bowen said all emotionally significant relationships involve third parties. Third parties could be people, such as relatives or friends; things, such as drugs or alcohol; or a situation, such as memories of past events and relationships. For example, a husband and wife could be discussing a current situation. The husband says, "you did the same thing five years ago and I think the same old thing is happening now." He's bringing in the past—a third party—which detours the conversation out of a problem solving mode. One cannot work on a solution for what was done five years ago. If a third person is brought into the discussion to side with one of the parties, that person is triangulated. He or she serves the purpose of detouring the current discussion away from problem solving.

Triangulating freezes conflict in place. It becomes a chronic diversion that corrupts and undermines relationships. Most family problems are triangular. For example, if a mother is over-involved with her son as compensation for her husband's indifference to her, no amount of behavioral instruction on how to handle the son will relieve the problem. Changes must be made in the relationship between the mother and father that enables them to relate as a team, before mother and son can relinquish their inappropriate coalition (over-involvement across generational boundaries). With the son as the focus (the third party), the parents are detoured from work on their relationship. When the parents are coached to become a team—a couple again—they can become more effective in improving their son's behavior.

3. **Nuclear family emotional system:** The unfinished business with one's family of origin is acted out within the nuclear family. Lack of differentiation in the family sometimes leads to cutoffs from one's parents, which leads to fusion in one's marriage. Some of the problems that could show up include reactive distancing between spouses (imitating the patterns that are unresolved in their families of origin), physical or emotional symptoms in one spouse (depression, anxiety, or psychosomatic symptoms), overt marital conflict, or projection of the problem onto one's children.

4. **Family projection process:** This process occurs when parents transmit their lack of differentiation onto their children. Spouses with unresolved family of origin issues create a family environment that necessitates an intense focus on one or more of the children (e.g., overprotection, coalitions between one parent and a child, or constant criticism of a child—the unspoken goal is to keep the child dependent). The child who becomes the object of the projection becomes the one most attached to the parents and the one with the least differentiation of self. A parent's focus of his or her anxiety on the child tends to limit that child's age-appropriate development and differentiation.

5. **Multigenerational transmission process:** Refers to the family's emotional process across multiple generations. In each generation, the child most involved in the family's fusion is less differentiated while the least involved child moves toward greater differentiation. This pattern suggests that problems of the identified patient reflect the relationship between his or her parents and grandparents and most likely can be traced back for several generations.

6. **Sibling position:** Children develop in relation to the child's sibling position in his or her family. Sibling position can be the basis for many of a child's personality characteristics (Toman, 1973). It is helpful to know whether a client is oldest, middle, youngest, as well as other family specifics, as a way of predicting family patterns. For example, was the role of the firstborn in the parents' families of origin similar to the expectations for the firstborn in the nuclear family or immediate family? (Bowen, 1966).

7. **Emotional cutoff:** This process shows up in a person who is a reactive emotional distancer. This person is relatively undifferentiated yet appears aloof and isolated from others. He or she tends to deny the importance of family, and even boasts of being emancipated and out of touch and out of reach of his or her parents. It is a facade of independence because it is emotionally reactive. Family issues remain unexplored

and unresolved. This person finds intimacy profoundly threatening. He or she may have physically moved far away from the family of origin, or may have decided not to have any contact with them and speaks of being his or her own person. This stance is often reactive, emotionally charged, and limits authentic individuation.

8. **Societal emotional process:** A prolonged increase in social anxiety can result in a gradual lowering of the functional level of differentiation within families. In times of external crisis, family members often cling closer together and discourage individuation. They need each other. This process appears in crises such as natural disasters or in war-torn communities. It may be useful for the time period involved in the crisis. If this **enmeshment** continues long after the crisis period is over, individuals tend to be stunted in their personal growth (Bowen, 1976; Kerr & Bowen, 1988).

A Surprise Shift

Bowen used his own family of origin story to define the uniqueness of his family systems theory. Until March 1967, the mental health profession saw his theory as but one more method of family therapy. In February of that year, he had made a detailed effort to learn about and resolve relationships with his own family of origin. That effort was described by Bowen as "amazingly successful" (Kerr & Bowen, 1988, p. 344). He was scheduled to do a major presentation a month later. It was an invitational meeting that included every important person in the family field. He wondered if he could do the same thing with the family of family therapists that had worked so well in his own family.

That month, he prepared a routine text and sent it in advance to participants. Then at the meeting, he did a sudden surprise shift and told of the effort with his own family. He reported that the result was electric. Not a single family therapist recognized his original goal, which had been to differentiate himself and his theory in his professional world. Instead the therapists guessed he was advocating a study of one's own family as a part of all good family therapy. That day started an international move to include extended family concepts in the understanding of any family. Since then, increasing numbers of family therapists have done historical genealogical surveys of their own families (Kerr & Bowen, 1988, p. 344).

Bowen began to utilize what he had experienced in the exploration of his own family of origin when working with any problem or symptom that developed in his staff. As he modified his part in the creation of the problem, the disharmony would automatically be corrected (Kerr & Bowen, 1988, pp. 346–347).

Bowen's Central Premise

The central premise of Bowen's theory is that unresolved emotional attachment to one's family of origin limits a person's ability to assume a mature, healthy personality. He spoke of two counterbalancing forces that exist in nature—togetherness and individuality. Too much emphasis in either direction suggests the system is out of balance. If there is too heavy an emphasis on togetherness, this could result in **fusion,** or lack of individual growth. If there is too much emphasis on individuality, emotional cutoff is the expected outcome. For relief of anxiety, and to develop a healthy personality, a balance of togetherness *and* individuality must be achieved. When a person achieves a balanced differentiation of self—a balanced way of thinking and interacting—he or she does not get caught up in **reactive polarities** (e.g., guilt- or anger-driven behaviors). He or she is not pulled apart by the emotional demands of the family of origin that pull against his or her individual needs (Bowen, 1960).

Symptom-Inducing Family Scripts

Bowen described a family script that he theorized as fostering schizophrenic symptoms in a child. It begins with a marriage of two immature individuals—one taking the role of being over-adequate and the other taking the role of being inadequate and in which conflict begins just weeks after the wedding. Each spouse had learned these roles in his or her family of origin. Anxiety grows as the reciprocal over-adequate/inadequate functions of each partner increases. The couple maintains a facade of a happy marriage. Their stress increases as they cannot decide on anything together, and distance themselves emotionally from one another. With the birth of a baby, the mother tends to project her own inadequacy onto the child, which the child accepts. As the child becomes an adolescent, any move to become independent is seen as a threat to the mother. She forces her child back into an inadequate role. The child is locked into the family's **emotional relationship system.** The unfortunate outcome, when this pattern persists, is often that the child may develop symptoms of schizophrenia (Bowen, 1978).

Differentiation and Resiliency

Symptoms of psychological distress in the family reflect the level of chronic anxiety and the level of differentiation in the family system. The more differentiated the person, the more **resiliency** he or she has, and the more flexible and able to sustain relationships. The less differentiated person is more emotionally reactive to stress and more apt to develop psychological and somatic symptoms. Stress created by life-cycle transitions often increases the level of anxiety (e.g., loss of a job, a child leaving for college) and may show up as a symptom in the most vulnerable (undifferentiated) child, adolescent, or adult.

Goal of Bowenian Therapy

Bowen's theory affirms the need to train oneself to control emotional reactivity, so as to better control one's behavior—to think before reacting. It does not suggest suppression of authentic and appropriate emotional expressiveness.

The goals of Bowenian therapy are to help clients to learn to connect emotionally by developing a personal relationship with every member of one's family and to develop an intellectual and emotional balance by increasing the client's ability to *distinguish between* thinking and feeling, and learning to use that ability to direct one's life and solve problems (Carter & McGoldrick, 1999).

How Clients Are Helped

Bowenian therapists often **coach** clients to meet with their family of origin to address the patterns and projections that represent their **unresolved emotional attachments** that have evolved into family **anxiety**. Therapists coach people to relate with one another without gossiping or taking sides, without counterattacking, or defending oneself. Bowenian therapists work toward helping individuals gain insight into the influence of their family system and how that influence has shaped the way they look at life. In tracing the pattern of family problems, therapists pay attention to process (patterns of emotional reactivity) and to structure (triangles, coalitions/alliances) within the family. Clients are also coached to address patterns that have been revealed as destructive for their differentiation. Lack of differentiation limits a person's ability to experience both intimacy with, and independence from, other family members, and it limits the potential for intimacy with significant partners in the present.

Family psychotherapy is family psychotherapy not because of the number of people in a treatment session, but because of *how* a therapist conceptualizes the problem (Kerr & Bowen, 1988, p. 286). Individual sessions are often most helpful for a person who is concentrating on individuating from his or her family of origin. Increasing factual knowledge about one's family of origin is an important component of becoming more of a self (Kerr & Bowen, 1988, p. 287).

Exploring the Family of Origin

Change is begun by helping clients learn about their family of origin, at least as far back as their grandparents. Clients are asked who was in their family of origin, what they knew about them, stories they have heard over the years, where they lived, what they did, what they were like, and what they knew about relationships among family members over more than one generation. They are then asked to think about what they have learned about the patterns and relationships in their family of origin, and to use what they learned when they approach family members in an effort to heal and resolve old wounds (Kerr & Bowen, 1988). Later in this chapter we cover how this process developed into a diagram of the family that is called a genogram.

Initial Questions Bowenian therapists believe understanding *how* family systems operate is essential. They regularly use questions designed to slow people down, diminish reactive anxiety, and start them *thinking* about how they are involved as participants in interpersonal patterns. Bowen suggested 10 initial evaluation questions:

1. Who initiated the therapy?
2. What is the symptom and which family member or family relationship is symptomatic?
3. What is the immediate relationship (usually the nuclear family) of the symptomatic person?
4. What are the patterns of emotional functioning in the nuclear family?
5. What is the intensity of the emotional process in the nuclear family?
6. What influences that intensity—an overload of stressful events and/or a low level of adaptiveness?
7. What is the nature of the extended family systems, particularly in terms of their stability and availability?
8. What is the degree of emotional cutoff from each extended family?
9. What is the prognosis?
10. What are important directions for therapy? (Kerr & Bowen, 1988, p. 290)

Each question is followed up with another related to the client's response and always directed toward highlighting the interactive nature of relationship issues (Guerin, Fay, Burden, & Kautto, 1987). These questions engage clients in thinking, rather than feeling, responses, as the therapist teases out specific descriptions of what is and has been happening in the client's life. Clients begin to learn to think about people and events, rather than simply reacting to them. This realization helps them decrease their repetitive emotional patterns of reaction. They can then begin to realize they can learn to change those reactions as they change the way they think about the people or events that have triggered their reactional and reciprocal responses in the past.

Bowenians suggest that a successful differentiation of self occurs when the client and his or her family members are able to see each other as people rather than emotionally charged images. This process allows people to make thoughtful decisions about how feelings influence their relationships.

The Family Diagram   The **family diagram** is an outgrowth of Bowen's family systems theory. The diagram reflects the ebb and flow of emotional process through the generations. It can be used to define interactions in the present, as well as the influence of the multigenerational family. From the information gathered in the initial interview, the principal pattern of emotional functioning can be ascertained. In Figure 5.2, drawn from a couple interview, the principal pattern of the wife's family of origin (B) is conflict, indicated by the jagged line. In the husband's family of origin (A), the principal pattern is over/under-functioning, indicated by the up and down arrows. Family C is the nuclear family the couple has created in which they have developed a family projection process (indicated by the arrow from the mother to the son). These symbols are highly simplified ways of diagramming the various patterns of emotional

FIGURE 5.2 | SAMPLE FAMILY EVALUATION

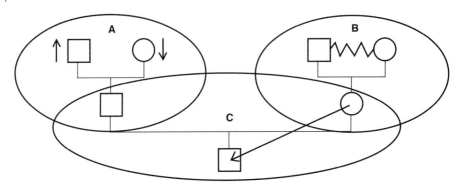

Family A is the husband's family of origin. The principal pattern of emotional functioning in his family was under-functioning by his mother (indicated by the arrow pointing
downward) and the over-functioning of his father (indicated by the arrow pointing
upward). Family B is the wife's family of origin. The principal pattern of emotional
functioning in her family was conflict between her parents (indicated by the jagged line
between the parents). Family C is the nuclear family of this husband and wife. The
principal pattern of emotional functioning in their family is the family project process
(indicated by the arrow from the mother to the son). These are highly simplified ways
of diagramming the various patterns of emotional functioning, but they are a useful
shorthand.

From *Family Evaluation: An Approach Based on Bowen Theory*, by Michael E. Kerr & Murray Bowen.
Copyright © 1988 by Michael E. Kerr and Murray Bowen. Used by permission of W. W. Norton &
Company, Inc.

function—a useful shorthand (Kerr & Bowen, 1988, p. 307). The family diagram in Figure 5.2 is but one possible configuration. Expanded to the family of
origin, it offers a simplified record of the information gathered by the therapist
about a clinical family, or his or her own family.

The Genogram   An essential Bowenian intervention involves obtaining the
history of three generations of family members in a diagram, which he later
named a **genogram**. It evolved from Bowen's idea of a family diagram.
Utilization of genograms and an expanded vision of what constitutes a family
are spelled out by Carter and McGoldrick (1999).

Genograms record the information gathered by the therapist about a
client family, or about the therapist's own family. Adaptations of genograms
are being used in business and government organizations. A family genogram
is a flow diagram, similar to a family tree, which depicts emotional and biological processes over generations. It follows a basic format with standard
symbols; for instance, males are represented by squares, females by circles.
There are specific symbols for marriages, pregnancies, deaths, households,
birth order, and many other life-cycle events and arrangements, as well as for

the emotional processes including conflict, closeness, distance, and emotional triangles. Genograms were an important part of the pioneering work of Dr. Bowen. Figure 5.3 is a sample genogram. As part of the experiential activities, students will have an opportunity to share parts of their genogram—as much as they are willing to share, as a part of class discussion.

BOWENIAN THEORY: FOUNDING PRINCIPLES

Therapy based on Bowen family systems theory, no matter what the nature of the clinical problem, is always governed by two basic principles: (1) a reduction of anxiety will relieve symptoms, and (2) an increase in basic level of differentiation will improve adaptiveness. Lack of differentiation in the family of origin leads to intimacy problems in the nuclear family. Undifferentiated couples are unable to feel connected, are defensive, argue, or withdraw. They are restricted in their ability to engage in mutually beneficial problem solving.

Bowen postulated there was ongoing tension in the balance between two forces—the forces of fusion, connecting with others, and the urge to be an individual and pursue one's own goals. Anxiety and emotional arousal in the family may produce symptoms in the most vulnerable family member: These symptoms occur when something stresses the family, such as a job loss, a child going off to school, or a chronic illness. One parent may enter into a coalition with a child to deal with the stress (triangulization). That parent uses the child as a buffer or ally against the other parent, who is perceived as not understanding or being supportive of the stressed parent. Triangulization diminishes the parents' ability to problem solve with one another. The involved child may develop symptoms, become the scapegoat for the family in the form of a psychological or behavioral problem, expressing the anxiety felt by all family members. The degree of distress and the level of differentiation in the parents will influence the intensity of the symptom (family projection process). Relationships are limited by family members' ability to balance both feeling and thinking processes.

The problems of the past are visited on the present and future. The way people interact in the nuclear family reflects the way the spouses' parents had interacted (multigenerational emotional system). If the spouses' parents had been enmeshed or detached, they tend to be the same in the nuclear family they create. Their children learn to relate the same way and continue the same patterns when they marry, unless or until some family member becomes aware of the possibility of change and acts on that awareness.

Meaningful change occurs for most family members as an individual or couple, capable of effecting change, changes. When clients recognize that their repetitive, emotionally reactive behaviors are interfering with their sense of well being and crippling their ability to be intimate and autonomous, and are motivated to address those issues, they can create new and more satisfying ways of living their lives. In therapy, this process may involve coaching

FIGURE 5.3 | SAMPLE GENOGRAM

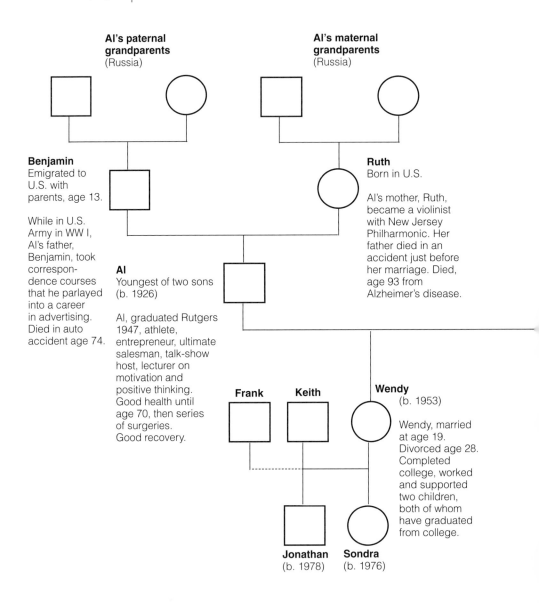

Al's paternal grandparents (Russia)

Al's maternal grandparents (Russia)

Benjamin
Emigrated to U.S. with parents, age 13.

While in U.S. Army in WW I, Al's father, Benjamin, took correspondence courses that he parlayed into a career in advertising. Died in auto accident age 74.

Ruth
Born in U.S.

Al's mother, Ruth, became a violinist with New Jersey Philharmonic. Her father died in an accident just before her marriage. Died, age 93 from Alzheimer's disease.

Al
Youngest of two sons (b. 1926)

Al, graduated Rutgers 1947, athlete, entrepreneur, ultimate salesman, talk-show host, lecturer on motivation and positive thinking. Good health until age 70, then series of surgeries. Good recovery.

Frank

Keith

Wendy
(b. 1953)

Wendy, married at age 19. Divorced age 28. Completed college, worked and supported two children, both of whom have graduated from college.

Jonathan
(b. 1978)

Sondra
(b. 1976)

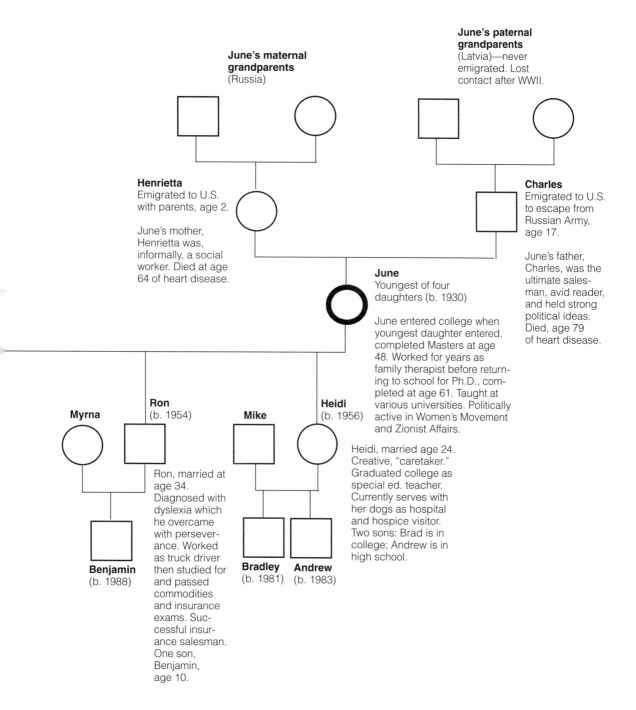

June's maternal grandparents (Russia)

June's paternal grandparents (Latvia)—never emigrated. Lost contact after WWII.

Henrietta
Emigrated to U.S. with parents, age 2.

June's mother, Henrietta was, informally, a social worker. Died at age 64 of heart disease.

Charles
Emigrated to U.S. to escape from Russian Army, age 17.

June's father, Charles, was the ultimate sales-man, avid reader, and held strong political ideas. Died, age 79 of heart disease.

June
Youngest of four daughters (b. 1930)

June entered college when youngest daughter entered, completed Masters at age 48. Worked for years as family therapist before return-ing to school for Ph.D., com-pleted at age 61. Taught at various universities. Politically active in Women's Movement and Zionist Affairs.

Myrna

Ron (b. 1954)

Mike

Heidi (b. 1956)

Ron, married at age 34. Diagnosed with dyslexia which he overcame with persever-ance. Worked as truck driver then studied for and passed commodities and insurance exams. Suc-cessful insur-ance salesman. One son, Benjamin, age 10.

Benjamin (b. 1988)

Bradley (b. 1981)

Andrew (b. 1983)

Heidi, married age 24. Creative, "caretaker." Graduated college as special ed. teacher. Currently serves with her dogs as hospital and hospice visitor. Two sons: Brad is in college; Andrew is in high school.

an individual or couple to learn how to separate feelings from thoughts to develop more satisfying ways of interacting within their family of origin. Clients can learn to modify their emotionally reactive responses with thoughtful consideration and then to act in ways that enhance their relationships and their individuality. Therapy may also involve preparing clients to meet with significant family-of-origin members to confront their issues. When they confront their issues successfully, their newly freed, differentiated self can interact in a more gratifying way within their own nuclear family.

Meaningful change by one family member—that is, differentiation—leads to differentiation among all family members. Reciprocally, these changes affect the way all the family members interact with each other. It is important to note that significant changes in physical and psychological functioning occur as a result of more ability to be a "self" in one's most emotionally significant relationships systems (Kerr & Bowen, 1988, p. 338).

SUGGESTED GENOGRAM QUESTIONS

These questions relate to the family of origin over at least to four generations, if available. They are guidelines only. A therapist may want to fit the questions to the specific family he or she is working with. As always, offer the questions in a friendly, conversational style.

1. What is your family motto or myth?
2. How do you "carry" or "display" or "act out" that myth or motto? How do other family members do it?
3. How do you help others in your family display and/or perpetuate their myths?
4. How do you hinder others in your family with their myths?
5. Who helped, helps, you?
6. Who hindered, hinders, you?
7. Who made the rules by which the myths were developed?
8. How were, are, those rules maintained?
9. Which parent are you most similar to or different from? List specifics.
10. What is the message in your family about "the women in the family are," "the men in the family are"?
11. What was expected of you as a man/woman in your family? List specifics.
12. What did you learn from that to expect from the opposite sex? List specifics.
13. What subjects were taboo?
14. Which family members were mostly in collusion with each other against another?
15. Which family members had positive, healthy alliances?
16. Which family members were habitually in conflict?
17. Which parent did you feel closest to? Why?
18. Which parent did you feel most distant from? Why?

19. Were there any family traumas as you were growing up? For example: medical problems, financial problems, school problems, relationship problems.
20. What was the history of alcohol or drug abuse through the generations?
21. Were any members in your family extremely obese, anorexic or bulimic?
22. What else would be helpful to know to understand the interactions over time, in your family and what was their effect on your worldview?

IVAN BOSZORMENYI-NAGY AND CONTEXTUAL THERAPY

Ivan Boszormenyi-Nagy describes himself as a therapist who went from being an analyst, prizing secrecy and confidentiality in his sessions with individual clients, to a family therapist, fighting the forces of pathology on an open battlefield (Nichols & Schwartz, 1998). "Open battlefield" refers to his inclusion of the *context* in which clients live. Contextual therapy encourages as many family members as possible to meet in the therapy sessions and explores the influences of three generations or more, even if they are not all available to participate in person.

Introduction of Ethical Considerations

Boszormenyi-Nagy adds **ethical obligations** and **accountability** to his therapeutic goals and techniques. He said that neither the pleasure-pain principle, nor transactional expediency, is a sufficient guide to human behavior. He believes that family members have to base their relationships on **trust** and **loyalty,** and they must balance the **ledger** of **entitlement and indebtedness.** According to the theory behind contextual family therapy, "the breakdown of trustworthiness of relationships through disengagement from multilateral caring and accountability sets the stage for symptom development" (Boszormenyi-Nagy & Ulrich, 1981, p. 171). When people in a family are not concerned about, or do not feel a sense of loyalty to, family members, people in that family lose their ability to trust one another, or to depend on one another.

Goals of Therapy

The goal of contextual therapy is to restore people's capacity to trust and to be fair within their relationships. The healthy growth of the individual is seen to include caring and giving. The added benefits of caring about the ethical implications of relationships actually help to strengthen a weak ego (Boszormenyi-Nagy & Ulrich, 1981).

In 1957, Boszormenyi-Nagy founded the Eastern Pennsylvania Psychiatric Institute in Philadelphia as a center for research and training. He was a highly respected scholar-clinician and was able to attract highly talented colleagues and students. In 1980, the institute was closed down and he and some of his associates moved to nearby Hahnemann University Medical School. His contextual therapy is the only family theory that leans heavily on ethical values.

An Integration of Interpersonal and Intrapsychic Ideas

Contextual therapy integrates interpersonal and intrapsychic thinking. Boszormenyi-Nagy's approach speaks to the continuity of family life through traditions that get passed on from generation to generation. His theory suggests that therapists need to help their clients focus on the personalities of people in their **relational context.** For Boszormenyi-Nagy, judging people out of context is not just. "People are as they are; they do the best they can in their circumstances" (Boszormenyi-Nagy & Ulrich, 1981, p. 146). Considering the context in which some people live, it is difficult to view their actions as perverse or malicious, or to assume they are totally responsible for their perverseness. Contextual theory offers a way of understanding behavior through a lens of morality and contextualized judgments.

Invisible Loyalties

Boszormenyi-Nagy contends that each spouse brings his or her heritage into the marriage. The new family they form will be built on **invisible loyalties** to their family of origin that extend across generations. Invisible loyalties are usually unconscious. As Boszormenyi-Nagy put it, "The struggle of countless preceding generations survives in the structure of the nuclear family" (Boszormenyi-Nagy & Ulrich, 1981, p. 162). He describes **relational ethics** built on a sense of equitability over the generations.

He speaks of a **ledger** as an interpersonal/relational account book. The ledger contains two ethical components. The first component he called **legacy.** Children acquire a legacy by being born to their parents, and by taking on the social role relative to their experience in the family. For example, the way the family thinks about sons and daughters may create a legacy of a son who feels entitled to approval and a daughter who feels entitled only to shame. These legacies fall with gross unfairness on both of them. The children become ethically bound to accommodate their lives somehow within those legacies (Boszormenyi-Nagy & Ulrich, 1981). This predicts a kind of destiny—a **revolving slate**—a continued enactment for the role acquired in the family of origin to be repeated when each, as an adult, creates his or her own nuclear family.

The second component of the ledger is the record of the individual's accumulated **merit** by "contribution to the welfare of the other" (Boszormenyi-Nagy & Ulrich, 1981, p. 163). This record of merit combines what one is due as parent or child, as well as what one merits or deserves from the way one interacts within the family.

For Boszormenyi-Nagy, one of the most problematic issues is a claim for loyalty by one parent at the cost of the child's loyalty to the other parent—

split-filial loyalty. His term, revolving slate, describes the legacy for good or ill that "patterns shall be repeated, against unavailing struggle, from one generation to the next" (Boszormenyi-Nagy & Ulrich, 1981, p. 166).

Multipersonal loyalty implies the existence of structured group expectations to which all members are committed. In this sense, loyalty pertains to what Buber called "the order of the human world"(Buber, 1951). Its frame of reference is trust, merit, commitment, and action, rather than the "psychological" functions of "feeling" and "knowing" (Boszormenyi-Nagy & Spark, 1984).

Boszormenyi-Nagy and Spark (1984) state, "The concept of loyalty is fundamental to the understanding of the ethics, that is, the deeper relational structuring of families and other social groups. Loyalty commitments are like invisible but strong fibers that hold together complex pieces of relationship behavior in families as well as in larger society" (p. 47). The internalized patterns of loyalty originate from something owed to a parent or to an internalized image of a parent representation. In a three generational system, the adults become the **creditors** in the dialogue of commitments, and the children become the **debtors.** The debtor will eventually have to settle his or her debt in the **intergenerational feedback system,** by internalizing the expected commitments, by living up to the expectations, and eventually by transmitting them to his or her offspring. Each act of repayment of **reciprocal obligation** will raise the level of loyalty and trust within the relationship, creating a balance of loyalty obligations from the maturing child toward the nuclear family.

Mature Love as Dialogue

Mature love, rather than being a **fusion,** as often stated in song and romance novels, is a true dialogue, in which each participant complements the other's needs. Fusion describes an undifferentiated family, as an amorphous "we" experience. Each member defines "self" as "other," projectively, and in general, speaking for the other (for example, "my wife thinks . . ."). In fused families, members think of others before self, sacrificing and living for others. If some other family member is unhappy, one blames oneself. Conversely one blames the other for one's own unhappiness. The "anyway you lose" character of such guilt-driven behavior suggests a self-inflicted double bind. The fused family is one in which the members have joined forces to help each other avoid the pain and challenge of emotional growth.

Life phenomena must be understood in their contextual frame. Healing pertains to a capacity for living and enjoying life. "The patterns of invisible loyalties determine the relational context in which the individual is either enabled or hampered in his or her life aspirations" (Boszormenyi-Nagy & Spark, 1984, p. 362). When those loyalties become visible—are no longer denied or avoided—the individual is free to pursue his or her life aspirations, consciously considering the merit of his or her actions in the context of the family.

How Families Are Helped   Boszormenyi-Nagy recommends that as many family members as are interested and willing should be included in the therapy sessions. He sees the therapist's initial role as engaging all family members present through the process of **multidirectional partiality,** his term for taking turns siding with one family member after another. This initial process allows everyone in the session a fair, impartial, nonjudgmental hearing. Contextual therapists explore historic factors in family of origin as well as events leading up to development of the current situation. They reframe and rename events with empathic understanding. They respectfully challenge people's perceptions of each other and of the problem (Boszormenyi-Nagy & Spark, 1984). For instance, if a parent labels a child as lazy, a contextual therapist could wonder, out loud, if that child had so many things on his or her mind, that activity would be too draining.

After the therapist clarifies the problems as perceived by the family, he or she begins the process of problem solving by encouraging family members to increase their options and expand their trust of one another.

Contextual therapy is not as short a process as many of the other family therapies. It not only looks for behavioral changes, it works toward altering injustices from previous generations, reinterpreting them, and then building interpersonal trust and respect in the present generation. As the ledger is balanced, credits, merits, debts, and loyalties are changed. The altered contextual climate opens the family members to more satisfying relationships, and improves individual self-esteem.

An Integration of Past and Present

Boszormenyi-Nagy encourages the use of a co-therapist. Boszormenyi-Nagy helps clients identify other resources to assist in making changes. He is careful to advocate for every member of the relational context. This advocacy includes the multigenerational extended family, even deceased family members who laid the groundwork for the legacy the present family members who need change. Family resources are the main focus of assessment, followed by the therapist's observations of family relationships among the people in the session. The process involves ongoing observations and attempts to discern current or past triangles, stages of development, and the effect of loyalties within and outside of the family. Family history and current observable and reportable family interactions are integrated into the sessions.

Founding Principles of Contextual Theory

Individuals are born and grow in a contextual climate of at least three generations, which projects **invisible threads** of **credits, merits, debts,** and **loyalties** through which family relationships are patterned. In human terms, grandparents model patterns of interaction. For example, Grandma may be hard working, long-suffering, and not show much warmth. She puts her work before her spouse or children. Grandpa may be fun-loving, eager to play with the children, and a hugger. The family members learned they could trust Grandma to keep things going smoothly, and they learned affection from Grandpa and returned it to him. When those children grow and become parents, they will have internalized beliefs about what they didn't get and apply it to the present (e.g., they believe they didn't get affection from a woman and don't expect it from women) and what they did get and apply it to the present (e.g., they did get dependability from a woman and expect it in women). They bring those beliefs and models into the nuclear family they form, reenacting the patterns and beliefs they experienced growing up.

The concept of loyalty is fundamental to the understanding of the deeper relational structuring of families. In human terms, loyalty generates a sense of obligation and offers a platform of security. Loyalty is fundamental for a solid foundation for any family. However, if children in a family are taught that no matter what, loyalty to the family comes first, and if this lesson is too tightly woven into the family members' belief systems, the children in this family could find it very stressful to enter personal relationships outside the family. The message is that any alliances outside the family constitute disloyalty to the family. This example describes an undifferentiated, or fused, family. Its members tend to be isolated emotionally, living only for the group, discounting individual development. A balance of loyalties and personal growth is a goal to be strived for.

FEMINIST FAMILY THERAPY: AN ACTIVIST APPROACH

Gender relations enter into and are constituent elements in every aspect of human experience (Flax, 1990, p. 40). In the early 1970s, feminists suggested that the traditional family and the social environment that promoted it may not consider the well-being of women. Rachel Hare-Mustin wrote the first paper challenging family therapy about issues of gender published in *Family Process* in 1978. But the push to address clinical issues from a feminist perspective really came from the Women's Project (Silverstein, 2000).

The Women's Project

The Women's Project came together in the late 1970s when a number of women trained in clinical social work came together to share their ideas. Elizabeth (Betty) Carter and Olga Silverstein had been fellow students at Hunter College. They had their first placement at the Ackerman Institute. Silverstein founded her own Family Institute in Westchester, NY, in 1977. Around the same time, Peggy Papp was working at the Center for Family Learning in New Rochelle, NY. Marianne Walters was working with Salvador Minuchin at the Philadelphia Child Guidance Clinic. They were all strongly influenced by Bowenian theory.

In 1977, Marianne Walters invited Peggy Papp, Betty Carter, and Olga Silverstein to present a small workshop looking at women's issues. The workshop went so well that they decided to offer it at a conference in New York. They were not on the program, so they just put a sign up in the hall. It said: After lunch—women who are interested can come to such and such a room and chat about women's issues. When they came back after lunch, they discovered more than 500 people in that room waiting for them.

"We knew that the time had come" (Silverstein, 2000, p. 18).

The group then held a series of open seminars. They held separate seminars on women as mothers, women as wives, women as mothers of sons, and women as mothers of daughters. They were a group of very vocal women and soon found a way to work together that they enjoyed very much. They wrote a book, *The Invisible Web: Gender Patterns in Family Relationships* in 1989, which is still selling. The Women's Project continued their workshops until they gradually realized that their ideas had spread into the field and become general knowledge (Silverstein, 2000).

The Metaphor of Power

Most prominent family theorists had not directly addressed concerns about the inequality of power between men and women in traditional families. Many systemic theorists were alienated by the feminist use of the metaphor of power to explain the exploitation of women in families and by the feminist instructive and educative style of clinical practice. They feared feminism would become a new dogma, as oppressive a social construction as the one it set out to replace.

Feminists have argued that an analysis of power is necessary to understand incest and battering, as well as other more subtle, less dramatic behaviors that undermine a woman's well-being. They believe power relations between husbands and wives, as well as between fathers and daughters, are strongly influenced by the structural realities of socially defined sex roles; the family systems interventions reinforce stereotypic sex roles. They suggest that when family therapists frame their interventions around traditional family structure, they reinforce the cultural concept that the woman should adapt herself to the family context and be primarily responsible for the tranquility of the domestic environment (Bagarozzi & Giddings, 1983).

Feminists criticized family therapy for participating in gender stereotyping and gender ignoring when it focused on the maintenance of the traditional family. They pointed out that economic inequity, violence, and other exploitations are as pervasive now as they were at the beginning of feminism and family therapy (Hare-Mustin, 1987).

Social Change Agents

Feminist family therapists see themselves as social change agents. They view family dysfunction as broader than the immediate family system. Feminist family therapy seeks to be consciousness-raising. It strives to increase the options available to women. It seeks to change the conditions in society that contribute to the maintenance of sexist behaviors. Both male and female clients are encouraged to examine how their communication patterns and stereotypical beliefs about gender roles perpetuate their presenting problem and interfere with their ability to achieve intimacy and mutual satisfaction within their relationship. Feminist family therapists do this by asking questions that help people examine their gender beliefs and how those beliefs affect satisfaction in their relationship. They work toward building a respectful, collaborative therapeutic relationship with both men and women (Hare-Mustin, 1978).

A FEMINIST PERSPECTIVE FOR FAMILY THERAPY TECHNIQUES

- When arranging a contract for therapy, the feminist therapist suggests all members share equal responsibility in making and arranging appointments; the woman should not be the only one to have to make babysitting arrangements. The man may have to arrange to take off from work.
- Foster explicit discussion of sex roles involving mutual consciousness-raising.
- Establish clear generational boundaries. Realize how women may form alliances with children out of frustration with their lack of power in the family, and encourage men and children to show more positive regard to the female members of their family.
- Encourage private time for both men and women. Suggest ways to share family responsibilities. The more each family member shares in the goals, responsibility, and service to the family as a whole, the more each member can also attain some space and privacy.
- Female therapists, by being who they are, model a significant difference from the traditional stereotypes (Hare-Mustin, 1978).

Postmodern Thinking on Feminism

Different forms of feminism have developed different positions in relation to the question of genders. It is important to recognize the philosophical underpinnings and practical consequences of particular stances. Postmodernists suggest that what people come to recognize as male or female is mediated by their relationship with others through language. Postmodernists assert people are defined through the dominant stories of their culture regarding their perceptions of self and of others. Through a narrative process, postmodern therapists help clients construct new stories to replace those dominant stories that may be undermining people's perceptions of themselves and their relationships. Postmodern and narrative theory and therapy are discussed in Chapters 10 and 12.

Summary on Feminist Family Therapy

Feminist family therapists broadened the arena in which family therapists had been operating by introducing concerns about the inequality of power between men and women in families. They became advocates for women and men by describing the negative impact of gender stereotyping on family relationships. Through a series of consciousness-raising workshops the Women's Project brought this message to family therapists. Specific practice methods evolved.

There has been some concern by some schools of family therapy, particularly the postmodernists, that by focusing on family issues from a feminist perspective and by introducing the metaphor of power, feminists family therapists are imposing their biases on their clients. Feminist family therapists take issue with the postmodern stance of neutrality that implies all family members are equal in their ability of fashion the way they live their lives.

EXPERIENTIAL ACTIVITIES

1. As a take-home project, instructors should ask each student to prepare a genogram. See genogram preparation questions. In the next class session, students may share what they have learned from this project. Instructors should allow ample classroom time to discuss both the preparation of the genogram and student concerns, in order for this project to have the impact needed to understand family of origin influences in the students' lives and to relate that to client families.

2. Form small groups to conduct 10–15 minute family and therapist role plays using Bowenian process questions, such as the following: What did you do? How did he or she respond? What happened next? The instructor may give a short demonstration of how to use the process questions and then serve as a coach to the students designated to play the therapist for each of the small groups. Roles include one student to play the therapist, two students play the couple, and one student to play a child with symptoms and behaviors reflecting his or her role within the family. As an example, that child may have been enlisted in a dependent alliance with the father. One student serves as an observer and will report at the end of the role play on his or her observations. The group should pick a topic they expect a family would present, and an ethnicity or religion for the family. Remember, the therapist's job is to ask for detailed descriptions by using process questions about interactions as a way of calming overheated emotions. After the role play, the observer reports on what was observed about the reacting or thinking processes of the role-play group. Then, the other members of the group report on their experience. Encourage group members to separate feeling and thinking when they report. Instructor can help students stay focused by asking "What did you think?" and "What did you feel?" Role plays can be set up depicting different backgrounds and lifestyles.

3. Instructors should divide students into small groups reflecting their birth order within their families: one group of oldest, one group of middle, one of youngest, and one of only children. Have each group discuss how they think their position in the family influenced their childhood experiences and how they think their birth order status affects their own self-perceptions and expectations for themselves. Return to a full class and

ask a spokesperson for each group to describe that group's experiences, noting any similarities or differences. Compare and contrast differences based on birth order.

4. Instructors should dictate open-ended questions related to student's family of origin. Some sample questions are listed below. Allow time for them to write a brief ending for each sentence. Answers can be discussed by the whole class or in small groups.

I would describe my family of origin as . . .

In my family, my mother/father was always the one who . . .

My family thought I was . . .

One topic we could never discuss was . . .

As a male/female in my family, I thought I was . . .

In my culture, the role of a wife is____ and the role of a husband is ____.
My family of origin was (proud, ashamed, fearful, etc.) of its heritage.

5. Instructors may ask students to divide into two groups: male and female. Have each group discuss how they believe males or females were perceived and valued in their family of origin and how they believe that affected their perceptions of themselves and the opposite sex. Then have groups come together to discuss those perceptions.

6. Set up groups of four or five students. Have each person in the group practice multidirectional partiality with other members of the group. The instructor should demonstrate this first. Each group decides a presenting problem to talk about. After 10 minutes, each member of the group describes how and when they felt included or excluded by the therapist, and how they felt in the role of therapist trying to demonstrate multidirectional partiality. A full class discussion can follow to process people's experiences.

7. Instructors may set up small groups of four or five students to explore the ways they think it would help to balance the ledger of debts, credits, and merits from their own family of origin that may get in their way as a family therapist. Report consensus on issues and what students think can be done to deal with those issues.

8. Instructors should lead a full class discussion of Boszormenyi-Nagy's statement: "People are as they are; they do the best they can in their circumstances." Is he suggesting there is some lessening of personal responsibility because someone grows up in poverty or some other distressing context?

9. Ask small groups of students to discuss among themselves how they believe Boszormenyi-Nagy's value-laden ideas would play within different groups. For instance, do students think they would be different for Irish or Chinese or Native American? Process those ideas through any understanding of expected group differences in their relationship with their traditions. Students should look for similarities between traditions and remember the fact that generalities do not define individuals or their families.

REFERENCES

Bagarozzi, D., & Giddings, C. (1983). Conjugal violence: A critical review of current research and clinical practices. *American Journal of Family Therapy, 11,* 3–15.

Bertalanffy, L. von. (1968). *Systems theory: Foundation, development, application.* New York: Brazillier.

Boszormenyi-Nagy, I., & Spark, G. M. (1984). *Invisible loyalties: Reciprocity in intergenerational family therapy.* New York: Harper & Row.

Boszormenyi-Nagy, I., & Ulrich, D. N. (1981). Contextual family therapy. In A. S. Gurman & D. P. Kniskern (Eds.), *The handbook of family therapy.* New York: Brunner/Mazel.

Bowen, M. (1960). A family concept of schizophrenia. In D. D. Jackson (Ed.), *The etiology of schizophrenia.* New York: Basic Books.

Bowen, M. (1966). The use of family theory in clinical practice. *Comprehensive Psychiatry 7,* 345–374.

Bowen, M. (1976). Theory in the practice of psychotherapy. In P. J. Guerin (Ed.), *Family therapy: Theory and practice.* New York: Gardner Press.

Bowen, M. (1978). *Family therapy in clinical practice.* New York: Jason Aronson.

Buber, M. (1951). Guilt and guilt feelings. *Psychiatry 20,* 114–129.

Carter, B., & McGoldrick, M. (1999). *The expanded family life cycle: Individual, family and social perspectives* (3rd ed.). Boston: Allyn & Bacon.

Flax, J. (1990). *Thinking fragments, psychoanalysis, feminisms and post modernism in the contemporary west.* Berkeley, CA: University of California Press.

Guerin, P. J., Fay, L. F., Burden, S. L., & Kautto, J. G. (1989). *The evaluation and treatment of marital conflict: A four-stage approach.* New York: Basic Books.

Hare-Mustin, R. (1978) A feminist approach to family therapy. *Family Process, 17,* 181–194.

Hare-Mustin, R. (1987) The problem of gender in family therapy theory. *Family Process, 26,* 15–27.

Kerr, M., & Bowen, M. (1988). *Family evaluation.* New York: Norton.

McGoldrick, M., Preto, N., Hines, P., & Lee, E. (1990). Ethnicity in family therapy. In A. S. Gurman & D. P. Kniskern (Eds.), *The handbook of family therapy* (2nd ed.). New York: Brunner/Mazel.

Nichols, M. P., & Schwartz, R. C. (1998). *Family therapy: Concepts and methods* (4th ed.). Boston: Allyn & Bacon.

Silverstein, O. (2000). Olga Silverstein, Margaret Newmark, & Chris Beebs: Glimpses of history and current concerns. In *Family therapy: The field's past, present, and possible futures, 1:1.* Adelaide, South Australia: Dulwich Centre Publications.

Toman, W. (1976) *Family constellation: Its effects on personality and social behavior* (3rd ed.). New York: Springer.

Walters, M., Carter, B., Papp, P., & Silverstein, O. (1989). *The invisible web: Gender patterns in family relationships.* New York: Guilford.

EXPERIENTIAL FAMILY THEORY AND THERAPY

KEY THEORISTS

Virginia Satir—provides a bridge between communication and experiential

Carl Whitaker—joins the "craziness"

Walter Kempler—Gestalt/experiential

TERMS TO KNOW

person of the therapist

use of self

frame of reference

conjoint family therapy

context

denotative level

metacommunicative level

congruent and incongruent messages

nurturing touch

placating

blaming

super reasonable

irrelevant

functional coping

sculpting

self-esteem

co-therapist

psychotherapy of the absurd

experiential/symbolic

family reconstruction

self-actualization

battle for initiative and structure

joining the craziness

Gestalt/experiential

observer as participant

encounter

EXPERIENTIAL FAMILY THEORY AND THERAPY

Emerging from humanistic psychology of the 1960s, experiential family therapy is largely ahistorical. It focuses on the here-and-now. The **person of the therapist** influences the process of the therapy session. It strongly emphasizes the **use of self,** in the immediate sense. That is, when something is happening that evokes a feeling response in the therapist, he or she uses that feeling as a prompt or challenge, calling those feelings to the attention of the clients. For instance, in a family session, a father makes a series of blaming statements such as, "It's my family's fault that I'm so grouchy. All of them pick on me." As the father makes this statement, the therapist observes other family members who appear nervous and stay silent, and begins to feel some of their anxiety. The therapist could say, "I'm feeling afraid, like I have to back off, because I worry that you're going to knock me down too." By expressing his or her feelings, the therapist may be reflecting some of the clients' feelings. Family members feel understood by the therapist and may begin to feel safe to talk about how they feel. By expressing his or her feelings at the moment, the therapist is attempting to place some personal responsibility on an individual for the effect he or she may be having on other family members.

Experiential therapy uses many of the techniques first developed in encounter groups. It draws from psychodrama, art therapy, Satir's communication and sculpting processes, and other feeling-expressive practices. It emphasizes unblocking honest emotional expression, largely by having the therapist serve as a model for expressing feelings and encouraging family members to do the same. Clients are encouraged to speak openly with one another to hear about each other's pains, pleasures, nightmares, and hopes. They are helped to accept each other empathically, without judgment or personalizing. Nonjudgmental empathy allows individual family members to gain more personal autonomy and allows the family to achieve more intimacy. All gain more freedom to relate to other important people in their lives in a more satisfying, growth-supporting way.

Experiential family therapy depends heavily on the person of the therapist and his or her ability to communicate freely and openly. The use of the client's language—utilizing words that connect to the kinds of words the client uses—is seen as especially important. For instance, if a client uses a phrase like, "It felt like such a *burden*," the therapist could reflect back, "Sounds like your problems feel so *heavy* to you." This client expresses problems in terms of *weightiness*. "Burden" and "heavy" are from the same sensory **frame of reference**.

Experiential family therapy offers a set of beliefs that form a framework for therapy. It suggests that the scapegoat, or symptom bearer, provides anxiety relief for the family. A symptomatic family is one that has little tolerance for differences and is stuck with rigid roles that are largely unexamined. If individual family members attempt to make changes, they are seen as threatening family stability. Symptoms offer nonverbal messages in reaction to the dysfunctional communication working within their system. Change begins when the family is in enough pain to seek help, or when the problems in the family become involved with community services such as schools, social services, or the police (e.g., positive feedback as described in previous chapters).

The immediate shared experience in the therapy session is often able to produce new responses, helping all the family members to move toward individual growth and greater family intimacy. The therapist models creativity, spontaneity, and the value of, and ability to be, playful. Satir believed by being caring and accepting, the therapist helps people to overcome their fears, open up to their experiences, and open their communication. She encouraged the therapist's use of self within the therapy session as important step toward bringing about congruence. For example, if a father is saying things to a child that express his despair, the therapist might comment, "I feel such sadness when I hear you. Does anyone else in the family feel so sad?"

Much of the learning from the therapy involves self-learning and self-rediscovery as the therapist journeys with the client. Satir believed in the human potential to change. The meta-goals of her therapy were to raise clients' self-esteem by supporting them to be their own change makers. Satir initiated **conjoint family therapy.** It was a revolutionary idea to include all family members in the treatment room for therapy. She joined with each family member and encouraged dialogue and loving reconnections within the session.

The Person of the Therapist

The experiential family therapist's approach to a session is guided by his or her own personal style in response to the **context** the client family offers him or her. In general, experiential therapists begin by joining with each family member and gathering information about what is happening with them and what they hope for from therapy. Experiential family therapists tend to push and confront families from the outset (Kempler, 1973). For example, the therapist may say, "I'm getting upset at the way you avoid giving clear answers to your daughter." They clarify communications and increase expressiveness by the open way in which they express their personal reactions in the session. They prefer to include as many family members and generations as possible in the therapy sessions. Therapy is terminated when the mutually agreed on goal is reached.

VIRGINIA SATIR

Satir, who began her professional life as a schoolteacher and later became a social worker, was one of the early members of the Mental Research Institute(MRI) in Palo Alto, California. As we noted in Chapter 4, this group studied the emotional impact of communications. She was the only female member of that initial group. As a social worker, Satir had begun seeing families in her private practice in 1951. In a training program she organized for residents of the Illinois State Psychiatric Institute, Boszormenyi-Nagy had been one of her students. In 1959, she was invited by Don Jackson of MRI to become the first director of training. She stayed with that group until 1966, when she became director of the Esalen Institute in Big Sur, California.

Satir projected warmth, nurturing, caring, and genuine involvement to the families she counseled. The warmth of her personality and authenticity of her responses, both in clinical sessions and during large group seminars, is legendary. She expressed belief in the healing power of love and spoke of the healing power of humankind. She wrote:

> The germ of my particular theory and practice grew out of a new appraisal of the meaning of relatives' calls to me about the patient I was seeing. These calls were ostensibly in the form of complaints about the patient, or about my handling of the situation, or reports about things they thought I should know. In traditional psychotherapeutic practice, I had been taught to view any attempt by a relative to communicate with the therapist as a potentially dangerous obstacle to the treatment relationship. As I began to try to understand the meanings of these calls, I saw there were at least two messages conveyed in them; one about the pain or trouble the relative observed in the patient, and one about the pain and trouble in the relative who was making the call.
>
> The next step was to see that the call contained not only an offer of help to the patient, but also a request for help for the relative, disguised as a threat. It was then impossible not to recognize there was an essential relationship between a patient and his (or her) family. While I had known this at some level, it now

was explicit. Furthermore it became clear that any individual's behavior is a response to the complex set of regular and predictable rules governing the family group, though these rules may not be consciously known to him or the family. From this point of view, we can begin to stop seeing activities only as dangers, and look at them as forces for growth and indications of the power of interactional transactions in relation to shaping the behavior of the individuals that are part of that family system.*

Symptoms as Shared Family Pain

Satir explained what has become the background tenet of all family theory: When one person in a family has emotional pain that shows up as a symptom, all family members feel this pain in some way. All communication occurs in context. She suggested that therapists recognize that people communicate simultaneously by gestures, facial expressions, body posture and movement, tone of voice, the way they dress, and their frame of reference, such as their use of feeling, seeing, or hearing words. Experiential family therapists ask all client family members, when, where, with whom, and under what circumstances does the problem occur? They ask, "What is understood, agreed on consciously, and what is expected between the persons involved in the interchange?" They ask other family members if they see those agreements and expectations the same way. They notice the reciprocal nature, patterns of the interaction, in the context of the session. They observe whether those patterns are familiar to the family members, often comment on what they see happening, and ask family members how they feel and think about the patterns.

Communication and Interpersonal Functioning

As Satir emphasized, humans cannot *not* communicate! (Erickson's influence.) Communication includes all those symbols and clues used by people giving and receiving meaning. Taken in that sense, the communication techniques that people use can be seen as reliable indicators of interpersonal functioning (Satir, 1983).

People communicate at two levels: (1) the **denotative level**—defined as the literal content, and (2) the **metacommunicative level**—defined as a comment on the literal content and on the nature of the relationship between the persons involved. These two levels can be observed in the nonverbal messages and the process by which the message is given. Satir wrote that all messages, when viewed at their highest abstraction level, may be characterized as "validate me" messages. By "validate me" message, she meant "Validate me by showing me you value me and my ideas" (Satir, 1983, pp. 103–104).

---

*From *Satir Step by Step: A Guide to Creating Change in Families*, by V. M. Satir and M. Baldwin. Copyright © 1983 Science & Behavior Books. This and all other quotations from this source are reprinted by permission.

She described the difference between **congruent** messages and **incongruent** messages as follows. A congruent communication is one in which two or more messages are sent via different levels, but none of these messages seriously contradicts any other. For example, a husband may say, "The dog is on the couch," in an irritable tone of voice in a context that tells the wife he is irritated and why he is irritated, and it fits with what she expects to hear from him—she knew he didn't like dogs, on couches or anywhere.

An incongruent communication is one in which two or more messages sent via different levels seriously contradict each other. One level of communication is context itself. For example, if a husband says, in a delighted tone, that the dog is on the couch, and the wife knows he doesn't like dogs, she could find this message confusing. The tone and the affect do not match with her knowledge of his feelings.

Love, Autonomy, and Interdependence

Satir believed humans are all autonomous, interdependent, unique beings. At times we are dependent on others to help us with specific things and to validate our existence and worth. She said that humans were insatiable, that they could never be loved or valued sufficiently, even as they strive to be safe and powerful enough on their own. The trick is to allow both the autonomy and dependency needs to coexist so that each enhances the other. She described a mature person as someone with the following characteristics: the ability to make choices and decisions based on accurate perceptions about self, others, and the context of their life; the ability to acknowledge these choices and decisions as belonging to him or her; and the willingness to accept responsibility for their outcomes.

Goals for Therapy

Satir's (1972) goal for family therapy was expressed in the following quote:

> We attempt to make three changes in the family system: First, each member of family should be able to report congruently, completely, and honestly on what he(she) sees, hears, feels and thinks about his (or her) self and others, in the presence of others. Second, each person should be addressed and related to in terms of his (or her) uniqueness, so that decisions are made in terms of exploration and negotiation rather than in terms of power. Third, differentness must be openly acknowledged and used for growth. (p. 120)

Satir defined her approach to therapy as dependent on three primary beliefs about human nature:

• Every individual is geared to survival, growth, and getting close to others, and all behavior expresses these aims, no matter how distorted it may look.

- What society calls sick, crazy, stupid, or bad behavior is really an attempt on the part of the afflicted person to signal the presence of trouble and call for help. In that sense, it may not be so sick, crazy, stupid, or bad after all.
- People are limited only by the extent of their knowledge, their ways of understanding themselves, and their ability to check out with others to be sure they understand what is being said. Thoughts and feelings are inextricably bound together; the individual need not be a prisoner of his or her feelings but can use the cognitive component of feeling to put those feelings in perspective. People can learn what they do not know and therefore can change how they respond to and understand people to improve relationships and situations that haven't been working for them (Satir & Baldwin, 1983).

The Importance of Nurturance in Therapy

Satir preferred everyday words and concrete images. No psychobabble. She engaged clients caringly, yet authoritatively, from the very first session. She actively clarified communications, turning people away from complaints of the past, by pointing them toward solutions. One of her trademarks was her **nurturing use of touch**, a hand on a shoulder or a gentle holding of the client's hand. She was approachable. She joined with each family member, naturally offering the assurance of human touch. Family members soon trusted her and their anxieties were disarmed by her obvious caring, acceptance, and validation for each of them. As a result, family members became more open to change and mutual validation of each other.

Communication Shorthand

Satir coined the term and developed the process of conjoint family therapy sessions. This meant she met with all family members together and helped them talk about their issues in caring, supportive ways, reframing negatives and listening to exploring feelings. She named five basic ways of communicating and demonstrated the body postures that depict them. For example:

1. **placating**—depicted by a sort of down-on-one-knee, begging-for-acceptance pose.
2. **blaming**—standing over the other person with an angry grimace and finger pointing.
3. **super reasonable**—intellectualizing, perhaps with arms crossed or nose up in the air suggesting this person just knows better and has all the truths.
4. **irrelevant**—flitting about, being silly, in some way drawing the attention away from the subject under discussion.
5. **functional coping stance**—a person is congruent, competent, appropriate.

Sculpting

Satir utilized nonverbal experiences to help the family visualize and understand their interactions. One nonverbal technique she developed was **sculpting.** To set up a sculpting experience, the therapist asks the family to stand and designates one person at a time to be the director (protagonist). The director is then asked something like, "Show us the way you are feeling right now about your (Mom, Dad, brother, sister). Without words, gently, lead him/her to a place in the room that reflects how close or distant you are feeling toward him/her."

To set up a sculpting experience, the director (the protaganist, or the client selected for that role) is asked to place each family member into various parts of the room, in various positions that represent the way the director feels closeness or distance toward that person and may pose them in a way meant to depict how they see that person's actions toward him or her. This step is done nonverbally. The director then is asked to stand back and reflect on the "picture" he or she has created of the family, and now verbally, express feelings about how it feels now, and what could change that would feel better.

The therapist then invites the other family members to express their feelings about where they had been placed (how close or how distant) and what they would like to change. Sometimes, the family moves on from there and change begins. Sometimes more than one family member needs the opportunity to perform as director to further clarify relationships between them. Sometimes the sculpting experience works in ways that are not immediately evident.

For example, I had a client family I invited to do a sculpting experience. The goal was for the mother to understand her son's pain. The mother complained about almost everything about the boy and refused to believe her condemnation was hurting him. The teenage son had threatened to commit suicide if the mother couldn't acknowledge how much he wanted her love and approval. The son, as the director in a sculpting experience, placed his mother to the far side of the room, pointing her finger at him in a blaming stance. His father was placed about halfway between mother and son, but facing away from both of them, arms crossed tightly across his chest (he was a silent blamer). The son lay down on the floor in a fetal position, with his hands covering the back of his head. The mother angrily said, "I won't be intimidated by threats of suicide," and walked out of the session. The father followed her, leaving the boy sobbing. I was shocked, angry, and worried. This had never happened in any sculpting session I had directed before. The boy and I talked for a while. Over time he came to realize he was worthwhile and lovable, and could give himself the care he wanted, and find support and love from other sources. I saw him a few more sessions by himself. He grew more optimistic about his life. About a year later, he came in to tell me how well he was doing. He had a new girlfriend. Her family was very loving to him. He had received a scholarship to college. So although at the time of the sculpting it felt like a disaster, and actually seemed to enlarge the terrible breach in the family, it did help the boy tap into his own resources and find other ways to get his needs met. He told me later, he had met with his parents, accepted their limitations, and had developed an acceptable relationship with them. I received a call from his mother about four years later telling me her son had just graduated from college with honors and how proud she was of him. It seemed that sculpting session had inadvertently induced a crisis that led to changes in perceptions, expectations, and actions.

Family Reconstruction

Satir also offered a method called family reconstruction. This method is often used in larger groups or where actual family members are unable or unwilling to be present. The protagonist (client, director) describes his or her family. People from the group are asked to act as a specific family member and to respond to the protagonist's complaints or requests, as they believe that person would, based on the protagonist's description of that person. The role playing often becomes very real, and through it, meaningful change can occur for the protagonist. Interestingly, the role players often seem to be typecast and learn something about themselves in the process.

Satir (1983) wrote:

> I see all people as representations of life, in whatever form that happens to be. When people are in need or are having some kind of problem, their manifestation of themselves—the way they look and sound and talk—can be pretty ugly, pretty beautiful, or pretty painful. Underneath all this I see the living human who, I feel, would use himself or herself differently if he or she were in touch with the life that he or she is and has. So with every human being that I encounter, I mentally take off his or her outside, and try to see inside, which is that piece of the self that I call self-worth or **self-esteem**. . . . There is in the person, that which probably he or she has not touched. That person not only hasn't touched it—he or she doesn't even know it's there. I know it's there. This conviction in me is so strong that it is a given for me. I never ask if that person has life; I ask only how it can be touched. (p. 246)

Since Satir's death in 1988, groups have sprung up in the United States and around the world that follow her teachings and philosophy. Some go under the name of Avanta Network. In Singapore and Malaysia, there are post-graduate diploma programs in Satir systemic brief therapy.

CARL WHITAKER

Whitaker grew up on an isolated dairy farm. A story is told about how that rural beginning influenced the way he thought about solving problems. Apparently his father had asked the young Carl to get a mule into the barn. Carl obediently led the animal by a rope and pulled and pulled and pulled. It would not budge. After a while his father noticed his son's futile efforts, went up to where he was struggling with the stubborn animal, and whacked it from behind. Immediately the mule moved forward into the barn. At that moment, it is said, Whitaker learned there was more than one way to solve a problem.

Whitaker trained in obstetrics and gynecology and then psychiatry. His explorations of the psychotic mind was done by listening and learning to understand language, crazy but human, learning to follow the lead of his patient's symbolic wordage and then, gaining their trust, leading them back through saner, more productive word paths. His initial hospital placements at the University of Louisville emphasized play therapy and behavior rather than an intrapsychic focus. As a staff psychiatrist at the Oak Ridge Hospital in Oak Ridge, Tennessee, from 1944 to 1946, he found the position stressful because of the pressures associated with living and working in the shadow of the U.S. Army's atomic plant just before the development of the bomb. He was young, inexperienced, and had been given a heavy client load in addition to teaching classes for medical residents.

Co-therapy

It was in this setting, at Oakridge, that he began the use of a **co-therapist** and began to involve spouses and children of patients as part of his treatment approach. From 1946 through 1955, he was chairman of the Emory University Department of Psychiatry. His work at Emory included more experimentation with family therapy and focused increasingly on the treatment of schizophrenia (Whitaker & Malone, 1953). In 1948, he initiated a series of 10 four-day weekend conferences on schizophrenia featuring a diverse array of researchers. Gregory Bateson and Don Jackson were in attendance at the final conference in Sea Island, Georgia, the first major meeting of the family therapy movement (Nichols & Schwartz, 1998, p. 51). The format of the conference included a demonstration by each participant of his or her approach to therapy with individual clients and client families. After the group observed the therapy, they debated the issues that arose from the demonstrations. A cross-germination of ideas was set in motion.

Whitaker and his entire faculty resigned from Emory in 1955 in the face of mounting pressure to make the program more psychoanalytic. They started the Atlanta Psychiatric Clinic, which fostered the growth of experiential psychotherapy. In 1965, Whitaker moved to the University of Wisconsin Medical School and opened a private practice in Madison. He now thought of himself as a family therapist and defined the way he worked as **psychotherapy of the absurd** (Whitaker, 1975). We cover more about what he meant by this phrase under the heading of "How Families Are Helped" later in this chapter.

In 1980, he retired, only to begin a rigorous travel schedule, providing seminars on his work at conventions and workshops. He died in 1995.

Authenticity Versus Theory

In a 1976 article entitled, "The hindrance of theory in clinical work," Whitaker stated that rather than theory, he used "the accumulated and organized residue of experience, plus the freedom to allow the relationship to happen, to be who you are with the minimum of anticipatory set and maximum responsiveness to authenticity and to our own growth impulses" (1976, p. 163).

Whitaker's (1976) approach to family therapy is deliberately atheoretical:

> My theory is that all theories are bad except for the beginner's game playing, until he gets the courage to give up theories and just live. Because it has been known for many generations that any addiction, any indoctrination tends to be constrictive and constipating. (p. 154)

For Whitaker therapy was an art, and he recommended using faith in one's own experience and the ability to allow the process of therapy to unfold in an authentic and genuinely responsive manner. He labeled his particular approach as **experiential/symbolic** family therapy. He wrote that experience, not education, is what changes families. While education can be immensely helpful, the covert process of the family is the one that contains the most power for potential changing. Most of our experience goes on outside of our consciousness. We gain best access to it symbolically. Symbolic implies that some thing or some process has more than one meaning. (Keith & Whitaker, 1988)

Therapist and Client Grow from Therapy

Under Whitaker's theory, therapy was seen as a growth process for both the therapist and the client. All participants become equally vulnerable, intimate, and interactive, in a parallel experience in which no one takes responsibility for another. The therapist must be committed to his or her own growth, personally as well as professionally, if he or she is to be able to encourage growth in others:

> It is intuitive, it aims at increasing anxiety within a caring environment. . . . It is experiential, intrapsychic and paradoxical. Good therapy must include the therapist's physiological, psychosomatic, psychotic and endocrine reactions to a deeply personal interaction system. (Whitaker, 1976, p. 162)

Goal of Therapy

Whitaker's goal for therapy was to help individuals grow and to help them to do so in the context of their families. Healthy family relationships were understood to be far more important than either insight or understanding. It is through a sense of belonging to the integrated whole of one's family that the freedom to individuate and separate from the family, and then to reintegrate as an authentic, autonomous family member, is derived. That was Whitaker's goal for the families he worked with.

Whitaker described healthy families as **self-actualizing** families that grow despite the pitfalls and problems in their lives. A healthy family has no rigid patterns or triangulation and offers freedom to join and separate, as is age appropriate. Healthy family systems are open and available for interaction with other systems in their network. They are not symptom free, but problems are handled successfully through a process of negotiation. Sex, passion, and playfulness are acknowledged as valued ingredients. It allows for both separation of the generations and the ability to transcend generational boundaries. It facilitates individual autonomy and personal development. The healthy family provides a context that is supportive of its individual members and their shared experiences. Dysfunction may arise from the battle between the spouses over whose family of origin will provide the model for their family of procreation. In this case, the aim of therapy is to enable the spouses to learn to accommodate to each other's differences.

How Families Are Helped

Initially, the therapist engages in a **battle for structure** (Napier & Whitaker, 1978). He insists on controlling the structure—the way the therapy process is conducted and who is to be included, from the very first phone call. Whitaker made it clear that his own autonomy was important, that he is interested in his own growth as a result of their work together, and that they need not be concerned about protecting him. He establishes what they can all expect from one another and often described himself as a coach, who is not interested in becoming a player on the team (member of the family), but helping them play more effectively (develop better ways of being supportive team members). If the therapist loses this initial battle for structure, the family will continue to replicate the behavioral patterns that were aggravating their current problems in the first place.

Whitaker framed his ideas about the integrity of the family with the term **battle for initiative** (Napier & Whitaker, 1978). He said it was the family that was in charge of their lives, and responsible for their decision and the direction they wish for their lives to go. Any initiative for change must come from and be actively supported by the family members involved. The therapist makes clear that it is the family's responsibility, not the therapist's, for changes in the family. When family members are able to take this initiative, the therapy is deemed to have achieved its basic goals.

The therapy process Whitaker espoused included the enhancement of creativity, or craziness, within the family, so that all are freed up to grow and change. Whitaker defined seven techniques he considered important to the therapy process (Keith & Whitaker, 1982):

1. Redefining and reframing symptoms as attempts toward growth.
2. Modeling fantasy alternatives to real-life stress.

3. Separating interpersonal stress and intrapersonal stress.
4. Adding practical bits of information.
5. Augmenting the despair of a family member.
6. Affective confrontation.
7. Treating children like children and not as peers.

The family is taught how to use fantasy and expand its emotional options. Members learn to take risks. They are offered ideas they may accept or reject. The absurdity of a family situation is heightened and both relationship and generational boundaries are affirmed as the therapist models appropriate parenting behaviors.

Whitaker created a highly personal and very successful type of approach uniquely suited to his own personality. He stressed the value of a co-therapist to augment both his strengths and weaknesses. He required the whole family be present and requested that three generations be included. It was not his purpose to impose his personal values on anyone else. He freely implemented intuitive tactics he believed would affect change for the particular family he was working with. Yet, he has stated that ultimately, therapy is to be a joint effort in which the client is encouraged to break old patterns, to expand him- or herself, and to create the possibility for alteration through reorganization and reintegration. It was not unusual for Whitaker to get down on the floor and play with the younger children in the family.

One technique he used when working with clients who exhibited schizophrenic behaviors was to join them in their language patterns—**join the craziness**—as if he too saw and heard the fantasies expressed by the patient. After a time, the client, feeling accepted and understood, would begin to challenge the confusing word patterns he was hearing from Whitaker and begin to talk with more reality. Whitaker was unpredictable, playful, and skilled in using the strength of his personality. It was obvious he had learned his childhood lesson well—there was more than one way to solve a problem.

WALTER KEMPLER

Kempler labeled his approach **Gestalt/experiential** family therapy. A here-and-now process, in which "treatment consists of bringing discordant elements into mutual self-disclosing confrontation" (Kempler, 1982, p. 141). He began his medical career as a general practitioner in 1948 and completed a residency in psychiatry at the University of California in 1959. In private practice, he developed an interest in working with families. Kempler meshes his Gestalt heritage with existential psychology/philosophy and phenomenology. His therapy is focused on expanding awareness, accepting personal responsibility, and unifying the individual who is recognized as capable of directing and living his or her own life. Acceptance of personal responsibility is necessary if the individual is to achieve maturity.

A Positive View of Human Nature

Gestalt therapy places a heavy emphasis on a positive view of human nature and potential. Experiments have revealed that individuals view reality in terms of meaningful wholes, or Gestalts, rather than as unrelated isolates. The **observer as participant** is a key element of this theory. Gestaltists emphasize the here-and-now, for only the present can be changed inasmuch as the past is gone and the future is yet to come.

Kempler views the whole family as the most appropriate focus for therapy. A family can be any two persons who are concerned about each other with the potential to support individual development. Like Whitaker, he minimizes the importance of theorizing. He speaks of psychological reality as a combination of experience and awareness in the here-and-now. Since our perceptions often differ from those around us, one of the basic aims of his therapy is to facilitate a recognition, acceptance, and awareness of individual differences in perception. It is the role of the Gestalt/experiential therapist to act as a guide toward more positive human interactions that restore mutually beneficial transactions between family members.

Therapeutic Encounters

Kempler describes **encounters** as people-sequenced experiences. Good encounters are those that lead to a sense of closure or completion. An effective therapeutic encounter focuses on the process of behavior in the here-and-now and is composed of the following four requirements:

1. A clear knowledge of "who I am" at any given moment. This knowledge requires a dynamic awareness of what I need from moment to moment.
2. A sensitive cognition or appraisal of the people I am with and the context of our encounter.
3. The development and utilization of my manipulating skills to extract, as effectively as I am capable, what I need from the encounter. This aspect is expressive.
4. The capability of finishing an encounter (Kempler, 1981, p. 38).

The therapist serves as a model of effective encountering. Incomplete encounters are the source of psychological misperceptions. Incomplete encounters reflect an inability to express feelings aroused during the course of the interpersonal interaction. They result in a sense of uneasiness that distorts current awareness, and in turn, inhibits present encounters.

Healthy Families

Kempler described the healthy family as offering a supportive context that allows members to express both their individual identity and their personal desires, to acknowledge their autonomy and accept differences, and to function in the here-and-now. He said that families become dysfunctional when the pressures for togetherness and loyalty to the whole interfere with personal responsibility and integrity. "Symptoms are seen as signals of a distressed process: that is, a process that is not evolving suitably according to one of the points or participants in the process"(Kempler, 1982, p. 148).

He saw symptoms as an expression of conflict between two polarities, with one as the victim of the other, and with the identified patient inevitably describing him or herself in the victim role. In this context, feelings are not acknowledged. The client's symptom is a way of saying "Ouch! I have a pain in my family" (Kempler, 1973, p. 19).

Goal of Therapy

The basic goal of Gestalt/experiential family therapy is to restore the ability of the family to act as a fundamental resource for its members' well-being and continued development. Achievement of this goal requires stimulating and releasing the potential in family members "to perceive, to negotiate, and to act" (Kempler, 1982, p. 159). Kempler believes the first issue presented is not *the* problem, rather it is a signal of pain in the family.

How Families Are Helped

The Gestalt/experiential family therapist serves as a catalyst, encouraging individuals to confront each other in a more open and direct manner. The therapist gives observations of what is happening, then challenges the way family members interact that aren't working, offers suggestions as to different ways for them to interact, and gives advice. If the client's response is negative or negligible, the therapist may become a passionate participant, acknowledging his or her own feelings and demanding they be paid attention to. This active participation and use of the therapist's own personality and life experience is seen as an important key to the effectiveness of this therapy. To paraphrase Kempler (1981), a therapist needs to meddle in other people's lives, insist on being heard, take risks, demand responsible behavior, tolerate differences, understand others, be contrary, self-critical, courageous, and acknowledge mistakes.

SUMMARY

Proponents of experiential family therapy pay attention to recursive patterns of communication and feedback in a context of wholeness in keeping with a cybernetic epistemology. They work in the here-and-now, offering their own feeling reactions to the family members' interactions within the session.

Virginia Satir focused on affect and communication. She demonstrated five communication stances: placating, super reasonable, blaming, irrelevant, and functional coping. Satir worked toward building self-esteem in all family members. She said a need for love was fundamental, and we could never get enough. She reframed the meaning given by the family for the problem, and used her personal feeling responses that modeled openness and caring. The goal of her therapy was self-actualization, taking personal responsibility for self and personal growth within the context of the family.

She was gentle, warm, and joined with all family members. Tapping into each person's frame of reference—responding with words that resonate with theirs, clients felt readily understood. She encouraged people to experience fully how the ways in which they were interacting with one another were impacting their relationships. She helped family members express feelings, check out the meanings of what the other was saying or doing by asking questions, and promoted a safe and nurturing environment in therapy.

Carl Whitaker saw dysfunction as a battle for initiative and structure. He was directive, alternately supportive and provocative. He created crises in the therapy session as a way to measure the family's competencies and motivate them to change. He was concerned with growth, interactions, and appropriate life-cycle behaviors. He wanted the whole family, including three generations, when possible, to be in the sessions. He believed symptoms occurred when family members were restricted by rigid rules that lead to separation or individuation difficulties. He was playful, creative, spontaneous, and joined the craziness. He preferred working with a co-therapist to create a contrast with his style and bring balance into the session. Whitaker saw a successful session as one in which the therapist, as well as the client, experienced growth.

Walter Kempler combines Gestalt therapy with experiential therapy. He sees the goal of therapy as personal growth in the context of family dialogue. Kempler helps clients to be more open, to know themselves and others better, and to accept differences. He challenges clients, often by expressing his strong feeling reactions to how and what they were doing or saying in the session. He believes that when people are not able to get in touch with or express their feelings to others, they are not able to make meaningful contact, or to grow, or to take personal responsibility for themselves or others.

EXPERIENTIAL ACTIVITIES

1. In class, instructors can set up small groups to form family units. Each group selects a different background or lifestyle. The instructors should define specific symptoms. Students role play therapist and family roles and demonstrate how they would join and enact sculpting following the ideas of Satir.

2. Set up a team of students to demonstrate the four communication roles described by Satir. Invite full class discussion about how they would work with clients to change those communication roles. Have students role play some of their suggestions.

3. Use the entire class to do a family reconstruction. The class will decide on who is involved and what issues are involved. Use class members to

represent three generations and respond to protagonist as he or she approaches each with his or her needs or concerns.

4. Instructors should ask small groups to design playful ways they could intervene with family members, as they think a Whitaker styled therapist would. Each group would then demonstrate.

REFERENCES

Keith, D. V., & Whitaker, C. A. (1982). Experiential-symbolic family therapy. In A. M. Horne and M. M. Ohlsen (Eds.), *Family counseling and therapy*. Itasca, IL: Peacock.

Keith, D. V., and Whitaker, C. A. (1988). The family's own system: The symbolic context of health. In C. J. Falicon (Ed.), *Family transitions: Continuity and change over the lifecycle*. New York: Guilford.

Kempler, W. (1973). *Principles of gestalt family therapy*. Oslo, Norway: Nordahls.

Kempler, W. (1981). *Experiential psychotherapy with families*. New York: Brunner/Mazel.

Kempler, W. (1982). Gestalt family therapy. In A. M. Horne & M. M. Ohlsen (Eds.), *Family counseling and therapy*. Itasca, IL: Peacock.

Napier, A. Y., & Whitaker, C. A. (1978). *The family crucible*. New York: Harper & Row.

Nichols, M. P., & Schwartz, R. C. (1998). *Family therapy: Concepts and methods* (4th ed.). Boston: Allyn & Bacon.

Satir, V. M. (1972). *Peoplemaking*. Palo Alto: Science & Behavior Books.

Satir, V. M. (1983) *Conjoint family therapy* (3rd ed.). Palo Alto: Science & Behavior

Satir, V. M., & Baldwin, M. (1983). *Satir step by step: A guide to creating change in families*. Palo Alto: Science & Behavior Books.

Whitaker, C. A., & Malone, T. P. (1953). *The roots of psychotherapy*. New York: Blakiston.

Whitaker, C. A. (1975). Psychotherapy of the absurd: With a special emphasis on the psychotherapy of aggression. *Family Process 14*, 1–16.

Whitaker, C. A. (1976). A family is a four-dimensional relationship. In: P. J. Guerin (Ed.), *Family therapy: Theory and practice*. New York: Gardner.

7 CHAPTER STRUCTURAL FAMILY THEORY AND THERAPY

TERMS TO KNOW

Salvador Minuchin—
from psychiatry to
family structure

boundaries, alliances,
and coalitions

subsets

problem-maintaining
transactions

symptom bearer
(scapegoat)

joining

context

hierarchically organized

complementarity

family subsystem

spousal subsystem

sibling subsystem

rigid boundaries

diffuse boundaries

enmeshment

disengagement

alignment

affiliation

triangulation

coalitions

detouring

identified patient

transformation

join

assess

restructure

family structure

enactment

one-way mirror

family life cycle

tasks

therapeutic contract

autonomy

interdependence

executive subsystem

cross-generational
coalition

exaggeration of a
symptom

de-emphasizing a
symptom

re-labeling

reframing

STRUCTURAL FAMILY THEORY AND THERAPY

The primary goal of structural family therapy is to work toward organizational changes in the dysfunctional family. It asserts that when the family's structure is transformed, each family member's experience changes, both in self-perception and in relation to other family members. The structural family therapist actively engages the family as a whole, introduces challenges that force adaptive changes, and supports and coaches family members as they attempt to cope with the ensuing changes (Colapinto, 1991).

Structural family therapy focuses on the idea that the whole family is organized in a functional way. It focuses on the family members' patterns of interaction in the present. These patterns include its rules, spoken and unspoken, and **boundaries, alliances, and coalitions** among family members and among **subsets** of family members, across generations and within the same generation. Psychosomatic disorders are seen as rooted in a particular family context. It emphasizes that the structure of the family needs to be changed in order to resolve the **problem-maintaining transactions** that demand a **symptom bearer (scapegoat)** for family stability.

Structure is not static or fixed. The family's transactional patterns regulate the behavior of its members and are maintained by two sets of constraints: generic, or universal, rules, and idiosyncratic, or individualized, rules (Minuchin, 1974). Structuralists contend that well-functioning families should be **hierarchically organized,** with parents serving as the executives in charge. There must be **complementarity** of functions, with the spouses operating as a team and accepting their interdependence. Complementarity takes the form of teamwork in well-functioning families. The rules that evolve, along with the behavioral patterns of its members, become the family's structure. Deviations from established rules that go too far, too fast, will be met with resistance. The healthier the family, the more easily they adapt to transitional circumstances such as a baby being born, a grandparent coming to live with the nuclear family, a child becoming an adolescent, parents changing jobs or losing a job, the chronic illness of one its members. Figure 7.1 shows Minuchin's symbols for family mapping.

SALVADOR MINUCHIN: FROM PSYCHIATRY TO FAMILY STRUCTURE

Born and raised in Argentina, Minuchin served in the Israeli Army as a physician in the late 1940s as Israel became a country. He then came to the United States where he trained in child psychiatry with Nathan Ackerman (child guidance movement). Upon completion of that training in 1952, he went back to Israel to work with displaced children. It was there that he began to pay attention to the importance of families in the development of mental health and mental illness in its members. He returned to the United States in 1954, where he was influenced by the interpersonal psychiatry of Harry Stack Sullivan. He then went to work at the Wiltwyck School for delinquent boys, just outside of New York City where he encouraged his colleagues to include families in their sessions. Minuchin developed new concepts and techniques for working with these multiproblem, lower economic families.

The idea of including families as an essential part of the therapy process was revolutionary for clinicians who had been trained in the medical model of individual psychiatry and psychology. In 1962, Minuchin visited Palo Alto, which had become the home base for family therapy, and met with Jay Haley. Their friendship afforded an important cross-pollination of ideas. Minuchin then renewed contact with Nathan Ackerman, and credits Ackerman with teaching him the importance of the personal passion of the therapist when engaged with the family. Like Ackerman, he used **joining**, plus active involvement with the family in the session. Along with his colleagues from Wiltwyck, he wrote "Families of the Slums" (Minuchin, Montalvo, Guerney, Rosman, & Schumer, 1967), which was both a clinical and conceptual success. It was the first of nine books he wrote on family therapy topics.

In 1965, he accepted the directorship of the Philadelphia Child Guidance Clinic. He recruited Jay Haley and Cloe Madanes, among others, to work with him there. We cover them in greater detail when we discuss strategic family therapy (Chapter 9). Under his leadership, the Philadelphia Child Guidance Clinic became one of the largest and most prestigious clinics of its kind in the world. In 1974, it became the first clinic where the majority of clients were inner-city families.

FIGURE 7.1 | MINUCHIN'S SYMBOLS FOR FAMILY MAPPING

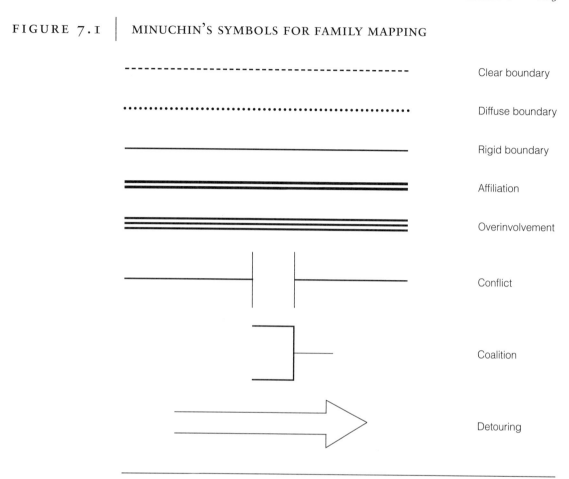

From *Families and Family Therapy*, by S. Minuchin, p. 53, Harvard University Press, 1974.

The Most Widely Practiced Family Systems Therapy

By the mid-1970s, structural family therapy had become the most influential and widely practiced of all systems of family therapy despite protests from the orthodoxy of the AMA and APA, who contested the validity of teaching family therapy to psychiatrists. Minuchin responded strategically, by not responding, and continued to expand the influence of family therapy.

In Philadelphia, Minuchin became interested in the role of family **context** in psychosomatic conditions. It came to his attention that no medical explanation could be found for the unusually large number of diabetic children who required emergency hospitalization for acidosis (a depletion of alkali in the body). These children did not respond to individualized therapy that focused on reducing stress. He and his colleagues researched the problem and developed successful interventions involving the entire family. He later expanded his research and treatment to asthmatic and anorectic children. The data confirmed for Minuchin that the locus of pathology was in the context of the family (Colapinto, 1982).

In 1976, Minuchin resigned as Director of Philadelphia Child Guidance but stayed on as head of training until 1981. He then started his own center in New York. He also had a private practice and provided training for family therapists. In 1996, he retired and moved to Boston. At the time of this writing, he was focusing his energies on the larger social contexts that contribute to family problems and serving as a consultant to the Massachusetts Department of Mental Health (Minuchin, Colapinto, & Minuchin, 1998).

In his book, *Families and Family Therapy* (1974), Minuchin told how the context of his family and community formed him, and his understanding of the "universality of human phenomena":

> My style is partly a product of a childhood spent in an enmeshed family with forty aunts and uncles and roughly two hundred cousins, all of whom formed, to one degree or another, a close family network. My hometown in rural Argentina, with only one main street had a population of four thousand. My grandparents, two uncles, a cousin and their families, lived on our block. Thus, I had to learn as a child to feel comfortable in situations of proximity, yet to disengage sufficiently to protect my individuality.
>
> As a young professional, I tended to empathize with children and to blame their parents. After I was married and had children of my own, and was making the mistakes that parents inevitably make, I began to understand parents and to sympathize with them. My life, both in Israel, where I worked with Jewish children from many cultural backgrounds, and in the United States, where I worked with black and Puerto Rican families, sensitized me to the universality of human phenomena, as well as to the different ways in which specific cultures prescribe a person's response to these phenomena. I became particularly aware of the manner in which societies coerce their underdogs.
>
> Through the years, I have had a number of successes and made innumerable blunders, which have given me a sense of competence and authority. In my worst moments, this sense of achievement expresses itself in an authoritarian stance, and at other times it allows me to operate as an expert. In the measure to which I have learned to accept myself and to recognize areas in which I will never change, I have developed a sense of respect for the diversity of people's approaches to human problems. (p. 120)

Complementarity of Roles

Family subsystems—spousal, parental, sibling—are usually made according to gender or generation, as well as common interests and functions within the family. Complementarity of roles is key: a child has to act like a son so his father can act like a father; a father has to act like a father, so his son can act like a son. The older son may take on a more executive role when he is alone with his younger brother and the younger brother must behave like a younger brother (Minuchin, 1974). The strength and durability of the **spousal subsystem** is central to family stability. How a husband and wife learn to negotiate differences and make accommodation to one another's needs tells us a great deal about their family stability and their ability to change as circumstances demand. Roles and rules must be renegotiated as children grow and require different parental responses. A family unable to be flexible during times of transitional changes tends to develop troubling symptoms in one of its members as a means for maintaining homeostasis—stability of the status quo.

The **sibling subsystem** offers the growing child his or her first experience of being part of a peer group. In a well-functioning family, all subsystems operate in an integrated way to protect the differentiation and integrity of the family system. Clearly defined boundaries between subsystems within a family help maintain separateness and, concurrently, emphasize belongingness to the overall family system. Boundaries need to be flexible enough so the family can accommodate to changing life circumstances.

Excessively **rigid boundaries** create impermeable barriers through which parents and children cease to make real, or affectional, contact. The child in such a family may gain a sense of independence and also feel isolated or unsupported by the rest of the family. **Diffuse boundaries** are easily intruded on. Parents are too accessible and overprotective. There is no privacy. Children have little opportunity to learn how to be independent, think for themselves, or gain the necessary skills to develop relationships outside the family. In families with diffuse boundaries, there is no clear generational hierarchy, adults and children exchange roles leading to confusion in personal identity.

Well-Functioning Families

In a well-functioning family with clear boundaries, each member gains a sense of "*I-ness*" along with a group sense of *we* or *us*. Family members feel more secure in knowing who is in charge as well as feeling accepted and respected as individuals. Most family systems fall somewhere along the continuum between **enmeshment** (diffuse boundaries) and **disengagement** (rigid boundaries) (Minuchin, et al., 1967). Boundaries of a subsystem are the rules defining who participates and what roles they will play to carry out a particular function.

Alignment suggests appropriate cooperation and **affiliation** between family members. It refers to how supportive or unsupportive family members are in carrying out a function. Power in a family is related to who is in charge in the context and the situation being dealt with. Structuralists use the term **triangulation** to describe a dysfunctional arrangement in which each parent demands the child side with him or her against the other. Every movement the child makes causes one or the other parent to feel neglected or attacked (Minuchin, 1974). **Coalitions** are alliances between specific family members *against* another member. A stable coalition is a fixed and inflexible union that becomes a dominant part of the family's everyday functioning. A **detouring** coalition is one in which two family members hold another family member responsible for their difficulties (Minuchin, Rosman, & Baker, 1978). The label of pathological refers to those families who, when faced with a stressful situation, increase the rigidity of their transactional patterns and boundaries, and refuse to adapt to changing circumstances and life cycle transitions. These families deny any exploration of alternatives (Minuchin, 1974).

Families in Their Larger Context

Minuchin emphasized that the definition of family had to include the social context in which it was embedded. This context includes extended family, community, treatment professionals, and government influences. His conceptual scheme of a normal family included three facets:

1. The family is transformed over time, adapting and restructuring itself so as to continue functioning.
2. The family has a structure that can be *seen only in movement.* Certain patterns are preferred in response to ordinary demands. But the strength of the system depends on its ability to mobilize alternative transactional patterns when internal or external conditions of the family demand it to restructure. The boundaries of the subsystems must be firm, yet flexible enough to allow accommodation and realignment when circumstances change.
3. The family adapts to stress in a way that maintains family continuity while making restructuring possible (Minuchin, 1974, pp. 65, 66).

Identified Patient's Symptoms Stabilize the Family System

When a family labels one of its members "the patient," it can be assumed that **identified patient's** symptoms are bringing some stability to that family. It can also be assumed that the symptom is being reinforced recursively, by the way the symptom bearer and the other family members interact with the symptom behaviors. When a family system responds to internal (developmental) or external (societal) pressures, by rigidly adhering to old rules and behaviors, those rigid transactional patterns block access to alternative ways of responding to the current stress. The stress is detoured and homeostasis (no change) is maintained as one person develops symptoms and becomes the identified patient. The identified patient's role offers the family a way to resist appropriate or adaptive change. This process is done *without conscious awareness* on the part of family members (Minuchin, 1974). As an example: A husband and wife may be having an ongoing battle over finances. When he gets frustrated that his wife doesn't understand his frustration, the husband threatens to leave. This interaction and threat is made many times. Their son, age 10, begins to regress, retreating into behaviors that were more like those of a child of 4 or 5. His mother cries, his father softens. He agrees he won't leave since the child needs both of them. The child resumes more appropriate behaviors. But shortly after, the parents repeat their arguments and threats. The child's symptoms return. This recursive pattern of behavior repeats itself again and again. The actions of all three reinforce each other's actions.

Goals of Therapy

The structural family therapist's function is to facilitate alternative responses necessary for the **transformation** of the family system that releases the identified patient from his or her role and symptoms. Learning more adaptive ways of interacting allows for the interpersonal and individual growth of all family members. As people relate differently, the need for the symptom, or for a symptom bearer, is reduced or eliminated. Transformation is defined as changes in the patterned sequences of interactions between family members (rules, boundaries, coalitions, alliances) that alter their reciprocal needs.

The process of therapy includes three *recurring* steps by the therapist:

1. **Join**
2. **Assess**
3. **Restructure**

These steps are inseparable and are an ongoing process throughout the therapy. Diagnosis begins with the interactional process of joining that continues throughout the therapy (Minuchin, 1974). The ongoing assessment focuses on six major areas:

1. The **family structure** and its usual transactional patterns and the available alternatives. The therapist observes the ways in which the clients interact during the entire session. One of his techniques, enactment, became a cornerstone of family treatment and diagnosis.

    Enactment involves directing family members to dialogue *with* one another in the treatment room utilizing an event already occurring between family members in the session as a point of intervention. For example, a mother came to a structural family therapist complaining her 2-year-old daughter had a tantrum whenever she didn't get what she wanted. The therapist intervened as soon as an enactment of the tantrum behavior presented itself in the session. This occurred when the girl asked her mother for candy and the mother said, "Not now." The structural therapist coached the mother to stay firm, stay in charge, and not give in. The girl began to cry, threw herself on the floor, and screamed. Staying in the background, the therapist supported the mother for a full half hour until the child finally stopped crying and screaming. The child seemed perfectly fine, as if nothing had happened. The mother, who had reported feeling overwhelmed with her own personal difficulties and inadequacies as a parent, felt strengthened as she realized she could be firm and both she and her child would survive. A short time later the mother reported that the tantrums had stopped (Rosenberg, 1983).

    During an enactment, the therapist backs out of the clients' talk, observes their transactions, coaches them to continue, and assesses how he or she will intervene. The therapist focuses on changing the way the clients interact and seeks ways to reduce or eliminate the presenting problem. Viewing each other's sessions from behind a **one-way mirror** afforded Minuchin and his colleagues the opportunity to observe one another's work, and thereby learn from each other how to do family therapy. Enactments help to make those interactions more immediately observable.

2. Evaluation of the system's flexibility and its capacity for broadening and restructuring. As the therapist observes the interactions among the clients, he or she assesses the way alliances, coalitions, and subsystems respond to changing circumstances. The therapist uses these observations in planning the next interventions to change the way family members interact into more productive, appropriate and satisfying relationships. He or she will direct family members to participate in specific tasks within the session, as well as to practice at home, to accomplish those goals.

3. The therapist observes the family's sensitivity to individual members. Enmeshment can be recognized when there is extreme sensitivity, that is, overpersonalization or overprotection in response to any small difference in the actions of any individual member. Enmeshed family members show intolerance of, resistance to, or rejection of, changes they regard as deviant behaviors (e.g., "That's not the way we do it in this family"). Extremely low sensitivity, or lack of notice or response to an individual member's input, suggests disengagement (e.g. "It's not my concern if my sister is in trouble").

4. The family life context, looking at the sources of support and stress in the family's environment (extended family, community resources).

5. The **family life cycle** and behaviors, rules, boundaries, and **tasks** appropriate for each of its members.

6. The patterns of interaction that maintain the identified patient's symptoms. The therapist creates tasks within the session that modify those interactions. (p. 130)

Paying Attention to Nonverbal Clues

An ongoing task for the therapist is to look for nonverbal cues. He or she observes who speaks *to* whom, who speaks *for* whom, *how* they speak (tone of voice, facial expressions, body language, etc.), and notes the family's responses to the therapist's suggestions of alternative perceptions and actions. The advantage of an evolving diagnosis related to context is that it provides constant openings for therapeutic intervention. *Diagnosis and therapy become inseparable* (Minuchin, 1974).

Therapeutic Contracts

After the initial joining, the therapist asks everyone present to tell how he or she sees the presenting problem. A **therapeutic contract** is agreed on for the course of therapy, which includes defining the family's goals. It specifies where, when, and how often they will meet and who will be at the sessions. It also specifies what is expected of each family member and of the therapist. The therapist then begins the process of restructuring the family. In joining, the therapist becomes an actor in the family play, part of the cast of players. In restructuring, he or she functions as a director as well as an actor. The therapist also uses him or herself by entering into alliances and coalitions; creating, strengthening, or weakening boundaries; and opposing or supporting transactional patterns. Through a position of leadership within the therapeutic systems, the therapist puts forth challenges to which the family must accommodate. Clients may attempt to get the therapist to side with one or the other, thereby pulling him or her into the family system to perpetuate its status quo (homeostasis). It is the therapist's responsibility to stay in charge of the process, not get pulled in, and to intervene to disturb family members' repetitive, unchanging patterns of interaction. When one family member begins talking *about* the behavior of another family member, the structural therapist directs the speaker to talk *with* the other member instead of about him (enactment). If family members resist entering into a dialogue with one another, the therapist must persist and have a number of techniques available to persuade clients to carry out those in-session dialogues. He or she persuades, teases, is playful, sits silently, and avoids making eye contact with anyone until someone begins the task. He or she moves back from the group, so as to be out of the line of vision, doesn't respond if addressed other than to redirect the speaker to speak with the other family member, or may even leave the room to observe from behind a one-way mirror.

Reward Competence

The therapist encourages family members to reward competence that occurs in the session and is generous with positive statements, supporting individuals as they make even minimal changes. The structural family therapist encourages and joins with the family underdogs, and supports the struggle of growing children for age-appropriate independence. He or she uses family members as co-therapists, making the larger family unit the context for healing. Structural family therapists do not make interpretations of individual difficulties. Problems are seen as developed and maintained by dysfunctional relationships (Minuchin, 1974).

Spatial Manipulation

Sometimes the manipulation of where people sit in relation to one another in the therapy room can be a metaphor for closeness or distance between people. For example, when family members seat themselves in the therapy room, if a child sits between the parents, the therapist may, at some point, ask the child to move so that the parents can sit next to each other. The therapist does this to enable more direct dialog between the parents without the buffer created when the child sits between them. This step could be an important one in beginning the process of helping the parents work as a team and defining the parental hierarchy for the family. "Spatial manipulation has the power of simplicity. Its graphic eloquence highlights the therapist's message" (Minuchin, 1974, p. 141).

Autonomy and Interdependence

The structural family therapist helps the family create the flexible interchange between **autonomy** and **interdependence** that promotes the psychosocial growth of its members. Interdependence is seen as a complementary component to autonomy. A balance between interdependence and autonomy is in the interest of the individuals in the family, as well as for a well-functioning family system. Rejection of either generates defects in intimacy skills and curtails personal growth. Simple rules can be established to promote autonomy for family members:

- Listen to what each family member says and acknowledge what you have heard.
- Family members should talk with, and not about, each other.
- Family members should not speak for others, or answer questions directed to another, or expect one member to act as the spokesperson for the family.

Therapist as Model and Teacher

It is the therapist's job to model and impose those simple rules within the session. He or she may offer information about differences to help the parents achieve age-appropriate responses related to each family member's developmental stage. The therapist initiates tasks that help subsystems, such as a spouse subsystem, define what each may want from the other, as spouses, as well as parents. He or she can help parents join in an **executive subsystem** that can make decisions regarding limits and privileges, in a way that promotes healthier growth-permitting boundaries. The therapist must work to reduce rigid **cross-generational coalitions** that blur parent/child distinctions. Strengthening the spouse subsystem helps spouses negotiate spousal issues without drawing in a third family member (triangulation). This strategy also protects the third member's autonomy. When boundaries around a subsystem are strengthened, the functions of that subsystem improve.

Instigating System Crises

The family therapist's skill at instigating stress in different parts of the family system gives the family an opportunity to experience its own capability to restructure—to do something different. The simplest maneuver the therapist can use to produce stress is to block the flow of communications along its usual channels. In an example offered by Minuchin, a parental child's usual role was to translate the mother's communications to the other children and then their responses to her. Minuchin intervened, saying, "Excuse me, Morris," to the parental child, and "Go ahead" to the interrupted child. He reported that five minutes later, Morris again tried to help his mother understand his sister, and the mother, imitating the therapist, told him not to interrupt (Minuchin, 1974, p. 148). A system change had occurred!

Another way a structural family therapist instigates a system crisis may be by temporarily joining with one family member or subsystem, excluding others in the room. He or she may do this sequentially, with one member or one subsystem at a time, then moving on to another. Rigid systems can be jarred into motion as their discomfort grows. The therapist must constantly be aware of the person he or she is currently allied with, and remain alert to that person's threshold of endurance, as well as the endurance of the others who are not engaged in that dialogue. Even as the therapeutic alliance is acted out, the therapist must offer some support to the others. When the reason for the alliance is over, either because the goal has been reached or the threshold of endurance has been reached, the therapist must shift his or her position and ally with another family member, maybe even against the former ally. The therapist must not go so far that he or she pushes anyone away or drives him or her into greater blaming or scapegoating (Minuchin, 1974). This process requires constant observation, alertness, and a delicate balancing act by the therapist to the ways the other family members are behaving while he or she is involved with one of their members.

Tasks for Assessment and Change

Structural family therapists use tasks, either within the session or outside the session. Tasks within the session help the therapist assess the family's processes and patterns and their abilities for change. Enactments, blocking interruptions, temporary therapeutic alliances, and repositioning people within have already been described. Tasks to be done at home are aimed at both the presenting problem and the structural problem. They provide the opportunity for the family to test out new ways of being together.

For example, if a mother has been in a coalition with a child, and the father has disengaged from both of them, the task could be, first, for mother and father to talk with each other to discuss reassigning a responsibility, such as preparing breakfast. Mom may have the task of instructing Dad (she sees this as her role) on how to prepare breakfast. What is different is that Dad now has to prepare breakfast and sit with the children as they eat and talk with them (perhaps his habit had been to hide behind a newspaper and wait to be waited on). The task could include an arrangement for Mom to sit out in the living room and do her crossword puzzle while the family eats, something she had said she wished she had time for. This task re-involves the father with the children. It develops a sense of being a team for the couple, since they plan it together. Old rigid roles and patterns of behavior are broken. It utilizes the mother's pattern of instructing, yet takes her out of the middle from interactions with the children and the father. He gets to do tasks around breakfast that involve him with the children, without her interference. He can feel more in charge. She gets to do something she wants to do which reduces her resentments of "having to do it all for everyone else." Since they plan it together (albeit coached by the therapist), it begins the establishment of an executive subsystem.

Exaggerating a Symptom

An **exaggeration of a symptom** often will change the usefulness of the symptom as the symptom bearer and other family members are forced to respond differently.

Minuchin offered an example of a middle-aged couple that came to therapy because the husband's depression was so severe he was unable to work. The therapist noticed there was a lack of mutual support between the husband and wife. He acknowledged the man's depression as a correct assessment of his wasted life, suggesting he mourn even more, for the part of himself that is sad. He also suggested that this Jewish man observe the mourning ritual of his religion and sit Shiva for eight hours each day. (Shiva is a tradition where people sit and mourn for the dead). His wife was instructed to be as attentive and sympathetic as she could. She was to bring him food and console him. Minuchin was telling this man to perform a ritual of mourning and to grieve for his own dead sense of himself, and was telling his wife to be actively involved in the process. The wife dutifully did her part. The man mourned and cried continually for three days. On the fourth day, he became bored. His depression left him and he returned to work. Both partners came to realize that they had become isolated from one another, and they both had been feeling depressed and uncared for. They were now motivated towards being more supportive of one another (Minuchin, 1974, p. 154). Here Minuchin exaggerated the man's depressed behaviors and involved the wife in the behaviors, giving her a caring role that helped to reconnect husband and wife.

De-emphasizing a Symptom

A symptom can also be **de-emphasized** by framing alternatives that incorporate something different for all family members. One way to de-emphasize the symptom is to change the way, time, or place in which it is done. The identified patient is instructed to do the symptom only at specific times, while other family members may be directed to avoid the patient completely while the symptom is being done. Sometimes clients are asked to do the symptom behavior in a different place or in a different way. Sometimes the therapist will move the focus to another family member, taking the attention away from the initial symptom bearer.

Relabeling or Reframing

Relabeling or **reframing** the symptom into interpersonal terms opens new pathways for change. Minuchin offered the example of an anorexic girl whose symptoms were relabeled as disobedience in an effort to punish her parents, so they would feel incompetent (Minuchin, 1974). This new label of disobedience rather than illness helped define her anorexia as a purposeful act on the part of the girl, which could be changed as family understandings and interactions changed, rather than as an eating disorder over which she had no control.

Using a Symptom Constructively

Minuchin suggests using symptoms as a basis for teaching competence. If a child has taken to throwing things when upset, and the mother is feeling helpless, the therapist could design a task to teach the mother *how* to teach the child to throw things better, perhaps setting up a target to practice on. This task is designed to give the mother a sense of competency and give the child the attention, respect, and guidance he or she is indirectly asking for with the destructive behavior.

SUMMARY

According to this model, an effectively functional family is an open system, in transformation, maintaining links with the extra-familial community, possessing a capacity for appropriate life cycle developmental tasks, and having an organizational structure composed of executive and sibling subsystems (Minuchin, 1974). Minuchin highlighted the concepts of enmeshment and disengagement and emphasized how they affected family problems. In the next chapter, we will cover how both structural and strategic family therapists see symptoms as developing from problem-maintaining interactions embedded in repetitive patterns. Symptoms are maintained as the family members rigidly do the same thing again and again, limiting their ability to adjust to life cycle transitions. Symptoms are also maintained by cross-generational coalitions that are demonstrated by dysfunctional hierarchies (i.e., parent/child in coalition against other parent). Symptoms are relieved when families become open to a larger variety of interactive problem solving skills that are life cycle appropriate.

Members of effectively functional families feel comfortable and safe in expressing feelings with other family members. Family members are flexible and adapt to each member's developmental stages. They feel a connection with their community, have flexible boundaries and rules, and are able to change roles as needed and change alliances as appropriate. The parents need to function as a team, accessible yet in charge. Problems are reframed in interpersonal terms. The structural therapist sets up enactments within the session and observes the way family members interact with one another. He or she then intervenes with tasks to be done at home or in the session, education about family roles, and directives geared toward establishing more functional and appropriate interactions between family members. Support, education, and guidance are joining and restructuring functions. Nurturance, healing, and support from the family is seen as vital for the well-being of each individual family member and for the healthy functioning of the family system. The therapist may have to teach all family members how to be mutually supportive, and teach the parents to strengthen their executive boundary and enact different responses to each other and to their children.

EXPERIENTIAL ACTIVITIES

Additional experiential activities for this chapter are included at the end of Chapter 8, Strategic Family Theory and Therapy, since they involve activities that examine the similarities and differences between structural and strategic theories and therapies.

1. Instructor arranges four students into a role play to demonstrate an enactment. At the same time the other students in the class are arranged in a circle around the role play. This larger group is to serve as observers. One role play student is a therapist. The other three are a family. The therapist asks the family members to decide among themselves as to whom they will be in the family, the problem they will present, and how they will act toward one another. The therapist will not know in advance what the family members will do. The therapist's task will be to get members of the family to enact their situation among themselves. The therapist will sit back and let the enactment unfold for a few minutes. Then he or she will offer observations to the family about the way they are interacting. For example, the therapist may say something like: "I wonder if you are aware that when your father begins to get emotional you try real hard to change the subject. I wonder what you think would happen if you let him express his feelings." At that point the observers will be invited to offer their ideas as to what was going on with the family and suggest some interventions they think could reduce the problem-maintaining interactions.

2. Using the interactions and problem presented in the above example, the instructor asks members of the class to make statements as if they were the therapist who was rewarding the competence of family members who had showed some movement toward change.

REFERENCES

Colapinto, J. (1982). Structural family therapy. In A. M. Horne & M. M. Ohlsen (Eds.), *Family counseling and therapy*. Itasca, IL: Peacock.

Colapinto, J. (1991). Structural family therapy. In A. S. Gurman & D. P. Kniskern (Eds.), *The handbook for family therapy* (Vol. II). New York: Brunner/Mazel.

Minuchin, P., Colapinto, J., & Minuchin, S. (1998). *Working with families of the poor*. New York: Guilford.

Minuchin, S. (1974). *Families and family therapy*. Cambridge, MA: Harvard University Press.

Minuchin, S., Montalvo, B., Guerney, B. G. Jr., Rosman, B. L. & Schumer, F. (1967). *Families of the slums: An exploration of their structure and treatment*. New York: Basic Books.

Minuchin, S., Rosman, B. L., & Baker, L. (1978). *Psychosomatic families: Anorexia nervosa in context*. Cambridge, MA: Harvard University Press.

Rosenberg, J. B. (1983). Structural family therapy. In B. B. Woman & G. Stricker (Eds.). *Handbook of marital therapy*. New York: Plenum.

8 STRATEGIC FAMILY THEORY AND THERAPY

CHAPTER

KEY THEORISTS

Jay Haley—power and control	**Cloe Madanes**—love and violence	**Milan Group**—power game to postmodern

TERMS TO KNOW

Jay Haley's Terms to Know

hierarchical structure	sequences of behavior	power and control
triads	paradoxical directives	stages of therapy

Cloe Madanes' Terms to Know

reverse hierarchies	family rituals	pretend technique
family intentions		

The Milan Group's Terms to Know

power game	circular questioning	alternating day ritual
team	respecting a system	invariant prescription
positive connotation	hypothesizing	systemic mutuality
family ritual	storytelling	universal prescription
neutrality	counter-paradox	
curiosity	therapeutic double bind	

Strategic theorists and therapists all suggest that emotional problems and symptoms of family members result from hierarchical structures in which the boundaries are unclear or inappropriate for healthy family functioning. This chapter describes three primary schools of strategic thought as expounded by Jay Haley, Cloe Madanes, and the Milan Group. Although each theorist explains somewhat different motivations for the problems that surface, they all see the repetitive sequences of behaviors as the process that maintains them. Each utilizes strategic methods designed to correct hierarchical distortions and improve more age- and role-appropriate interactions. Strategic therapists work toward solving the presenting problem.

HALEY: POWER AND CONTROL

As discussed earlier, Jay Haley trained with the Bateson's MRI group in Palo Alto. They studied how communications occurred in families when a family member exhibited schizophrenic symptoms. During that time, Haley was strongly influenced by the renowned hypnotherapist, Milton Erickson. In 1973, Haley wrote, *Uncommon Therapy,* a book about Erickson's techniques. It was just one of many books Haley has written, the others primarily describing his own strategic theories. He was not a psychiatrist nor trained in psychoanalysis. He was a researcher who was initially interested in communication patterns. In 1967, he became director of family therapy research, working with Minuchin at the Philadelphia Child Guidance Clinic.

Strategic Theory

Haley's theories evolved through his diverse background. Although systemic in his thinking about family reciprocal interactions, he believes strongly in the importance of a **hierarchical structure,** with parents in charge. He describes **triads** as the family unit that maintains its stability. He defines family therapy, not as a different way to treat individual problems, but rather as offering a *different perspective on the concepts of change and stability* (Haley, 1976).

Haley focuses on **sequences of behavior**—communication patterns in the here-and-now. He uses directives and action plans and creates strategies to fit the uniqueness of each family. His use of **paradoxical directives** has been criticized by some as manipulative (Cade & O'Hanlon, 1993). Yet the paradoxical directives are the hallmark of strategic therapy. Haley explained that paradoxical directives are not ploys to outsmart families—they are thoughtful suggestions derived from long experience (Haley, 1984). We will talk more about paradox and manipulation a little later in this chapter.

Haley describes the struggle for **power and control** as central to family patterns. He defines symptoms as resulting from repetitive, unproductive attempts to control or influence other family members. Here he disagreed with Erickson, who said that control was an illusion and not congruent with systems theory. Erickson said the pursuit of control leads people to engage people in ecologically and interpersonally destructive behavior (M. Erickson, personal communication, 1979).

The Metaphor of Control

Haley uses the concept of control as a metaphor to describe patterns that seem to characterize all systems and families. He said people engage in reciprocal attempts to control and define the nature of their relationships: "It must be emphasized that no one can avoid being involved in a struggle over the definition of his or her relationships with someone else" (Haley, 1963, p. 9).

Symptoms and Hierarchical Organization

Haley wrote that family organization is in trouble when coalitions occur across the generations—between a member of the parental hierarchy and one of the children—especially when those coalitions are covert, or denied. Problems are viewed as resulting from inappropriate triads or triangles. He said symptoms were clues that the hierarchical structure of the family is confused and needs restructuring (Haley, 1976). He has described pathology as a "rigid, repetitive sequence in a narrow range" (Haley, 1976, p. 105).

Role of the Therapist

The strategic therapist becomes part of the family system with which he or she is working. Therapeutic change is seen as "a change into a system of greater diversity" (Haley 1976, p. 105). The strategic therapist asks, "What is being done that maintains the symptom?" Haley wrote that changes in behavior change feelings and perceptions. Strategic therapists focus on process, rather than content. They intervene to disrupt covert hierarchical structures—hidden rules and patterns that control couple and family interactions. They interrupt the problem-maintaining patterns of behavior. Haley differs from other strategic family therapists in that he describes therapy and change as a series of **stages,** creating new symptoms along the way as steps leading toward more adaptive behaviors.

How Families Are Helped

1. Whole families are seen together to observe their patterns—sequences of behavior—with one another. These observations give the therapist information with which to redefine the problem as belonging to the family system, rather than the identified patient.
2. One therapist is in control of the process so he or she could be more immediate and decisive. This reasoning precludes the use of a cotherapist.
3. Other therapists may view the process from behind a one-way mirror to serve as consultants, to offer insights, suggest directives, and help the primary therapist to maintain control. (The one-way mirror room is connected to the therapy room by a telephone. Consultants can call in observations and suggestions.)
4. Strategic therapists have a specific, structured format for the first interview. Haley (1976) stresses the importance of structure in defining the therapy. It must include:
    a. Social engagement (joining) with all family members. This step lays the groundwork for establishing the importance of each family member and for redefining the problem as systemic. It also puts the therapist in control of the process of therapy.

b. Next, the therapist explains why he or she has asked all family members to attend and tells them they are all to serve as resources for problem solving. Everyone is asked to give his or her perspective about the presenting problem. At this point, all conversation is directed toward the therapist, who validates each family member's opinion. The therapist discourages discussion between family members during this phase. After listening to all family members, the therapist redefines the problem as one shared by all of them rather than belonging to an individual symptom bearer.

c. The therapist then asks the family to discuss the problem among themselves and observes their patterns of interaction (i.e., who talks the most; who interrupts, who says the least, who is calm, who is tense) and the family structure (i.e., who takes charge, who rescues whom, who is in a coalition with whom).

d. After observing the family's interaction, the therapist defines the changes he or she perceives as needed by the family, and describes them in terms of solving the presenting problem in specific interactional, behavioral terms.

e. The therapist ends the interview with clearly spelled out directives—tasks to be done at home. The therapist describes the directives in painstaking detail as to when, where, and how they will be done, and exactly what each family member is assigned to do. Directives can be paradoxical or direct assignments for changes to be made. Paradoxical directives may take the form of suggesting that the clients do more of the same—more of the behaviors that have been maintaining the problem. Or they could be something that may seem contradictory or opposite of the family's stated goals. For example, if the family complains a child is not going to bed at a parent-prescribed time, the family members may each be given a task designed to keep the child up past the designated bedtime.

f. The next appointment is set.

In the next session, the therapist asks the family to describe how they did on the tasks and what outcome resulted from their efforts. The therapist neither blames nor praises the family for doing or not doing the assigned tasks. The therapist uses the information gained from whether or how they complied to the plan and design subsequent interactions that will again be assessed in each session.

Stages of Change

Following the idea that changes need to be made in stages, Haley promotes more extreme changes first, such as putting parents in charge in an almost tyrannical way, which will usually be even more uncomfortable for the family than the presenting problem. In subsequent sessions, he might tell them to keep doing things that more extreme way, or suggest they lighten their rules, as the parents become more adept at modifying behaviors, while still remaining in control. The therapy is considered complete when the presenting problem is resolved.

CLOE MADANES: LOVE AND VIOLENCE

Cloe Madanes was born in Argentina and serves as codirector with Haley of the Family Therapy Institute. As a researcher, she compared the hierarchies in three different kinds of black families—families where a member was using heroin, families with a member with schizophrenic behaviors, and those with high-achieving young members. She found the families of heroin users had the largest number of hierarchical reversals, in which one parent was put down to the drug abuser's level in the hierarchy. The families where one member had schizophrenic symptoms also had a large number of reversals. Only the high achievers had a small number of reversals. She explained that **reverse hierarchies** are not bad in certain situations, such as when children need to take care of a sick parent. "It's when there is incongruity in a hierarchy—for example, when an addict appears weak because of his addiction, but also derives power from it by being threatening and dangerous— that families are at risk" (Madanes, 1981).

Basic Intentions of Relationships

Madanes has written a number of books about strategic family therapy, the latest in 1990, *Sex, Love, and Violence: Strategies for Transformation*. This book builds on ideas that differ from Haley's notion that power and control issues motivate all relationships. She wrote, "All problems brought to therapy can be thought of as stemming from the dilemma between love and violence" (p. 5). Family problems were categorized according to four basic **intentions** of the family members:

1. First, the intention to dominate and control, which show themselves as delinquency and behavioral problems. Madanes suggests parents learn to work together to take charge of their problem children.
2. The second intention is to be loved. She associated psychosomatic symptoms, depression, anxiety, and eating disorders with this motive. Therapists are to encourage **family rituals** and mutual interactions intended to initiate and reinforce loving behaviors between family members.
3. A third intention is to love and protect others; related symptoms include suicide threats, abuse and neglect, and thought disorders. Reframing the children's symptomatic behaviors, Madanes would ask the children to find better ways to protect or care for their parents.
4. Finally, the intent to repent and forgive, and she finds these families have problems like incest, alcohol and drug abuse, sexual abuse, and sadistic acts. Families are taught to form appropriate boundaries and hierarchies.

Goal of Therapy

Madanes (1990) wrote, "A goal of therapy is to bring harmony and balance into people's lives. To love and be loved, to find fulfillment in work, to play and enjoy: All are part of a necessary balance" (p. 13). She said people will often do something they wouldn't ordinarily do, if it is framed as play or pretend, and she developed a whole range of **pretend techniques.** One such strategy is to ask a symptomatic child to pretend to have the symptom and encourage the parents to pretend to help. The child is able give up the actual symptom now that pretending to have it is serving the same family function (Madanes, 1981).

THE MILAN GROUP

In the late 1960s, Mara Selvini-Palazzoli of Milan, Italy, introduced eight of her psychoanalytically trained colleagues to the work of Bateson, Haley, and Watzlawick. The Milan model emerged, adopting systems theory, the MRI interactions model, and the strategic model. The Milan group's model is most consistent with Bateson's original ideas concerning *circular epistemology* (MacKinnon, 1983). Four members of the group, Mara Selvini-Palazzoli, Luigi Boscolo, Gianfranco Cecchin, and Guiliana Prata, formed the Center for the Study of the Family. Over the next decade, they developed new theories and strategies (Boscolo, Cecchin, Hoffman, & Penn, 1987). They continue to develop and distill new ideas and methods into the Milan model, adapting postmodern thinking and process. The Milan therapy process involves the use of team members in addition to the primary therapist. Their postmodern work will be described later in this chapter. In Chapter 10, postmodern ideas are described in greater detail, and in Chapter 12, specific postmodern therapy practices are discussed.

Power-Game Aspect of Family Interaction   The initial focus of the Milan group was on the **power-game** aspect of family interaction and the protective function symptoms serve for the whole family. Power games are unacknowledged patterns used by the family to control each other's behavior. These patterns maintain the family as a self-regulating system that controls itself according to rules formed over time (Selvini-Palazzoli, Boscolo, Cecchin, & Prata, 1978). The Milan group pursued a systematic search for differences in behavior, relationships, and beliefs among family members, to uncover the connections that keep the family system in homeostatic balance. They interviewed families about their history over several generations, searching for evidence to confirm their hypothesis about how the children's symptoms came to be necessary. They hypothesized that the patient developed symptoms to protect one or more other family members so as to maintain the delicate network of family alliances (Selvini-Palazzoli, 1986). In 1974, in their first article written in English, they introduced a **team** approach and a set of powerful interventions such as **positive connotations** and **family ritual** (Selvini-Palazzoli, Boscolo, Cecchin, & Prata). The role of the team will be described when the structure of their sessions is outlined later in this chapter. The Milan model continues to evolve.

How Families Are Helped

The Milan model stresses **neutrality** and **curiosity** and generates a hypothesis through **circular questioning**. It moves people away from cause-and-effect linear thinking, to thinking of multiple patterns and possibilities in relationships. Curiosity is enhanced through telling, and considering, the myriad applicable stories describing one interaction. There is no right or wrong story. There is no story that is more correct than another. The therapist makes no judgment or moral stance toward the position taken by family members. The therapist keeps the focus on the pattern of the interactions in the stories of family members, and how those stories fit with the therapist's descriptions.

Neutrality is described as a way to leave oneself open to being curious. Since neutrality belies judgment, one is free to inquire and learn about the many points of view different family members hold about a given situation. The act of asking about the patterns or relationships of ideas, people, events, and behaviors, perturbs (shakes up) the system with which the therapist is interacting. Curiosity and concern for patterns generates respect for all participants, even as respect generates a sense of curiosity. **Respecting a system** means the therapist acts toward a system with the understanding that the system is simply doing what it does—no right or wrong label tied to what it does. For example, the client family may talk about a particular belief of how children should treat their parents. Using the concepts of neutrality and curiosity, the therapist asks questions that help both clients and therapist understand how those beliefs work for this family. The therapists ask the questions in a nonconfrontational and nonjudgmental manner, in a way that the family can feel the therapist's respect.

Milan strategic family therapists don't profess to know which specific script will be successful for a specific family. It is their job to flush out problem-maintaining patterns by asking questions that challenge the way family members have been thinking about their problems.

Curiosity encourages all participants to look for different descriptions and explanations, even when one cannot immediately imagine the possibility of any other way of thinking about the problem.

Hypothesizing feeds, and is fed by, curiosity. Each hypothesis offers the base from which to ask questions. Milan therapists believe that the therapist must come to the family session prepared with hypotheses. Having a ready hypothesis as a catalyst for their questions reduces the possibility that the family will impose its own definition of the problem that will probably support the game-perpetuating behaviors that maintain the problem.

Hypothesizing begins in the pre-session with the team as they discuss their ideas of what might be responsible for maintaining the family's presenting symptoms. They formulate a map of the family game. Hypotheses orient the therapist to ask the kinds of questions that confirm, necessitate revision, or refute the hypothesis.

Within the family session, useful hypotheses are created through **storytelling.** Families are wonderful storytellers and have such interesting stories to tell. Their scripts are often well practiced over many years by the time they come into therapy. Sometimes they have gotten stuck in scripts that have not kept up with their changing circumstances, such as life-cycle stages.

Milan therapists join the family, with new stories, new scripts based on the therapists' hypotheses, which the family may choose to respond to by changing their scripts into more appropriate resolution-oriented stories. The therapist may also adjust his or her hypotheses as the stories change, and so on, until a script is developed that meets the family's needs.

Putting It All Together

Circular questioning, along with hypothesizing, is a technique nurtured by curiosity and neutrality. By using the language of the relationship, circular questioning undermines the family's belief system that says an individual is the problem. For example, a therapist could ask, "If your mother decided to stop worrying about you, what would your father do?" Questions like that imply patterns, not facts. The moment a question undermines the belief system of family members about the problem, it creates opportunities for new stories.

More examples of circular questions:

- To learn about relationships, subsystems, alliances, "Who do you confide in the most in your family?"
- To check on degree of concern, "On a scale of 1 to 5, how much do you think that worries others in your family?"
- To note changes over time, "Are you closer now than you had been?"
- To learn about a person's a sense of control over another's actions, "If you were to leave, what would he do?"
- To help people recognize how one's reactions, behaviors, and feelings link with other family members, "How would your daughter describe your discipline style?"
- To help look for new insights, "Do you see your shyness as a way of not getting close to others or as a way of being selective about who you want to be friends with?" (Prevatt, 1999, p. 191).

The three principles, hypothesizing, circularity, and neutrality are recursively interlinked. As multiple hypotheses are offered by various team members about the client family, they provide a context for seeing circular patterns occurring between family members (as opposed to linear, cause-and-effect thinking).

Reframing Relationships

The therapist intervenes in the family's system by reframing issues in the context of relationships. The family is simultaneously intervening in the therapist's system as members share their ideas about their dilemma. The idea of recursive relationships calls on therapists to be more curious about the symptoms presented in therapy by the family. It also calls on the therapist to stay alert to the way he or she is affected by, and responds to, family interactions.

A Variety of Interventions

The Milan group devised interventions to break homeostasis using **counterparadox.** They might tell the family, "Although we as therapists are change agents, we think you should *not change* because it is a good thing that Johnny has tantrums and that mother feels hopeless, as this pulls father in to help her." This statement creates a **therapeutic double bind** (Selvini-Palazzoli et al., 1978). If the family changes, they disobey the therapist. If they don't change, they maintain the status quo and the pain that comes with it. The therapist is telling the clients, "Don't change," and is specifying how the symptom behavior is serving a useful purpose (positive connotation) that might not continue if the symptom is stopped.

Positive connotations are reframes of the family's problem-maintaining behaviors. Symptoms are described as having a positive or good purpose because they help maintain the system's balance and facilitate family cohesion. A Milan therapist could suggest, "The reason your child refuses to go to school is he knows his mother is lonely for companionship because his father is always so busy." This statement changes what had been seen as school truancy, to something well-intentioned—keeping mom from being lonely and less focused on dad's absence. It redefines the problem as one involving family relationships and implies that if the relationship between mother and father improves, the child will go to school. Therefore, instead of seeing the child as out of control and defiant, he is seen as a helpful member of the family, helping to maintain family stability.

Note that it is not the symptomatic behavior—not going to school—that is given the positive connotation. It is the intent of the behavior—maintaining the family stability—that is being praised. As a result of reframing the symptomatic behavior with a positive connotation, that behavior is seen as voluntary. A voluntary behavior is something one can change. In addition, when the behavior of family member is described as positive, it becomes easier for them to view one another as cooperative, and they become more willing and able to join together in complying with tasks offered by the therapist.

Utilizing and Creating Family Rituals

Transitional family rituals such as weddings, birthday parties, baptism, and bar and bat mitzvahs are central to a family's life. The therapist designs new rituals that challenge rigid family behavioral patterns that the therapist and the team view to be problem maintaining. Rituals promote new ways of doing things, which may alter the family's thoughts, beliefs, and relationship options (Imber-Black, 1988). The therapist goes into great detail as to what is to be done, by whom, when, and in what sequence. Rituals are ceremonial acts proposed as tentative suggestions, as an experiment for the family to try out. Rituals are not expected to remain a permanent part of the family's life. Their purpose is to provide clarity to a confused family relationship: the clarity is gained as the family enacts of the ritual directive (Tomm, 1984). A frequently used ritual is the **alternating day ritual**. For example, the therapists may hypothesize that one reason the child seems out of control is the parents have not been able to come up with a consistent parenting style. To the Milan therapist, this lack of cooperative parenting reflects a problem within the marriage. These parents may be asked to be in charge of discipline on alternate days—mother on even days, father on odd days. This ritual is prescribed for a specific number of days. On the off days, the parents are each told to behave spontaneously. (Obviously a paradox, since once one is told to do something it no longer is spontaneous.)

Goals of Therapy

The goal of a Milan therapist is to stimulate a process in which the family creates new patterns of behavior, along with new beliefs that are supportive of the creation of new patterns (Tomm, 1984). Milan therapists see emotional problems as problems of social interaction. They understand family members as being caught in recursive patterns and view them with compassion and without judgment (Tomm, 1984). Milan therapists introduce new meanings directly through reframes and positive connotations, and indirectly through circular questioning and by prescribed rituals.

The goal of a ritual is to draw attention to crucial distinctions that maintain the problem. Doing a prescribed ritual points out to the parents how their differences confuse their child, and that his or her misbehavior is a plea for consistency and for the security a healthy marriage offers to a child. The goal is for the parents to realize the importance of two-parent cooperation as a goal. As they become parenting partners, they are actually working on improving their relationship. The therapist accepts responsibility for the process of therapy, but not for what the family chooses to do (Tomm, 1984).

Pre-session Preparations—Teamwork

Milan systemic therapists believe that unless the therapist comes to a session prepared with a hypothesis to be checked out in the session, there is a risk the family may impose its own definition of the problem on the therapist. A team of Milan therapists serves as a planning committee with the primary therapist before and during and after the actual therapy session. They offer alternative voices for the family, responding to what they hear during the session. In pre-session, therapist and team hypothesize what they believe might be responsible for maintaining the family's presenting problems. The therapist tests those ideas in the session, through techniques such as positive connotation, paradoxical interventions, rituals, and circular questioning (Goldenberg & Goldenberg, 2000). Mid-session the family is asked to wait in another room. They are not given any instructions other than to be told that the team is talking with their primary therapist about ways to help them. A team member is designated as a voice of support for each family member. A team could be two or more therapists who sit behind a one-way mirror and a primary therapist who works in the therapy room with the family:

1. The team holds a 5–20 minute pre-session to form hypotheses. They discuss the information gathered in the initial phone call.
2. Next, the primary therapist holds a 50–90 minute family interview as the others observe, usually behind the one-way mirror. The session will confirm or disconfirm the initial hypotheses. New ideas may surface during this interview.
3. Third, the team has a 15–40 minute mid-session where they discuss what they heard. During that time, the therapist asks the family to wait in another room. They cannot hear the team discussion.
4. Fourth, the primary therapist returns to the family for a 5–15 minute intervention in which the primary therapist shares the various conclusions of the team with the family. The therapist reports the various responses given by the team. One team response may be especially supportive of one family member or one idea. Another would then offer a differing response or suggestion. The primary therapist usually offers a positive connotation to the symptom, as well as a paradoxical task, or ritual. In the initial session, the therapist usually prescribes maintaining the status quo, "Continue to do what you've been doing."
5. After the family leaves, the team concludes with a 5–15 minute post-session. Team members sum up their observations and develop hypotheses in preparation for the next session.

All therapists have a legal obligation to act as agents of social control in specific circumstances, such as reports of abuse or threats of violence. Since this requires judging, it can sometimes feel counterproductive to the therapeutic process. The Milan therapists get around that conflict by using their supportive team of therapists to deal with legal responsibilities. This strategy allows the primary therapist to stay removed from those issues and stay focused on the interactional patterns.

Selvini-Palazzoli and Prata sought and developed an **invariant prescription** they said fit universally for all families. Their research focused on finding similarities in the games that symptom-producing families play and then formulating countermoves so the therapist could interrupt those games, forcing a family to change their interactive patterns (Pirrotta, 1984).

They developed an invariant prescription based on a six-stage model of psychotic family games. Selvini-Palazzoli contends that these stages takes place in all schizophrenic and anorectic families. The stages are as follows:

1. A stalemated marriage in which a child attempts to takes sides.
2. The child sides with the passive parent that he or she considers is the *loser.*
3. The child develops symptoms, disturbed behaviors that require parental attention. This behavior is labeled as a demonstration to the passive parent of how to defeat the *winner.*
4. The passive parent, or *loser,* sides with the *winner* and disapproves of the child's behavior.
5. The child feels betrayed and escalates the disturbed behavior.
6. The system stabilizes around the symptomatic behavior, with all participants resorting to psychotic family games as each tries to turn the situation to his or her advantage (Pirotta, 1984).

Establishing Appropriate Boundaries

An invariant prescription consists of a fixed sequence of directives the parents must follow if the therapist is to help them interrupt the family game. For example, if after the initial interview, the therapist and team hypothesize that the hierarchical boundaries of the family are being breached, the therapist will see the parents separately from the child and may give them the following prescription intended to introduce a clear and stable boundary between generations:

> Keep everything about this session absolutely secret at home. Every now and then, start going out in the evenings before dinner. Nobody must be forewarned. Just leave a written note saying, "We'll not be home tonight." If, when you come back, one of your (daughters/sons) inquires where you have been, just answer calmly, "These things concern only the two of us." Moreover, each of you will keep a notebook, separately, and will register the date and describe the verbal and nonverbal behavior of each child, or other family member, which seems to be connected with the prescription you have followed. We recommend diligence in keeping these records because it is extremely important that nothing be forgotten or omitted. Next time you will again come to your session without the children, with your notebooks, and read aloud what has happened in the meantime. (Selvini-Palazzoli, 1986, pp. 341–342)

Previously existing alliances and family coalitions are interrupted by the joint action and secretiveness directed by the prescription. The overall therapeutic goal is to first strengthen the boundary around the parental subsystem, and then to reunite the family in a more stable alliance (Selvini-Palazzoli, Cirillo, Selvini, & Sorrentino, 1989; Prata, 1990).

Milan therapy process is carefully orchestrated:

1. In the first phone call the therapist receives, he or she establishes a stance of neutrality and curiosity to avoid any implication of a coalition with

the caller. After listening to the initial complaint, the therapist may ask a circular question: "When did you start having problems with your son?" instead of "When did your son start to have problems?" This wording immediately directs the thinking to the idea that the problem involves more than one person.

2. Only 10 sessions are planned—each one month apart. The time between sessions is explained to the family as time needed for a therapeutic change to develop.

3. Family members who phone the therapist between sessions are told, unless it's an emergency, to bring it up at the next session.

4. If along the way, the team or therapist decides the therapy is not effective, the therapist may ask for additional family members, who are actively involved with the family, to come to the sessions and may also invite support from additional team members.

Termination of therapy may be made by mutual agreement, initiated by the therapist or the family. The team respects the family's decision. Whatever the circumstance of termination, the family is alerted to possible relapse and doubt is expressed about maintaining change. Family members are told that small setbacks can be expected and are normal.

Early Milan Theory Versus Postmodern Milan Theories

The early Milan therapists prescribed highly structured prescriptions for therapy. The postmodern Milan therapist is seen as a nonhierarchical facilitator, curious and impartial, who encourages family members to investigate different points of view in relation to their presenting problem. Family members are encouraged to decide about their future in their own way and at their own pace. As the therapist and family work together, the postmodern Milan therapist serves as a facilitator who opens the idea of possibilities. Both early and postmodern Milan therapists ask circular questions that suggest to family members that they are *all* involved in the problem and in the decision-making process. This position of **systemic mutuality** empowers the family to choose *whether or how* to change. The therapist is seen as a part of the therapeutic system. He or she is both the observer and the observed, and brings a subjective view of the family, as do all the other participants. The postmodern Milan therapist does not serve as an expert who knows what is best for the family.

SUMMARY

Structural and strategic therapists see symptoms as developing from problem-maintaining interactions embedded in repetitive patterns. Symptoms are maintained as the family members rigidly do the same thing again and again, limiting their ability to adjust to life-cycle transitions. Symptoms are also maintained by intergenerational coalitions that are demonstrated by dysfunctional or reverse hierarchies, that is, parent/child in coalition against other parent. They are also maintained by triangulation, which means that instead of dealing with a problem between the two people involved, a third member is pulled in to support or demean another. Symptoms are relieved when families become open to a larger variety of interactive problem-solving skills that are life-cycle appropriate.

Change occurs as family members develop more flexibility in the way they respond to one another and experience new transactions between them.

- Appropriate permeable boundaries are formed between generations.
- Executive and sibling hierarchies are established.
- Triangles and coalitions are eliminated.
- Family members learn to focus on resolving problems in the present, together, in age-appropriate subsystems.

In general, the stages of therapy include:

- A structured initial interview.
- Mutual definition of goal of therapy.
- Observation of interactions by therapists as family members discuss problems.
- Tasks and directives—in the sessions and at home.
- Termination occurs when symptom relief is achieved or when initiated by therapist or family.

Therapy is brief, ranging from 8 to 12 sessions in most cases. The therapist is active and deliberate and takes responsibility for the *process* of the therapy. The initial joining is key to building trust and cooperation. The therapist focuses on the presenting problem, using the language of the family. Problems are reframed in interactional terms.

There are specific differences between structural and strategic theories and therapies, and among strategic theories and therapists. The structural theory of Minuchin emphasizes the concepts of enmeshment and disengagement and empowering the parent. Haley focused on the power and control aspects of family dysfunction and emphasized the importance of putting the parental team in charge of the family. Madanes saw family dilemmas as a struggle between love and violence aggravated by reverse hierarchies. She saw family member's intentions as clues toward how to address their difficulties. She developed pretend techniques and family rituals as tasks to effect change. The research of the Milan group convinced them that there were **universal prescriptions** that could apply to family difficulties. They developed a tightly defined process of therapy and saw a family only once a month over 10 months. Milan therapists work as a team, with all team members having a role in creating hypotheses. Over the years, they have leaned toward a less directive, more egalitarian process in keeping with the social constructivist, postmodern philosophy permeating the field.

The personality and perceptions of the therapist guides his or her adaptations of the theory they are most comfortable with. Therapists need to learn how others have developed their theories and therapies, and eliminate what doesn't fit for them. For therapists, comfort, or discomfort, with a personal therapeutic process is essential, and directly related to their ability to achieve authentic therapeutic relationships with clients and to become effective change agents.

EXPERIENTIAL ACTIVITIES

1. What are the similarities and differences between structural and strategic theory and therapy? Compare the initial sessions of Minuchin, Haley, Madanes, and the early Milan group.

2. The instructors should designate a small group to create a family and a presenting problem. The team will designate the family as from a particular ethnic/religious/racial background. Students will map the family according to Minuchin's structural symbols and explain the map to the full class, hypothesizing what changes they believe the family needs to make and how the map would change when the structural therapist accomplished designated goals. Minuchin worked with troubled children of lower economic backgrounds. Role play with that group could be useful to demonstrate his ideas on empowerment.

3. The instructor should assign a small group to create a family and a presenting problem. Group members choose a therapist and family members. The therapist role plays how he or she would work with this family as a structural therapist. Other students act as observers behind a one-way mirror (pretend if one isn't available). They can call in suggestions during the session or can offer post-session hypotheses as if planning for the next session. Here again, since Minuchin worked with psychosomatic symptoms, it would be useful to use the role play to demonstrate how to work with psychosomatic symptoms.

4. The instructor should designate a small group of students to create a family and a presenting problem to be worked with in a strategic mode, as Haley or Madanes would work. An immigrant family with an authoritarian father and submissive mother might be a good example with which to demonstrate Haley's power and hierarchy concepts. The group should describe the hierarchy as it is now, and how it should change to relieve the presenting problem. The class helps the designated therapist devise a paradoxical intervention directed toward making that hierarchical change. Other students serve as observers, as if behind a one-way mirror. They can call in suggestions during the session. The full class may join a post-session discussion about what they would expect to happen in the next session, and how they would handle what the family brings in.

5. A student is selected to act as a therapist receiving a first phone call to demonstrate how a Milan therapist would handle that initial call. The instructor may show how to reframe the presenting problem into an

interpersonal one. What would that therapist then do before the initial session? Another student could demonstrate how a strategic therapist would handle a between session call from a family member wanting to talk about the identified patient.

6. The instructor should designate a small group to create a family and a presenting problem. The group selects a therapy team and devises a session as would be done by the Milan group. The group should select one person to be the primary therapist. The others serve as team members and act their roles at the appropriate sequences. Provide for a team planning session in which they devise hypotheses for the next session.

REFERENCES

Becvar, R. J., & Becvar, D. S. (1982). *Systems theory and family therapy: A primer.* Washington, DC: University Press of America.

Boscolo, L., Cecchin, C., Hoffman, L., & Penn, P. (1987). *Milan systemic therapy: Conversations in theory and practice.* New York: Basic Books.

Cade, B., & O'Hanlon, W. (1993). *A brief guide to brief therapy.* New York: Norton.

Campbell, D., Draper, R., & Crutchley, E. (1991). The Milan systemic approach to family therapy. In A. S. Gurman & D. P. Kniskern (Eds.), *The handbook of family therapy* (Vol. II). New York: Brunner/Mazel.

Fisch, R. (1978). Review of problem-solving therapy by Jay Haley. *Family Process, 17,* 107–110.

Goldenberg, I., & Goldenberg, H. (2000). *Family therapy: An overview* (5th ed.). Pacific Grove, CA: Brooks/Cole.

Haley, J. (1963). *Strategies of psychotherapy.* New York: Grune & Stratton.

Haley, J. (1973). *Uncommon therapy: The psychiatric techniques of Milton Erickson, M.D.* New York: Norton.

Haley, J. (1976). *Problem-solving therapy.* San Francisco: Jossey-Bass.

Haley, J. (1984). *Ordeal therapy.* San Francisco: Jossey-Bass.

Imber-Black, E. (1988). *Families and larger systems: A family therapist's guide through the labyrinth.* New York: Guilford.

MacKinnon, L. K. (1983). Contrasting strategic and Milan therapies. *Family Process, 22,* 425–440.

Madanes, C. (1981). *Strategic family therapy.* San Francisco: Jossey-Bass.

Madanes, C. (1990). *Sex, love, and violence: Strategies for transformation.* New York: Norton.

Pirrotta, S. (1984). Milan revisited: A comparison of the two Milan schools. *Journal of Strategic and Systemic Therapies, 3,* 3–15.

Prata, G. (1990). *A systemic harpoon into family games: Preventive interventions in therapy.* New York: Brunner/Mazel.

Prevatt, F. F. (1999). Milan systemic therapy. In A. M. Lawson & F. F. Prevatt (Eds.), *Casebook in family therapy.* Pacific Grove, CA: Brooks/Cole.

Selvini-Palazzoli, M. (1986). Towards a general model of psychotic games. *Journal of Marital and Family Therapy, 12,* 339–449.

Selvini-Palazzoli, M., Boscolo, L., Cecchin, G. F., & Prata, G. (1974). The treatment of children through brief therapy of their parents. *Family Process, 13,* 429–442.

Selvini-Palazzoli, M., Boscolo, L., Cecchin, G. F., & Prata, G. (1978). *Paradox and counter paradox.* New York: Jason Aronson.

Selvini-Palazzoli, M., Cirillo, S., Selvini, M., & Sorrentino, A. M. (1989). *Family games: General models of psychiatric processes in the family.* New York: Norton.

Tomm, K. M. (1984). One perspective on the Milan approach: Part I. Overview of development, theory, and practice. *Journal of Marital and Family Therapy, 10,* 113–125, 253–271.

9

BEHAVIORAL COUPLES/FAMILY THEORY AND THERAPY

KEY THEORISTS

Cognitive/Behavioral Theory

J. Thibault and H. H. Kelly—social exchange theory

Gerald Patterson—behavioral parent training

N. Jacobson and **A. Christensen**—integrative couples therapy

Albert Ellis—rational-emotive therapy (RET)

Aaron Beck—thoughts and depression

F. M. Dattilio—family schemata

W. H. Masters and **Virginia Johnson**—sensate focus

Helen Singer Kaplan—deconditioning sexual anxiety

John Gottman—marital researcher

TERMS TO KNOW

learning theory

operant conditioning

positive reinforcement

extinguished

contingency of reinforcement

intermittent reinforcement

generalized

naturalistic reinforcers

social exchange theory

rewards and costs

positivistic tradition

testable

objectively measured and replicated

social learning theory

modeling

symbolic

cognitive

cognitive processes

reciprocal determinism

cognitive/behavioral

reciprocity

written contracts

reciprocal reinforcement

contingency management

mutual reinforcers

role rehearsal

behavioral parent training

conflict resolution

problem-solving skills

learned responses

consistency

positive expectations

collaboration strengths

power sharing

accommodating

collaborative

A-B-C model, theory of Albert Ellis

rational-emotive therapy (RET)

dispute irrational beliefs

family schemata

functional family therapy

conditioned anxiety about performance

systematic desensitization

sensate focus

disorders of desire

arousal disorders

orgasm disorders

OVERVIEW OF LEARNING THEORIES

Although there are differences between the processes of cognitive/behavioral, psychoeducational family therapy, sex therapy, and marital/couple therapy, **learning theory** is a concept underlying them all. Learning theory is the bond that brings them together into this one chapter.

According to Albert Bandura, behavior—in its normal as well as abnormal manifestations—is learned. Bandura's approach involves a social kind of learning theory that investigates behavior as it is formed and modified in a social context. He recognizes that much learning takes place as a result of behavioral reinforcement, but stresses that virtually all forms of behavior can be learned through observation. He believes individuals do not automatically copy or reproduce behaviors he or she sees other people doing. Rather, Bandura assumes people can fashion, regulate, and guide their own behavior and make a conscious decision as to which observed behaviors to make a part of their own behaviors (1977). Bandura is on the faculty of Stanford University and has studied and written many articles on various aspects of social learning theory since 1969 (Schultz, 1986).

The Individual Foundations of Behavior Therapies

Individual behavioral theory is the grounding on which cognitive/behavioral family therapy is based. It began with Ivan Pavlov, a Russian physiologist who developed the theory and process of classical conditioning. Later, Joseph Wolpe introduced the concept of systematic desensitization used for the treatment of phobias (1948). Perhaps the greatest influence on behavioral family therapy can be seen in B. F. Skinner's **operant conditioning.** Operant conditioning refers to voluntary behavioral responses, as opposed to involuntary or reflex behavior. The frequency of operant responses is determined by their consequences. Responses that are **positively reinforced** will occur more frequently; those that are punished or ignored will be **extinguished** (Skinner, 1953). After carefully analyzing the function of a behavior, the clinician notes the consequences of the behavior to determine the **contingencies of reinforcement.** An important discovery was how inconsistency, or **intermittent reinforcement,** made a troubling behavior more resistant to change. For example, if a child has temper tantrums and most of the time the parents are able to ignore them, but every so often they give in and respond to the tantrum, all their prior hard work of ignoring it could be wiped out by this inconsistency. Inconsistency serves as an intermittent reinforcement of the tantrum behavior.

Questions arose as behavioral therapists were able to accomplish their goals within a short span of treatment: Would the changes last? Could they be **generalized** into the home, work, and school settings? To address those concerns, behavioral family therapists incorporated **naturalistic reinforcers,** by involving other family members as therapists, gradually decreasing the external influence of the therapist. By enlisting the cooperation of family members, they strengthen the probability of generalization (Nichols & Schwartz, 1998, p. 273).

Families are more complicated than individuals. Behavioral family therapists have developed a variety of powerful, pragmatic, effective, and testable techniques, such as parent training, behavioral couples therapy, communication skills and problem-solving skills training, and treatment of sexual dysfunction. This chapter will discuss various cognitive behavioral therapies as they relate to families and couples.

COGNITIVE/BEHAVIORAL FAMILY THERAPY

Cognitive/behavioral family therapists also lean on **social exchange theory,** as developed by Thibault and Kelly (1959). This theory helps the therapist understand the motivations underlying family interactions by analyzing interactions in terms of the relative amounts of supposed **rewards and costs** to each person in a relationship. The assumption is that people in a relationship seek to maximize rewards and minimize costs, and that in long-term relationships, an equilibrium of rewards and costs is established. Social exchange theory is less systemic than most of the theories covered in this book, since it relates more to dyads and tends to see one person as having the problem. It looks for the cause and effect of each behavior.

However, when related to behavioral marital therapy it bears some of the features of a systemic description since it focuses on the transactional nature of relationships: "the marital relationship is best thought of as a process of circular and reciprocal sequences of behavior and consequences, where each person's behavior is at once being affected by and influences the other" (Jacobson & Margolin, 1979, p. 13).

Dyads Versus Triads

Behaviorists hardly ever treat whole families. They usually think of and work with dyads. Systemic therapists suggest this practice could deter successful treatment since often a child's problem behaviors are reflections of more complex triangulating marital discord. However, family behavioral therapists don't seem to consider this a problem. Perhaps the greatest strength of behavior therapy is its insistence in observing and measuring change. It is testable. This characteristic is obviously an advantage for doing replicable studies.

A Testable Process

All behavioral therapists are committed to the scientific approach in the **positivistic tradition,** and behavioral family therapists adhere to that tradition. That means base lines are set for acceptable behaviors, and outcomes are **testable** and explicit. In general, treatment is consistent with the methods of experimental psychology. Techniques are described precisely and can be **objectively measured and replicated.** The process has evolved from rigorous experimental evaluation of treatment methods and concepts (Becvar & Becvar, 1982, p. 235).

Behavioral family therapy incorporates Bandura's **social learning theory.** Social learning theory emphasizes the effect of **modeling** and **symbolic** and **cognitive processes** on self-regulation, and **reciprocal determinism** that describes the dynamics of relationships (Bandura, 1982). Reciprocal determinism reflects the circularity of systemic thinking.

The Importance of Client/Therapist Relationship

Behavioral family therapists of all bents now consider the importance of the client/therapist relationship, a condition early individual behavioral therapists did not originally think important. The client decides specific goals. Symptom relief is the desired outcome. Therapists work toward establishing desired behaviors to replace those defined as undesirable by the clients. The therapist decides the *process* of therapy. The ultimate goal of all cognitive-behavioral family therapy is the understanding, prediction, and control of behaviors in the present.

Behavior Changes Plus Understanding

Cognitive/behavioral family therapists work, not only to alleviate symptoms, but also to teach skills and foster understanding so that families will be able to solve their own problems in the future. This theory fosters no implicit values, but in keeping with social exchange theory, infers that a good relationship is one in which there is a higher proportion of rewards relative to costs for both parties (Becvar & Becvar, 1982). The therapy is action oriented and includes *measurable* homework tasks. Cognitive behavioral concepts were introduced to couple and family therapy about 25 years ago (Goldenberg & Goldenberg, 2000).

Assessing Interactional Consequences

The assessment process pays detailed attention to the interactional consequences of a behavior. For example, it asks, "What do *you* do when Johnny doesn't eat?" How clients describe their responses to the undesirable behavior helps the therapist see how the family may be inadvertently rewarding the undesired behavior. The focus is generally on increasing positive behaviors rather than on decreasing negative behaviors and uses positive reinforcement and reward within the sessions. Progress is carefully monitored and documented. The therapist has the responsibility for the therapy process.

In the initial assessment, the client is asked about any physical or psychological problems. The client's self-esteem is evaluated. The therapist attempts to learn the purpose served by the problem. For couples, behavioral therapists look at how their interactions regulate intimacy. Therapists assess family functioning at two levels:

- Problem analysis—to zero in on specific behavioral deficits (e.g., school problems, defiant behaviors).
- Functional analysis—to uncover the relationship between behavioral deficits and the interpersonal environment in which they are functionally relevant. The goal is to understand what happens—how family members interact, just before and after the problem behavior occurs (e.g., inconsistent or exaggerated responses).
- Emphasis is on the environmental, situational, and social determinants that influence behavior (Falloon, 1991; Kazden, 1984).

The Function of Symptoms

Cognitive family therapists add a functional analysis of thoughts, attitudes, expectations, and beliefs. They see individuals as interactive participants, interpreting, judging, and influencing one another, in concert with systemic thinking. They use three methods: self-report questionnaires, clinical interviews, and direct observations of family interactions (Epstein, Schlesinger, & Dryden, 1988). Therapists methodically analyze behavioral sequences before treatment, assess the progress as therapy moves along, and evaluate the final outcome of the therapy.

The Development of Behavioral Family Therapy

Three theorists played particularly important roles in the development of behavioral family therapy: Richard Stuart focused on how the exchange of positive behavior could be maximized. This theory led to the principle of **reciprocity** and introduced the concept of **written contracts.** He applied **reciprocal reinforcement** to distressed couples. Participants learned to list the behaviors they desired from each other, record the frequency with which the spouse displayed the desired behavior, and specify what they would exchange for the desired behavior, all based on written contracts (1969). In 1970, Robert Liberman presented a paper, "Behavioral Approaches to Family and Couple Therapy." He offered an application of an operant-learning framework to the family problems of four adult patients with symptoms of depression, intractable headaches, social inadequacy, and marital discord. He used **contingency management** through **mutual reinforcers** and the use of **role rehearsal** and modeling, behavioral concepts that had been earlier described by Bandura and Walters (1963).

Gerald Patterson (1971) while working at the University of Oregon developed a program of **behavioral parent training.** He observed that behavior in the sessions is often very different from behavior in the home. He developed methods for sampling periods of family interaction in the home, trained parents in the principles of social learning theory, developed programmed workbooks, and worked out careful strategies for eliminating undesirable behavior and substituting desirable behavior.

Other behavioral applications were developed, such as charting, teaching spouses how to shape positive behavior in one another, analyzing negative interaction chains, behavioral contracts with children, and the extinction of negative behaviors by ignoring them. During the 1970s three major directions for behavioral family therapy were introduced: parent training, behavioral couples therapy, and sexual therapy.

Family Systems and Behavior Theory

Family systems theory has influenced behavioral family therapists. For example, Gerald Patterson studied with Salvador Minuchin. Patterson and a number of other behavioral family therapists have written on, and become adept with, the handling of family systems dynamics even as they apply their behavioral treatments. Many family therapists of other disciplines routinely include behavioral tasks as part of their treatments.

Behavioral family therapists do not look into family history, except to elicit information about current sequences of behavior involved in the presenting problem that may be influenced by that history. Although they are not inherently value oriented, some theorists have recently described the characteristics of successful marriage. For example, Thibault and Kelley's behavior exchange model describes a good relationship as one in which giving and getting are balanced—having a high ratio of benefits relative to costs (1959). Wills, Weiss, and Patterson (1974) said a good relationship is one in which there is a high exchange of pleasant behaviors but even more important, minimal unpleasant behaviors.

Conflict Resolution and Problem-Solving Skills

Most behaviorists see the ability to talk about problems—good communication skills—as key to satisfactory relationships. Couples are taught **conflict resolution** and **problem-solving skills** to maneuver successfully through the normal experiences of family life. In a satisfying relationship, the partners are able to speak openly and directly about conflicts. They are able to do the following:

- Stay focused on the current issue
- Describe their own feelings
- Be able to request specific behavior changes of others

They do not criticize one another, nor demand compliance with requests. The other party listens, attempts to understand what is being said, and checks it out by feeding back that understanding before giving his or her own point of view. This kind of communication fits the model for assertiveness training. Behaviorists do not believe that satisfying relationships naturally occur, but rather develop over time, as relationship skills are refined. They also emphasize the importance of being adaptable and flexible and open to learning.

Problem-Maintaining Learned Responses

Behavioral family therapists see symptoms as **learned responses,** involuntarily acquired and reinforced. They look for environmental responses that reinforce problem behavior. They note that people often inadvertently reinforce those behaviors that cause them distress. They also note that punishments often have the opposite effect from what is intended, as can be most clearly seen in the example of temper tantrums. When parents respond to a problem behavior by scolding or lecturing, those responses, even from an angry parent, can be powerful social reinforcers (Skinner, 1953). Behavioral family therapists stress the importance of **consistency** based on the effect of intermittent reinforcement that actually makes the undesired behavior more resistant to change (Ferster, 1963).

Tools to Measure Improvement

Behavioral family therapists have developed a number of specific measurement tools and workbooks. For couples therapy, they often start with a standard couples questionnaire. These questionnaires are designed to reveal strengths and weaknesses in the relationship and the way in which rewards and punishments are exchanged. Examples include the ability to discuss problems, current reinforcement value of their interactions, skill in pinpointing relevant reinforcers, sexual competency and satisfaction, child-rearing behaviors, financial management, distribution of roles, and decision making. After the couple completes the questionnaire, the therapist analyzes their relationship from the point of view of social learning theory. They carefully emphasize **positive expectations** and **collaboration strengths.** Too often clients are able to express what they *don't* want more easily than what they *do* want, so therapists assign tasks designed to elicit things their partner does that pleases them. When these lists of pleasing behaviors are reviewed in sessions, the therapist explains that when clients tell each other what they are pleased with, it helps to reinforce those behaviors. Reinforcing pleasing behaviors by telling the other person what he or she does that pleases you, provides all parties to the interaction the opportunity to increase those pleasing behaviors. Once goals are established, the therapist works toward teaching the skills necessary to achieve those goals, in very specific behavioral tasks. Couples are taught how to express themselves in explicit behavioral terms. They are taught new behavior exchange procedures, emphasizing the importance of positive reinforcement rather than aversive control. Communication skills are honed and practiced. Couples are taught effective **power sharing,** decision making, and problem-solving skills useful for future difficulties (Stuart, 1975).

Integrative Couples Therapy

Integrative couples therapy, a behavioral-based therapeutic strategy for promoting more **accommodating** and **collaborative** attitudes between partners, was developed by Neil Jacobson and Andrew Christensen in the early 1990s. Integrative couples therapy incorporates strategic techniques such as reframing and experiential techniques such as empathic joining to the usual behavioral methods. The goal is to promote intimacy and understanding in place of anger and blame (Jacobson & Christensen, 1996). Integrative couples therapy is designed to help couples see certain differences between them as inevitable. It works toward helping partners become more tolerant about behaviors they are seeing as negative or troublesome in a partner, and to accept those behaviors that resist change. Integrative behavioral therapists promote emotional acceptance in situations where behavior change either fails to occur, or else occurs but not to the extent the partner would like. Instead of demanding more of the requested change, partners are encouraged to change their *reactions* to the behavior that had been upsetting and balance change with acceptance of what seemed unchangeable. This emotional acceptance occurs when they are able to look at the problem in a new way. For example, they might be coached to see the troubling behavior as a common enemy each could be empathic about, or could detach from, or they could learn to reduce reactivity to the behavior through more tolerance and the increased ability to take care of oneself when the partner's disturbing behavior was happening (Christensen, Jacobsen, & Babcock, 1995). They may still wish the undesirable behavior were different. Couples are taught to see an undesirable behavior as just one part of the whole package of who the partner is and balance that behavior with all the other things the partner does that pleases them. When emotional acceptance is accomplished, the undesirable behavior becomes less aversive and less disruptive to the relationship (Eldridge, Christensen, & Jacobsen, 1999). Acceptance of what cannot be changed is especially helpful for long-term relationships where chronic health conditions or aging changes limit one partner's ability to alter their behaviors.

Albert Ellis—Rational Emotive Therapy

Albert Ellis was a pioneer in the area of cognitive therapy. In the 1960s he developed the **A-B-C model**. It describes the sequence of events that ultimately lead to a person's experienced feelings. By breaking down their experiences into the following A-B-C segments, people can discover if distortions or "irrational beliefs" are at play.

A = *Activating event.* These are a person's actual experiences. These events are described in objective, behavioral terms—"what happened" without describing any opinions about what happened.

B = *Belief.* What the person believes about what happened. The client is asked to list what he or she believes to be true about the event.

C = *Consequent emotion*. The feelings that result from the client's interpretation of the event.

Ellis contends that people differ with regard to their feelings associated with events because each has a different way of interpreting what happens to them (Ellis, 1962, 1977).

People may be strongly influenced by events in early life. Much of people's philosophy of life—what they think about themselves and their values—is learned from past experiences. These experiences stay with them in the form of beliefs they carry in their head in the present. The past cannot be changed, but people can change how they let the past influence the way they think and feel today and the way they want to think and be and feel tomorrow. **Rational-emotive therapy (RET)** is an optimistic, direct approach to solving problems.

Albert Ellis adapted his individually focused "A-B-C" rational-emotive model to family therapy by stating that family members largely create their own world by the phenomenological view they take of what happens to them (Ellis, 1977). The focus of his therapy is on how the particular problems of one family member affect the well-being of the family as a unit. Family members are viewed as individuals, each with a particular set of beliefs and expectations (Huber & Baruth, 1989; Russell & Marrill, 1989). The goal of the rational-emotive family therapist is to help family members realize that illogical beliefs and distortions serve as the foundation for their emotional distress, and to modify behaviors by making their thoughts about events more rational. The therapist actively and directly teaches the family that emotional problems are caused by irrational beliefs and that when they change those self-defeating ideas, the quality of family relationships for all of its members is improved (Ellis, 1978).

Example: A family comes in for therapy. Mom and Dad have been arguing about how to deal with their 15-year-old daughter. Dad complains that she is isolating herself from the family and that worries him. He says she used to like to take walks and talk with him and now finds every excuse not to be with him. She wants to be with her friends. She is hostile when he restricts her from being with them.

Mom says Dad is being too strict. That it's time to let her go out more. And their arguments have been getting hostile. Using the A-B-C model in Table 9.1, we could outline the situation like this:

Notice that both Mom and Dad state the other parent *"should"* agree—an irrational belief that is present in most relationship conflicts. Each person's emotions are largely dependent on how he or she evaluates what happens to him or her. Each person establishes a basic understanding of him- or herself, and that affects how he or she understands events. This understanding is often beyond the person's awareness. RET helps people pay attention to their automatic thoughts (beliefs) and to recognize those that are distorted (irrational) and cause distressing emotions. The therapy process involves **disputing the irrational beliefs** until more realistic and balanced interpretations are found. When people are able to think more rationally about what happens to them,

TABLE 9.1 | A-B-C MODEL

	A: Activating Event	B: Beliefs	C: Consequent Emotions
Dad	Daughter should want to be with me as she always did.	She's going astray.	Fear, sadness, anger
	She's hiding something.	"I'm losing my daughter."	
	I restrict her from her friends.	My wife should back me up.	
Mom	Same event	He's being unreasonable.	Anger, frustration
	Dad complains daughter doesn't want to be with him.	Teenagers need to be with their friends. We have to let go.	
	He restricts her from friends.	My husband *should* listen to me.	

they are able to see multiple ways to view a situation and can begin to alter the irrational beliefs that have been creating distressing emotions.

Every time a person identifies a distorted thought and modifies it, he or she is strengthening a new way of thinking that may eventually replace the distressing ways of thinking. This new way of thinking does not mean people have to scrutinize their every thought. That would be more distressful than the original problem. The key is to become aware of those thoughts that create distortions about events and recognize that there are other ways of interpreting events that will reduce a person's distress.

Aaron Beck—Cognitive Therapy for Depression

In many ways, Aaron Beck's ideas tie in with Ellis's ideas. Aaron Beck did a lot of work with cognitive therapy that disputed the thoughts (beliefs) that led to depression. He focused more on individual therapy. However, the outline he recommends for monitoring those thoughts and beliefs is different from the way Ellis outlined his individual and family rational-emotive therapy. Beck (1976) suggested the following way to chart the interaction of emotions and thoughts:

Event   Emotions   Thoughts   Logical Comeback

As you can see his chart shows emotions before thoughts, whereas Ellis puts the thoughts or beliefs ahead of the emotions. Ellis uses the term "irrational beliefs." Beck refers to distressing thoughts as "distortions." Although they may word them a bit differently, some common distortions and irrational beliefs that lead to distressing emotions, such as depression, anxiety, and anger, are applicable to both Ellis's and Beck's work. Here are six of them:

1. The mental filter: Taking the negative details of an event and magnifying them while filtering out all positive aspects of a situation.
2. Dichotomous thinking: There is no middle ground. Either/or, good/bad.
3. Mind reading: Believing you know exactly what people are thinking, especially in regard to their thoughts about you.
4. Catastrophizing: Thinking the worst case scenario is going to occur, and that it will be intolerable.
5. Blaming: Others are solely responsible for your problems.
6. Control: (a) Out of control. "I am at the mercy of external forces." (b) Need for control. "I must control everyone and everything or the results will be disastrous" (Beck, 1976).

Beck and his colleagues recommend several questions to help determine whether a person's belief is accurate or distorted. Beck suggested the client ask him- or herself these questions. Ellis actively challenges the client to respond to similar questions. Some of those questions are:

"What evidence do I have to support that belief?"

"What evidence do I have that refutes that belief?"

"How else could I word my automatic (distorted) thoughts?"

"What would my spouse, best friend (or someone I admire) say to themselves in this situation?"

"What would I say to my spouse, best friend (or person I admire) if they were thinking the same thing?"

"How could I look at this situation so I would feel less depressed (angry, anxious)? Is that a more reasonable way of thinking?" (Beck, 1976).

By teaching people to confront and dispute irrational thoughts, both Ellis and Beck work toward helping people become aware of how their thoughts and beliefs are the sources of their distress. They then can help them find alternate ways of thinking and believing that will relieve their distress.

Family Schemata—A Way of Viewing the Family's Beliefs

Cognitive/behavioral family therapy views family relationships, cognitions, emotions, and behaviors as exerting a mutual influence on one another, meaning a cognitive inference can evoke emotion and behavior, and emotion and behavior can influence cognition (understanding). It is compatible with systems theory because it is based on the premise that family members simultaneously influence one another. Interactions can become ingrained into patterns that recursively impact family dynamics. The process of therapy involves correcting irrational beliefs as a way of changing dysfunctional behaviors. Some cognitive/behavioral therapists examine the cognitions among individual family members as well, on what has been termed a **family schemata** (Dattilio, 1997). A family schemata is a jointly held belief about the family formed through the years of interactions among members of the family unit:

All of the cognitions that individuals hold about their own family life and about family life in general. . . . The family schemata contains ideas about how spousal relationships should work, what different types of problems should be expected in marriage and how they should be handled, what is involved in building and maintaining a healthy family, what responsibilities each family member should have, what consequences should be associated with failure to meet responsibilities or to fulfill roles, and what costs and benefits each individual should expect to have as a consequence of being in a marriage. (Baucom & Epstein, 1990, p. 50)

Dattilio contends the family of origin of each partner in a relationship plays a crucial role in the shaping of immediate family schemata. The family schemata is subject to change as major events occur such as the birth of a child, a death, or a divorce, and continues to evolve as a result of ordinary day-to-day experiences over the family life cycle (1997).

The Importance of Context

Cognitive/behavioral family therapists look at affective and behavioral responses, and incorporate thought processes and belief systems as they work with parents to improve child/parent relationships. They take into consideration the different ethnic, socioeconomic, and cultural backgrounds of the family, and whether or not there are developmental or physical problems in the children. Therapists intervene by teaching parents behavioral strategies for diminishing or extinguishing undesirable behaviors in the children, such as bed-wetting, temper tantrums, or chore completion (Dangel, Yu, Slot, & Fashimpar, 1994).

Functional Family Therapy

Functional family therapy is designed to bring about both cognitive and behavioral changes in individuals and their families. It integrates learning theory, systems theory, and cognitive theory. It says clients must first get help understanding the function the problematic behavior plays in regulating their relationships (Barton & Alexander, 1981; Alexander & Parsons, 1982). Functional family therapists see all behavior as adaptive and serving a function. Symptoms are seen ultimately, as efforts to achieve one of three interpersonal states: contact/closeness (merging), distance/independence (separating), or a combination of the two (midpointing). The functional family therapist makes an effort to comprehend why the behavior exists and how and why it is maintained by others in the family (Alexander & Parsons, 1982).

SEX THERAPY

Sex and affection elevate and promote intimacy and provide a bond that helps couples move past the inevitable hurts and disappointments of everyday living. Sometimes, sexual problems can be treated by working indirectly on other interpersonal problems by improving communication and assertiveness skills. Sometimes focusing on specific sexual problems will repair a troubled relationship, and of course, sometimes both sexual and nonsexual areas of a couple's life need to be addressed. Wolpe (1958) suggested that **conditioned anxiety about performance** was behind most sexual problems and introduced **systematic desensitization** as a treatment. This treatment involved instructing couples to engage in a graded series of progressively more intimate encounters, avoiding thoughts about erection or orgasm. Assertiveness training and teaching and encouraging people to express their needs and feelings also became an effective treatment for sexual disorders (Lazarus, 1965; Wolpe, 1958).

In 1970, Masters and Johnson introduced a procedure they called **sensate focus.** It adapted the ideas of systematic desensitization. Masters and Johnson included a complete medical examination to rule out organic problems, along with an in-depth interview to determine the specifics of the dysfunction and establish goals for treatment. They carefully selected couples who would be most responsive to their treatment plan. These couples were usually ones in which the lack of information about human sexuality, poor technique, and poor communication in the sexual area were evident. Helen Singer Kaplan (1979) elaborated on Masters and Johnson's notion that anxiety interfered with a couple's ability to relax into arousal and orgasm. She said there are three stages of the sexual response and therefore three types of problems: **disorders of desire, arousal disorders,** and **orgasm disorders.** Treatment focuses on:

1. Deconditioning anxiety.
2. Helping clients identify and stop negative thoughts that interfere with sexual desire.
3. When decreased emotional arousal and difficulty in achieving and maintaining an erection, and dilating and lubricating interfere with sexual satisfaction, couples are helped with a combination of relaxation techniques and learning to stay focused on the physical sensations they are experiencing from touching and caressing, rather than worrying what comes next (Kaplan, 1979).

The Effect of Attitudes and Beliefs on Sexual Satisfaction

Clients are told how anxiety develops and how it is maintained in their relationship. Changing their attitudes about sex is seen as essential to successful treatment. According to Kaplan (1974), attitudes may be changed by confronting clients with discrepancies between their attitudes and reality; by subtly fostering behavior changes (sometimes where the body goes the heart follows); and by facilitating the cathartic expression of feelings. Helping clients talk about and understand how each partner's beliefs and attitudes toward sex affect sexual responses is fundamental to successful treatment.

How Couples Are Helped

Although the needs of each couple are unique, most treatments begin with sensate focus. Sensate focus is a form of *in vivo* desensitization. Couples are taught how to relax and then touch, at first nonsexually. The demand for performance is put aside. Each takes turns caressing the other, and informing the other of where and how they enjoy being touched. At first they are told not to touch sexually sensitive areas like the breasts or genitals. After they learn to relax, and become comfortable with the nonsexual touch, they are encouraged to gradually touch each other in more intimate ways—and to slow down if either begins to feel anxious. After the couple experiences satisfaction with the sensate-focus process, other more specific techniques may be introduced to deal with specific difficulties. Too often the anxiety has built up from one partner's reluctance to tell the other what he or she does or doesn't like the partner to do. Treatment involves learning to talk with each other about how they feel about how they are being touched. By not talking about these feelings, the unhappy partner may withdraw or get angry. So, as each partner becomes more relaxed, and anxiety about performance and response is diminished, couples are encouraged to tell, and to show, each other what feels good and what doesn't.

Goal of Sex Therapy

Sex therapy is considered successful when the couple's sex life is much improved, *but not as fantastic as their prior frustrated expectations had led them to imagine.* Therapeutic gains are strengthened and maintained by reviewing the changes that occur in the course of the therapy, anticipating future trouble spots, and planning how to deal with problems according to principles learned in treatment. Sexual therapy is considered brief therapy and takes anywhere from 5 to 20 sessions (Nichols & Schwartz, 1998).

PSYCHOEDUCATIONAL THERAPY

All behavioral therapies use educational techniques. Educational techniques are the mainstay of psychoeducational therapy. In the therapy room, therapists tend to accept the parent's view that the child is the problem, and usually meet with only one parent and the problem child. They use programmed workbooks to teach parents behavioral skills and how to apply learning theory. A lot of psychoeducational work is offered as preventive education and includes classroom-type group experiences on such topics as parent training, assertiveness training, and couples communication courses.

COUPLES/MARITAL THEORY AND THERAPY

Marriage counseling began outside the psychiatric arena and was originally offered by clergy, teachers, medical doctors, and attorneys. In the 1930s, the

American Psychiatric Association convention heard a report that married couples have interlocking neuroses and are best treated conjointly. Around the same time, Paul Popenoe opened the first professional marriage clinic, the American Institute of Family Relations in Los Angeles. Abraham and Hannah Stone opened a similar clinic in New York. Other centers followed, and in 1941 the American Association of Marriage Counselors was formed (Broderick & Schrader, 1991; Oberndorf, 1938). In 1948, a truly revolutionary view was published by Bela Mittleman of the New York Psychoanalytic Institute suggesting that husbands and wives could be treated by the same analyst. She said this would help them reexamine their irrational perceptions of each other (Mittleman, 1948). Then in 1956, Mittleman wrote an article describing a number of complementary marital patterns, including aggressive/submissive and detached/demanding. She said these personality combinations often led to divorce because courting couples distort each other's personalities through the eyes of their illusions. She also suggested that a couple's reactions to each other may be shaped by their relationships with their parents. With insight, she believed, unconscious motivations would have less control over the current relationship.

In the same time frame, in Great Britain, the Tavistock Clinic formed the Family Psychiatric Unit. The courts referred divorcing couples to help reconcile their differences (Dicks, 1964). And, as previously discussed, in the 1950s Don Jackson and Jay Haley were writing about couples therapy and communications. Their ideas brought marriage counseling into the larger family therapy movement.

Patterns That Reinforce Marital Discord

A number of defective patterns of reinforcement have been identified in cases of marital discord:

- Receiving too little reinforcement from the marriage.
- Too few needs given marital reinforcement.
- Marital reinforcement no longer provides satisfaction.
- New behaviors are not reinforced.
- One spouse gives more reinforcement than he or she receives.
- Marriage interferes with extramarital sources of satisfaction.
- Communication about potential sources of satisfaction is not adequate.
- Aversive control predominates over positive reinforcement (Azrin, Naster, & Jones, 1973).

Research: Which Marriage Will Endure?

John Gottman, a prolific researcher of marital behaviors, produced a number of studies looking for common characteristics found in happy or unhappy married couples. His team videotaped couples, used EKGs, galvanometer sensors, and specially designed observational instruments. They compared how couples communicate, both verbally and nonverbally, microsecond by microsecond. They studied body movements, facial expressions, gestures, even heart rates during conflicts, and attempted to identify those behavioral and physiological responses essential to a stable marriage as well as those that predict the couples headed for divorce. They found it was not the exchange of anger that predicts divorce, but rather four forms of negativity. Gottman called them "The Four Horsemen of the Apocalypse":

- Criticism (attacking the spouse's character).
- Defensiveness (denying responsibility for one's own behavior).
- Contempt (insulting, abusive attitudes toward a spouse).
- Stonewalling (withdrawal and unwillingness to listen to one's partner).

Women were found more likely to criticize, and men were likelier than women to stonewall (Gottman, 1994). Gottman and his team identified three types of stable couples:

- Volatile, emotionally expressive couples who may bicker frequently and passionately *and* are more romantic and affectionate than most couples.
- Validating couples who are harmonious and less emotionally expressive—they listen to one another's viewpoints.
- Conflict-avoiding couples, low in emotional expressiveness, who resolve problems by minimizing or avoiding them and emphasize the positive aspects of their relationship. Partners are able to accept negative aspects of each other as unchangeable.

Gottman and Krokoff (1989) did a longitudinal study and determined that although direct expressions of anger and dissatisfaction between partners might cause marital distress in the short run, those confrontations were likely to lead to long-term improvement in marital satisfaction if couples then followed up by talking together to examine their areas of disagreements.

SUMMARY

All behavioral family and couple therapies emphasize the development of behavioral skills that will improve relationships. They generally work with dyads in the therapy sessions. An in-depth assessment of the client's physical health and environmental supports is made before talking about the presenting problem. Very specific, measurable behavioral goals are set. The results can be clearly evaluated and tested since the therapists set tasks and use ongoing evaluations of the progress as they move through specific steps of the therapy. The general goal is symptom relief.

Ongoing reciprocal interactions between behavioral and social conditions affect personal functioning. Cognitive/behavioral therapists attempt to increase positive interactions between family members, alter the environmental conditions that strain such interactions, and train people to maintain their newly acquired positive behavioral changes (Goldenberg & Goldenberg,

2000). Clients are educated in behavioral techniques and consequences. Psychoeducation is done within the sessions as well as in group or classroom settings. Functional family therapy views all behavior as serving the interpersonal function of creating specific outcomes in behavior sequences. Functional family therapists do not try to change those functions. They work toward changing the disturbing behaviors used to maintain the functions.

Conjoint sex therapy focuses on reducing anxiety about sexuality and performance, teaching assertiveness, and other communication techniques to enhance sexual interactions and to help clients examine their sexual expectations, which may be contributing to feelings of frustration. Sex therapy is successful when the couple's sex life is much improved, but not as fantastic as their prior frustrated expectations had led them to imagine.

EXPERIENTIAL ACTIVITIES

1. Describe some distinctions between Bandura's social learning theory and Thibault and Kelly's social exchange theory.
2. Instructors may set up a role play of a parent/child presenting problem and create an assessment process as a cognitive/behavioral family therapist. The goal for the session is to describe specific behavioral problems in relational terms. Include observers who will report on the process.
3. Using the relational descriptions created by the previous role play, design tasks with measurable goals as a cognitive/behavioral family therapist. Include observers to report on the process.
4. Instructors should set up a role play representing a couple in which each partner is from a different ethnic group. Those differences have developed into serious misunderstandings between the partners. Using Ellis's "A-B-C" process, have the therapist challenge the client's irrational beliefs about the defined problem. Include observers to report on the process.
5. Discuss the functional family therapy idea that all behaviors serve a function. Describe how the functional family therapist would work to relieve the presenting problem.
6. What are the three basic steps in sex therapy enumerated by Helen Singer Kaplan? What does she define as a successful outcome for sex therapy? Discuss how you think that is important as a determinant of satisfaction for the couple.

REFERENCES

Alexander, J. F., & Parsons, B. V. (1982). *Functional family therapy.* Pacific Grove, CA: Brooks/Cole.

Azrin, N. H., Naster, J. B., & Jones, R. (1973). Reciprocity counseling: A rapid learning-based procedure for marital counseling. *Behavior Research & Therapy, 11,* 365–383.

Bandura, A. (1977). *Social learning theory.* Englewood Cliffs, NJ: Prentice Hall.

Bandura, A. (1978). The self-system in reciprocal determinism. *American Psychologist, 33,* 344–358.

Bandura, A., & Walters, R. (1963). *Social learning and personality development.* New York: Holt, Rinehart & Winston.

Barton, C., & Alexander, J. F. (1981). Functional family therapy. In A. S. Gurman & D. P. Kniskern (Eds.), *The handbook of family therapy* (Vol. II). New York: Brunner/Mazel.

Baucom, D. H., & Epstein, N. (1990). *Cognitive-behavioral marital therapy.* New York: Brunner/Mazel.

Beck, Aaron T. (1976). *Cognitive therapy and the emotional disorders.* Connecticut: International University Press.

Becvar, R. J., & Becvar, D. S. (1982). *Systems theory and family therapy: A primer.* Washington, DC: University Press of America.

Broderick, C. B., & Shroder, S. S. (1991). The history of professional marriage and family counseling. In A. S. Gurman & D. P. Kniskern (Eds.), *The handbook of family therapy* (Vol. II). New York: Brunner/Mazel.

Christensen, A., Jacobsen, N. S., & Babcock, J. C. (1995). Integrative couples therapy. In N. S. Jacobsen & A. S. Gurman (Eds.), *Clinical handbook of couples therapy.* New York: Guilford.

Dangel, R. F., Yu, M., Slot, N. W., & Fashimpar, G. (1994). Behavioral parent training. In D. K. Granvold (Ed.), *Cognitive and behavioral treatment: Methods and applications.* Pacific Grove, CA: Brooks/Cole.

Dattilio, F. M. (1997). *Integrative cases in couples and family therapy: A cognitive-behavioral perspective.* New York: Guilford.

Dicks, H. V. (1964). Concepts of marital diagnosis and therapy as developed at the Tavistock Family Psychiatric Clinic, London, England. In E. M. Nash, L. Jessner, and D. W. Abse (Eds.), *Marriage counseling in medical practice.* Chapel Hill, NC: University of North Carolina Press.

Eldridge, K., Christensen, A., & Jacobsen, N. S. (1999). Integrative couples therapy. In D. M. Lawson & F. F. Prevatt (Eds.), *Casebook of family therapy.* Pacific Grove, CA: Brooks/Cole.

Ellis, A. (1962). *Reason and emotions in psychotherapy.* New York: Lyle Stuart.

Ellis, A. (1977). The nature of disturbed marital interactions. In A. Ellis & R. Greiger (Eds.), *Handbook of rational-emotive therapy.* New York: Springer.

Ellis, A. (1978). Family therapy: A phenomenological and active-directive approach. *Journal of Marriage and Family Counseling, 4,* 43–50.

Epstein, N. B., Schlesinger, S. E., & Dryden, W. (Eds.) (1988). Concepts and methods of cognitive-behavioral family treatment. In *Cognitive-behavioral therapy with families.* New York: Brunner/Mazel.

Falloon, I. R. H. (1991). Behavioral family therapy. In A. S. Gurman & D. P. Kniskern (Eds.), *The handbook of family therapy* (Vol. II). New York: Brunner/Mazel.

Ferster, C. B. (1963). Essentials of a science of behavior. In J. I. Nurnberger, C. B. Ferster, & J. P. Brody (Eds.), *An introduction to the science of human behavior.* New York: Appleton-Century-Crofts.

Goldenberg, I., & Goldenberg, H. (2000). *Family therapy: An overview* (5th ed.). Pacific Grove, CA: Brooks/Cole.

Gottman, J. M. (1994). *What predicts divorce?* Hillsdale, NJ: Erlbaum.

Gottman, J. M., & Krokoff, I. (1989). Marital interaction and satisfaction: A longitudinal view. *Journal of Consulting and Clinical Psychology, 57,* 47–52.

Huber, C. H., & Baruth, L. G. (1989). *Rational-emotive family therapy: A systems perspective.* New York: Springer.

Jacobson, N. S., & Christensen, A. (1996). *Integrative couples therapy: Promoting acceptance.* New York: Norton.

Jacobson, N. S., & Margolin, G. (1979). *Marital therapy: Strategies based on social learning and behavior exchange principles.* New York: Brunner/Mazel.

Kaplan, H. S. (1974). *The new sex therapy: Active treatment of sexual dysfunctions.* New York: Brunner/Mazel.

Kaplan, H. S. (1979). *Disorders of sexual desire and other new concepts and techniques in sex therapy.* New York: Brunner/Mazel.

Kazden, A. E. (1984). *Behavior modifications in applied settings* (3rd ed.). Homewood, IL: Dorsey.

Lazarus, A. A. (1965). The treatment of a sexually inadequate male. In L. P. Ullmann & L. Krasner (Eds.), *Case studies in behavior modification.* New York: Holt, Rinehart & Winston.

Liberman, R. P. (1970). Behavioral approaches to family and couple therapy. *American Journal of Orthopsychiatry, 40,* 106–118.

Masters, W. H., & Johnson, V. E. (1970). *Human sexual inadequacy.* Boston: Little, Brown.

Mittleman, B. (1948). The concurrent analysis of married couples. *Psychoanalytic Quarterly, 17,* 182–197.

Mittleman, B. (1956). Analysis of reciprocal neurotic patterns. In V. W. Eisenstein (Ed.), *Neurotic interactions in marriage.* New York: Basic Books.

Nichols, M. P., & Schwartz, R. C. (1998). *Family therapy: Concepts and methods.* Boston: Allyn & Bacon.

Oberndorf, C. P. (1938). Psychoanalysis of married people. *Psychoanalytic Review, 25,* 453–475.

Patterson, G. R. (1971). *Families: Application of social learning theory to family life.* Champaign, IL: Research Press.

Russell, T., & Marrill, C. M. (1989). Adding a systematic touch to rational-emotive therapy for families. *Journal of Mental Health Counseling, 11,* 184–192.

Schultz, Duane (1986). *Theories of personality* (3rd. ed.). Pacific Grove, CA: Brooks/Cole.

Skinner, B. F. (1953). *Science and Human Behavior.* New York: Macmillan.

Stuart, R. B. (1969). An operant-conditioning treatment for marital discord. *Journal of Consulting and Clinical Psychology, 33,* 675–682.

Stuart, R. B. (1975). Behavioral remedies for marital ills: A guide to the use of operant-interpersonal techniques. In T. Thompson & W. Dochen (Eds.), *International symposium on behavior modification.* New York: Appleton.

Thibault, J. W., & Kelley, H. H. (1959). *The social psychology of groups.* New York: Wiley.

Wills, T. A., Weiss, R. L., & Patterson, G. R. (1974). A behavioral analysis of the determinants of marital satisfaction. *Journal of Consulting and Clinical Psychology, 42,* 802–811.

Wolpe, J. (1948). An approach to the problem of neurosis based on the conditioned response. Unpublished M.D. thesis. University of Witwatersrand, Johannesburg, South Africa.

Wolpe, J. (1958). *Psychotherapy by reciprocal inhibition.* Palo Alto, CA: Stanford University Press.

LANGUAGE AS REALITY

PART IV

POSTMODERN, SOCIAL CONSTRUCTIONISM

CHAPTER **10**

TERMS TO KNOW

cybernetics of cybernetics   postmodern

cocreate   deconstructing the problem

same domain   saturated, dominant stories

social constructionism

FROM CYBERNETICS TO CYBERNETICS OF CYBERNETICS

Early in this book we described cybernetics as fundamental to the understanding of systems. The two basic elements of a cybernetic system are self-
correction and relationships. Meaning is derived from the mutual reciprocity
of the relationship between individuals. Feedback (self-correction) refers to
the process through which information from past behaviors is fed back into
the system in a circular manner. The terms "positive" and "negative" feedback are not based on value judgments. They refer to the impact of behavior
on the system, and the response of the system to that behavior. Negative feedback maintains the status quo (stability, homeostasis). Positive feedback indicates something has perturbed or interfered with the usual recursive pattern
of interactions. Positive feedback promotes change. Change can be both disruptive and constructive. Change and stability are necessary aspects of any
system's survival. "Cybernetics proposes that change cannot be found without a roof of stability over its head. Similarly stability will always be rooted
to underlying processes of change" (Keeney, 1983, p. 70).

Systems operate under a number of rules that create boundaries. These
boundaries act as gatekeepers for the flow of information into and out of the
system. Boundaries define a system's openness or closedness. Within the
framework of cybernetic ideas, most family therapists serve as experts and
offer interventions based on their understanding of the context within which
a problem fits, and the patterns that maintain the problem. They focus their
attention on attempted solutions and current communications about the
problem.

Another level of understanding of systems is introduced when the therapist is *included* as part of the system rather than as an outside expert observing the system. Called **cybernetics of cybernetics,** or second-order cybernetics,
it suggests another level of involvement and a different role with clients. As
an integral part of the client/therapist system, therapists examine the impact
of their behaviors (interventions) in terms of client reactions (feedback), and
respond to those reactions in an ongoing, circular, mutual modification
process. The goal is to **cocreate** a new context—a new environment—that
encourages the client's desired outcome as a logical response to their alternate
perceptions. All participants (including the therapist, who is now part of the
system) are part of the problem as well as the solution. Therapists introduce
new information intended to interrupt the system and change the communi-

cation patterns and rules of the relationships within that system. The therapist understands he or she is part of the system, part of the **same domain,** and needs to be speaking from within the system he or she is exploring, together with the client. This relationship results in a more egalitarian, cooperative dialogue among all participants in the therapy meeting. This stance is seen as empowering for the client.

The basic difference of these concepts:

First-order consensual domains are those where therapists are objective observers—looking in as experts, outside of the system.

Second-order consensual domains are those in which therapists become a part of the system they are in communication with.

In a text about cybernetics of cybernetics, Maturana (1974) explained:

A problem is a question. A question is a perturbation that the questioned system must compensate for by generating a conduct that satisfies certain criteria specified in the same domain as the perturbation. Therefore to solve a problem is to answer a question in the same domain in which it is asked. (pp. 457–469)

Clients are influenced as the therapist's worldviews interact with their worldview. Therapists are also influenced through their interactions with their clients. The relationship creates a sense of shared responsibility for the world and community in which the client and therapist live. (Becvar & Becvar, 1996)

POSTMODERN, SOCIAL CONSTRUCTIVIST IDEAS
CONSIDER LARGER SYSTEMS

Social constructionism encourages people to notice that things are different in different cultures. It helps people envision better and more satisfying ways of relating to one another. It helps them become aware of how their ordinary daily ways of doing things is affecting others and is being affected by others. It gives them clues as to how they might change things (Gergen, 1985). For therapists, limiting their thinking to family systems may limit their ability to think about the flow of ideas in the larger culture. "The social constructionist metaphor leads us to consider the ways in which every person's personal and interpersonal reality has been constructed through interaction with other human beings and human institutions and to focus on the influence of social realities on the meaning of people's lives" (Freedman & Combs, 1996, p. 1).

Post-modern, social constructionist ideas draw attention to larger systems. These ideas address the full environment, everything from government to talk shows, television to schools, and everyone from newspaper editorial writers, bosses, grandparents, parents, ethnic and religious groups to friends, who tell us how to think and who to be. The suggestion is that people define themselves through those ubiquitous messages, many of which may be destructive and discouraging. In response to those messages, some people feel oppressed, disempowered, and unable to help themselves. When therapists, in keeping with cultural dictates, allow themselves to be seen as *experts* who know what is right for their clients, it tends to reinforce that disempowerment. **Postmodern** therapists believe people are the experts of their own lives, and that the therapist's role is to provide the context that will enable them to empower themselves and to activate their innate expertise. Although the therapist may be the expert on the *process of therapy,* the client family is the expert on how and what will work best for them.

Postmodern, social constructivist approaches blur the distinction between politics and therapy. They bring issues of racism and sexism down to the personal level, focusing on the insidious effects of oppressive ideas and practices, habits of thought and action, to which all people are subject. When people learn that much of what they do or feel has been strongly influenced by messages they have internalized from the dominant culture, and then recognize they are not locked into those messages and beliefs, they feel liberated and more capable of acting on their own behalf. Social constructivist ideas open clients to different ways of thinking about themselves and their position in their environment.

Postmodern therapies offer an egalitarian, conversational approach. These therapies are founded on the idea that most of the beliefs and thoughts people cling to are nothing more than cultural brainwash and not etched in stone. All ideas can be challenged and replaced with other more empowering ideas. If people consciously learn to recognize the disturbing effects of certain cultural messages, and see them *not* as inherent in themselves, they can free themselves from them. This kind of liberating conversation is what postmodern therapists hope to have with their clients (O'Hanlon, 1994). Postmodern therapists would probably not even use the word "client" but would rather talk of "people" in session, of which he or she is one.

PARTICIPATE *WITH* THE CLIENT

The postmodern, social constructionist therapist is one who is wary of any all-encompassing theories "because no social theory can make claims to validity outside a particular context and value system" (Doherty, 1991, p. 40). In postmodern thinking, the role of the therapist is to participate *with* the client in **deconstructing the problem saturated, dominant stories** that the client brings to therapy, and to *collaborate* with the client in constructing new stories that solve or dissolve the problems defined by those problem saturated stories. The focus of the therapeutic conversation remains on the client's story rather than on some preconception of what is really going on in the client's system. The goal is *not* to impose some normal standard about how the client system should be. Therapy in this tradition is more likely to resemble a conversation, with each participant reacting to the information provided in the context of the meeting.

SOCIAL REALITY—A FUNCTION OF ONE'S BELIEF SYSTEM

In the postmodern stance based on the ideas of social constructionism, reality is understood to be a function of the belief system a person brings to a particular situation that guides his or her actions. The concern is with the *context* in which the presenting problem is embedded. Therapists and clients are *not discovering* behavior as something "out there," they are *creating* it as they participate. How people speak about their situation becomes crucial. All people have the right to develop their personal expertise relative to their own lives.

These changes in assumptions about the role of the therapist, and the creation of a mutual reality, are said to comprise a far more ethical perspective since they encourage the equal engagement of client and therapist as cocreators of a shared reality (Becvar & Becvar, 1996). Therapy is understood as a dialogue whose goal is the creation of a context that accommodates the needs and desires of *all* the participants. *All* includes the therapist.

"The main premise of social constructionism is that the beliefs, values, institutions, customs, labels, laws, division of labor, and the like, that make up our social realities are constructed by the members of the culture as they interact with one another from generation to generation and from day to day" (Freedman & Combs, 1996, p. 16).

Four ideas that summarize the social constructivist worldview:

1. Realities are socially constructed.
2. Realities are constituted through language.
3. Realities are organized and maintained through narrative.
4. There are no essential truths (Freedman & Combs, 1996, p. 22).

LANGUAGE AS CENTRAL TO HOW WE KNOW WHAT WE KNOW

A fundamental premise in the postmodern era is that the role of language is central. Postmodernists understand language as the means by which people interpret their world—while simultaneously constructing it. If humans can only know reality by way of their perceptions, then that which people perceive is a function of their mental processes or mind. People experience, and then interpret and express their knowing, through a system of language. Words express the conventions, symbols, and metaphors of a particular group.

> The terms in which the world is understood are social artifacts, products of historically situated interchanges among people. From the constructionist position the process of understanding is not automatically driven by forces of nature, but is the result of an active, cooperative enterprise of persons in relationship. In this light, inquiry is invited into the historical bases of various forms of world construction. (Gergen, 1985, p. 267)

Social constructivist, postmodern ideas opened the door to new, innovative, and somewhat revolutionary therapeutic processes. Specific therapies that are motivated by postmodern thought will be described in Chapter 12.

MODERN AND POSTMODERN TENSIONS

There was, and still is, an ongoing tension between the theory and practice of those who work consistent with first-order cybernetics and those who work consistent with second-order cybernetics. Tension is ongoing between those who hold to a modern stance of a structured or a given reality and those who propose a postmodern stance. Postmodern therapists understand reality as an evolving, language-generated system involving the relationship of all the participants in a larger context. Although some purists in each way of thinking may deny the validity of the other, this tension is what keeps family theory evolving and seeking more and different ways to help families and communities. To speak in terms of either/or is inconsistent with the systemic/cybernetic, both/and perspective. "The postmodern argument is not against the various schools of therapy, only against their posture of authoritative truth" (Gergen, 1992, p. 57).

SUMMARY

This chapter traces the change in the role of the therapist from the *expert* about what the clients need to improve their lives, to the *consultant* who becomes part of the client system and to the *collaborator* in rewriting the story brought in as a problem. The therapist remains the expert on the *process of therapy* but people are seen as experts on their own lives. These changes in roles are intended to empower family members and dilute the effects of disempowering messages within the dominant culture.

Postmodern, social constructionist ideas are used to explain how people create reality through internalized societal messages. The language used to talk about ideas reflects the participant's perception of a problem. The therapist acknowledges the participant's worldview and asks questions designed to open the conversation to alternative points of view. These concepts also look at how the therapist's worldview interacts with the other participants' worldviews. All participants may gain a sense of shared responsibility for themselves and their community. The next two chapters will describe some of the ways these ideas are used in therapy.

EXPERIENTIAL ACTIVITIES

1. The instructor will set up two teams to debate in class about how the students feel about the changes in the role of the therapist in postmodern theory.

2. The instructor may lead a brainstorming session about the future for systemic therapy as it adapts to a more collaborative, egalitarian stance.

REFERENCES

Becvar, D. S., & Becvar, R. J. (1996). *Family therapy: A systemic integration* (3rd ed.). Boston: Allyn & Bacon.

Doherty W. J. (1991). Family therapy goes post-modern. *Family Therapy Networker, 15,* (5), 36–42.

Freedman, J., & Combs, G. (1996). *Narrative therapy: The social construction of preferred realities.* New York: Norton

Gergen, K. J. (1985). Social constructivist movement in psychology. *American Psychologist, 40,* 266–275.

Gergen, K. J. (1992). The post-modern adventure. *Family Therapy Networker,* Nov/Dec., pp. 52–57.

Keeney, B. P. (1983). *Aesthetics of change.* New York: Guilford.

Maturana, H. (1974). Cognitive strategies. In H. von Foerster (Ed.), *Cybernetics of cybernetics* (pp. 457–469). Urbana, IL: University of Illinois.

O'Hanlon, B. (1994). The promise of narrative: The third wave. *Family Therapy Networker,* Nov/Dec., pp. 1–29.

11

SOLUTION FOCUSED
THEORY AND THERAPY

KEY THEORISTS

Insoo Berg—codeveloped solution focused theory

Steve deShazer—codeveloped solution focused theory

Eve Lipchik—used with domestic violence clients

Bill O'Hanlon—developed presuppositional questioning

Michelle Weiner-Davis—"Do a one-eighty."

TERMS TO KNOW

naturalistic trance

matches the client's language

exceptions

possibilities

customer

complainant

visitors

formula tasks

observe

presuppositional questions

miracle questions

exception questions

compliments

scaling questions

distinctions

difference that makes a difference

normalize

naturalistic trance

ROOTS AND DEVELOPMENT OF SOLUTION FOCUSED THEORY

Solution focused theory was a front-runner in the adoption of the social constructivist thinking that became prominent in the late 1980s and early 1990s. It offers a bridge between strategic theories and language theories.

The roots of this theory were developed at the Mental Research Institute (MRI) in Palo Alto and mutated from a problem-solving focus to a solution focus. Most of the innovators of solution focused therapy came from the Brief Therapy Center (BFTC) in Milwaukee in the late 1970s. The initial partners at BFTC were a married couple, Insoo Berg and Steve deShazer. deShazer, a researcher, is credited with being the primary developer of solution focused theory. Berg, a clinician, trained most of the current leaders of solution focused therapy. She is an advocate of its use with alcoholics. Another notable early clinician is Eve Lipchik who, among other things, developed a controversial model for working with domestic violence. Some of her ideas differ from most other therapy models, in that she often includes the batterer in conjoint sessions. Another solution-focused pioneer is Michelle Weiner-Davis, who trained with deShazer and is in private practice in Woodstock, Illinois. She is largely known for her upbeat seminars on solution focused concepts and therapy and her book *Divorce-Busting,* which is addressed to couples, and is useful for therapists and clients alike. One of her typical suggestions is "Do a one-eighty." It is her way of saying, if what a person has been doing isn't working, he or she should do something very different, often opposite of what he or she has been doing (Weiner-Davis, 1992). Bill O'Hanlon, who was a student of the hypnotherapist Milton Erickson, adapted Ericksonian ideas into the solution focused model. One of those ideas builds on the phenomena of **naturalistic trance.** This idea suggests people are all just naturally in a trance (entranced) when in a relationship. The therapist builds on this phenomenon by using language that **matches the client's language.** For example, if a client uses words such as "I *see* him failing," the therapist could reflect, "It *looks* bleak to you." Or if a client says, "I'm *confused*," the therapist may feed back, "It all seems so *mixed up* to you."

O'Hanlon and Weiner-Davis have collaborated on many seminars and coauthored *In Search of Solutions* (1989), a step-by-step guide to solution focused therapy.

AN OPTIMISTIC APPROACH TO THERAPY

As with most psychotherapies, the first few minutes of the session are spent joining, talking about anything except what might be related to the fact the clients are there because they have a problem. It is general, friendly talk, about their jobs, the weather, school, or even artwork on the therapist's wall. Confrontation or disagreements are avoided. The therapist shows nonjudgmental interest in helping clients feel comfortable being there. Because it has been recognized that clients often makes useful changes even before the first therapy session, the therapist often begins by asking, "What has changed between the time you called for an appointment and the time you came in?" Just the act of calling for help often activates people's skills at finding solutions. And, of course, the fact of the therapist calling that to their attention strengthens the idea that they can make changes and be more hopeful. Therapists will then ask, "So what brings you in?" The therapist may interrupt the description being given of the problem if it goes on longer than he or she feels is useful.

The solution focused therapist then asks a series of questions designed to extract information about **exceptions** to the problem. Exceptions are times when things had been progressing smoothly. The therapist is looking for past solutions clients have tried that have worked—what they have done in the past that was successful. Solution focused therapists are listening for strengths and resources in their clients that they can build on (O'Hanlon & Weiner-Davis, 1989). The initial goal is to change the *language* in the session from problem talk to solution talk.

Solution focused therapy is pragmatic, cognitive, and easily teachable. It emphasizes brevity and a non-pathological view of people. It projects optimism, uses praise of people's strengths and accomplishments, and refers to the past only to search for exceptions. Therapy sessions can include one or more persons.

PROBLEMS MAINTAINED BY "MORE OF THE SAME"

Solution focused therapy pays little attention to the intricacies of family dynamics and is oriented toward seeking future solutions. Therapists acknowledge clients' perceptions of reality and their descriptions of the presenting problem, but they quickly begin looking for solutions, rather than dwelling on long histories of the problem. The solution is seen as unrelated to *how* the problem developed. Solution focused therapists assert that when people are stuck in their complaint, they are constrained by narrow, pessimistic views of their problem and keep trying to fix it by doing "more of the same." People are seen as stuck in rigid repetitive patterns of thinking and behavior that maintain the problem. Those patterns limit their ability to seek alternatives. As long as the *meanings* they have given to their dilemmas are not questioned or challenged, nothing changes. When those meanings are questioned, new meanings can be generated which offer new, more effective approaches toward solutions (O'Hanlon & Weiner-Davis, 1989).

Solution focused therapists do not believe problems or symptoms serve a function for the family, or that people are ambivalent about wanting to change or are resistant to change. deShazer denies the existence of resistance as a concept, and suggests that when clients don't follow the therapist's directives, it's their way of cooperating and teaching the therapist to find better ways to help them (deShazer, 1984).

They believe that the way a problem is approached affects the outcome of the therapy. They seek **possibilities** for, and strengths in, the client. They focus on how the clients' lives will be improved in the future when they implement new solutions. They see people as basically competent, needing only slight shifts in their thinking or behaviors to activate that competence.

"Language constitutes the human world and the human world constitutes the whole world" (deShazer & Berg, 1993, p. 73). If nothing exists outside of language, deShazer (1993) asserts, "There are no wet beds, no voices without people, no depressions. There is only talk about wet beds, talk about voices without people, talk about depression" (p. 89). If one accepts that language is reality, therapy becomes a relatively simple procedure. All that's needed is to change the talk.

BASIC QUESTIONS FOR THE SOLUTION FOCUSED THERAPIST

On first meeting clients, therapists ask themselves some basic questions:

"Who is the **customer**?" They note which person is open to and eager for change.

"Who is the **complainant**?" This is the person who usually focuses on the problem and perceives it as something someone else needs to fix.

"Who is the **visitor**?" This is generally a family member who was invited to come along to the session but is not invested in either the problem or the possibility of change.

"What are the clients' goals and how will they and the therapist know when their goals have been achieved?"

For example, if a mother brings a child in to be "fixed" because he is rude and disobedient at school, the mother may be the customer or complainant or both. She is the one who is disturbed by the child's behavior and wants to see the child changed. At some time the mother may become the customer when she realizes there are parts of her beliefs and behaviors she needs to change. The child may begin as the visitor, and over time becomes the customer, as he or she perceives the benefits to be gained from changing behaviors. Or perhaps, the school principal is the customer, and the parents and child are the reluctant participants (visitors) of the principal's referral, and do not believe there is a problem. The *customer* may change as the therapy progresses, so therapists need to recheck themselves as the therapy proceeds, rethinking their own perceptions of each participant's ideas about the problem, especially if they are not making the expected headway in the therapy (O'Hanlon & Weiner-Davis, 1989).

MAINSTAYS OF THE SOLUTION FOCUSED APPROACH

Solution focused therapists created certain **formula tasks** that can be offered regardless of the content of the described complaint. One such formula task is offered at the very first session:

> Between now and the next time we meet, I would like you to **observe,** so that you can describe to me next time, what happens in your (pick one: family, life, marriage, relationship) that you want to continue to have happen (deShazer, 1985, p. 137).

This task was developed at BFTC and has proven useful with individuals, couples, and families alike. This question comes as a surprise to most clients, since they usually don't expect the therapist to ask about what is working. They are sent home looking for good things and much to their surprise, they often discover quite a few things they want to continue to have happen. They just had not paid attention to them since they had become distracted by their problem. This task directs clients' attention into a positive frame that enables them to realize there is good in their lives. Clients often come to the second session more encouraged, wanting to build on those good things. They are usually eager to describe to the therapist what they have found. They report how much just observing helped them, and often tell what they have already initiated to maintain those positives in their lives. Therapists often hear how differently a client's partner or child has begun acting toward them, although the client may not yet be aware of the connection of those differences to his or her own new attitude. Often, what clients discover, and have begun to do differently, is precisely the kind of changes they need to solve their problem. Realize, they were not instructed to change anything except *observe* what was good, what was working, in their relationships.

deShazer's group developed **presuppositional questions** that may be considered as the mainstays of the solution focused approach and can be used effectively with most presenting problems:

1. The **miracle question:** "Suppose one night while you were asleep, there was a miracle and this problem were solved. How would you know? What *will* be different?"

It appears that the mere act of constructing a vision of the solution acts as a catalyst for bringing it about. Through the use of the word *will* there is the implication that a solution is imminent. As they think about this question and answer it, clients begin to picture a better life. They are able look beyond just solving the problem. They begin to see how they will be able to do things they've felt unable to do because the problem had been getting in their way.

2. The **exception question:** "Tell me about those times in the past or present when you didn't have the problem, or when it wasn't quite so bad. What was different about those times? What were you doing differently?"

Therapists keep encouraging clients to expand on those differences, those exceptions, times when the problem was more manageable or less troublesome, and what they were doing at those times that was contributing to that difference. They use **compliments** for anything they note as helpful toward the described goal. They call attention to the smallest changes and ask clients how they managed to make it happen. They normalize through anecdotes, acknowledging the described behavior as an expected or familiar one. They are careful in their use of language, using past tense when referring to a problem, using "will" instead of "would," and interject everyday language rather than psychobabble. If a client describes a pathological relationship the therapist may say, "Sounds like you're in a rut."

Therapists check out progress by asking **scaling questions,** "On a scale of one to five how different are you feeling about _____ now?"

Seeking Exceptions

Looking for exceptions—times when the problem did not exist or was not seen as a problem—is essential for the therapy to progress. Regardless of the magnitude or chronicity of the problems, there are usually situations or times when the problem simply does not, or did not, happen. Bed wetters have dry nights, combative couples have peaceful days, and even teenagers sometimes comply without argument. Solution focused therapists examine what was different during the times the problem occurred and, when it did not occur, look for useful information that can lead toward solutions. Often, the solution simply is that the client needs to do more of what is already working during those exception times, until the problem becomes extinct. The solution could be in increasing those activities that have achieved, even briefly, the desired goal.

Being asked about exceptions offers a challenge to many clients. They are so used being worried about the problem that had not considered that it really isn't *always* that the problem is happening. When they discover that, in fact there are times it is not happening, they can begin to think about it differently. The very fact of asking questions that seek what is good in their lives, or exceptions from their problems is, at first, confusing to clients. Most people come in to therapy expecting to discuss the pain involved with the problem, as well as its history, in depth. Asking about exceptions not only redirects people's attention to what is already working, but also orients them to what is important to know and talk about in therapy that will lead to solutions (O'Hanlon & Weiner-Davis, 1989).

Presuppositional Questions

When they return for the second session the therapist asks, "So what is happening that you would like to continue to have happen?" Notice the solution language in the formula intervention (to observe), the follow-up question (would like to continue), and the miracle and exception questions all indicate that the therapist is certain that good things do happen, and will happen. Once the good things are described, the therapist asks the series of presuppositional questions to elicit information that amplifies and maintains the changes (O'Hanlon and Weiner-Davis, 1989, p. 137). The use of various solution-oriented interviewing techniques helps clients experience significant shifts in their thinking about their situations. These shifts free people to act in more productive ways. The task assigned at the end of each session serves to reinforce changes that occur within the session (O'Hanlon & Wilk, 1987).

Presuppositional questioning is designed to influence the clients' perceptions in the direction of solutions, through the careful use of solution language. As the clients reflect on these questions, they begin to consider their situations from new perspectives. As clients respond to these questions, they are opened to the underlying premise that change is inevitable. Sometimes the questions themselves are so powerful in the **distinctions** they make during the session, a response is not necessary for them to be effective (O'Hanlon & Weiner-Davis, 1989).

A presuppositional question is open ended, and avoids a "yes or no" answer. For example, rather than ask, "Were there any good things that happened?" the therapist asks, "What good things happened?" With that wording, the therapist implies, or presupposes, that good things happened. That kind of question, and the timing of specific questions, depends on the goals at the time they are being asked.

Presuppositional questions are designed to bring out information about exceptions. These questions, and many of the comments about them are adopted from the book *In Search of Solutions* by O'Hanlon and Weiner-Davis (1989):

1. What is different about the times when _____ (you are getting along, there are dry beds, he goes to school)? Any and all differences between the times the problem is active and the times it is not are explored. The therapist assumes a stance that indicates he or she would be surprised if there were no exceptions. The question is phrased in positive terms, asking for those times, "When you are getting along," not "When you aren't fighting." This approach encourages people to think about "getting along."

2. If clients insist there are never times the problem doesn't happen, the therapist asks, "When is it less severe, frequent, shorter, or different in any way?"

3. When the therapist gets any response that indicates even the smallest difference (an exception), the client is asked, "How did you get that to happen?" Clients are encouraged to take credit for whatever is working. Even if they deny that they did anything different to make a change happen, the therapist asserts, "You must have done something different. What could it have been?"

4. The therapist then asks the clients, "How does it make your day go differently when the exception happens?" This question suggests how good things happening in one area of a person's life are connected to good things happening in other areas of their life.

5. Recognizing other people are usually involved in the complaint, the therapists then asks the client, "Who else noticed that _____ (whatever the difference was)?" "How did you know that?" "What did he or she do or say?" These questions continue to reinforce the idea of the interconnectedness of events and of involvement with significant people. Clients get to hear what is pleasing to one another and that information is useful toward influencing future behavior.

6. Building on a client's strengths, the therapist asks, "How did you get her to stop (throwing a tantrum, nagging)?" Thinking about it, most everyone can explain how nagging goes on, but few have tried to focus their attention to how it stops. When asked, the person who sees his or herself as being nagged might say, "I try everything, and eventually I just give up and do what he wants, and then it stops." Somehow, the connection has not been made that what they did was a solution. The therapist then asks, "How did you figure that out, that in order to solve your problem and stop the nagging, you needed to do what they asked?" This question gives a clear suggestion about how they can stop the nagging should it happen again. That might not be the ultimate solution, but it does suggest that what one person does influences what the other does, and vice versa. Other ideas to change the nagging behavior could then be explored.

7. When a different action is noted, the next question is "How is that different from the way you might have handled it _____ (one week, one

month) ago?" This question is asked whenever clients report anything that appears to be new or different. It is an extremely important one, since clients often do not recognize their own movement toward solutions. Not asking this question may let their new behaviors go unnoticed and not viewed as a **difference that makes a difference.** Making this distinction is an invaluable step toward constructing future solutions. Having been asked this a number of times during therapy, clients often begin to volunteer this information, demonstrating they are becoming aware of their role in developing more effective ways to handle their lives then they did in the past.

8. "What do you do for fun?" "What are your hobbies or interests?" Asking these questions elicits information about people's abilities and how they problem solve, in the context of their everyday lives. Most clients have participated in some kind activity where they functioned well, yet they fail to generalize those skills to help problem solve or improve family relationships. For example, a husband complained, "We just don't communicate at home so nothing gets done and we're always angry with each other." The therapist had previously asked the "fun/hobby" question and learned about areas in which the man felt more competent. The husband had answered that he coached a ball team. The therapist could now follow up by asking how he and the team agreed on what signals to use. He was asked how he, as coach, rewarded team members for small changes and successes as they learned to play together. After getting more specific details of how he communicated with his team to motivate them and get better cooperation, the therapist suggested that the husband pretend the family was a team, and that he could use some of the communication skills he was using with the ball team with his family. He was cautioned not to tell his family what he was doing, just try it out, and see what happened. The next session, the husband arrived back at the office with a big grin, eager to report how much fun his family had become and stating he was sure he could keep things going on his own and didn't need more therapy.

9. Another important question to ask is "Have you ever had this difficulty in the past?" If the answer is yes, then the therapist asks "How did you resolve it then?" "What would you need to do to get that to happen again?" These questions are looking for past solutions that could apply to the present difficulty. It may be that all this client needs to do is reapply what worked before. Sometimes people say something like, "It worked, but only for a little while, so it really didn't work."

Solution focused therapists disagree. The solution may have stopped working because people stopped doing it, and returned to the old, less effective ways of doing things. So the problem returned. What they probably need to do is remember what they did that had worked, and do it again. It may be they just need to be more consistent with the new way for a longer period of time so that it becomes a more natural way. It helps when people become aware they are backsliding and then decide to pull themselves up with more of what had been working. The follow-up question, after identifying past solutions, is "What would *you* need to do to get that to happen again?"

Normalizing the Client's Story

What causes most of the difficulties that bring people into therapy? Most often something has been happening that gets repeated and repeated. The same ineffective effort to change it is done over and over. At some point the client (or the person or agency who refers the client) recognized the behavior as a problem the client has not been able to fix. The clients feel stuck, incompetent, and discouraged. Generally these things are not pathological. These behaviors are responses to events that occur as part of the ordinary difficulties of life. Solution focused therapists **normalize** everyday stressors. They might say something like "That's understandable," or "So what else is new?" or "That sounds familiar." Normalizing comments have a calming effect. From the client's point of view, having a person perceived as an "expert" view the difficulty as normal means maybe it's not as bad or unsolvable as it seems to the client.

It's important the therapist doesn't just listen silently for a long time as the problem is described. Clients could take this uninterrupted silence as meaning the therapist thinks the problem is really bad. So the therapist interjects normalizing comments like the ones above, or tells stories or anecdotes that place the client's situation in a normal context, like stories from their own or others experiences. Stories to which the client could say, "Yeah, me too." Another normalizing technique could be to anticipate the client's situation by asking questions like, "Does he ever do this," and then give a description of another child's behavior that fits with the client's story. As the therapist identifies with a number of behaviors as familiar to him or her, the context of the client's complaints changes from abnormal to commonplace. Client and therapist can smile together with recognition of their common experiences. This change in context begins to normalize the client's experiences and reduce the client's concerns.

Another helpful way to normalize the client's story is to say, "I'm a bit confused," and then ask "How can you tell the difference between your son's depression (which is seen as frightening by the parents) and normal teenage moodiness, or between his being quiet because he's mad at you, or being quiet because he's thinking about his day?" By making these distinctions the therapist is introducing an element of doubt as to what the behavior they've complained about actually means. This doubt affects how they respond to the behavior being discussed.

Naturalistic Trance

Bill O'Hanlon, a master of the **naturalistic trance,** described a typical mono-logue he uses with clients who come in complaining about being depressed:

> If I were going to do a real depression, I would reduce the amount of stimulation from the environment and from inside myself. I would go to my bedroom, pull the shades, and stay under the covers. . . . It would be essential to avoid anything that made me breathe deeply or move physically, because it is difficult to maintain a good depression that way. I would dwell on the past and all the things I should or shouldn't have done. I would compare myself with other people and lose by the comparison. I would think I had always felt this way and would always feel this way in the future. (O'Hanlon & Weiner-Davis, 1989, p. 98)

Clients are captivated by this kind of monologue. They are "entranced." They experience what is described by the term, naturalistic trance. Most people begin to recognize they are using repeated actions, behavioral patterns for *doing* their depression, and they see there are choices—they can choose to act differently to change those patterns that have been maintaining their depression.

GOALS OF THERAPY

The process of achieving therapeutic goals (solutions) is to resolve the presenting complaints by accessing the clients' strengths and resources. Sometimes a simple shift in the focus from what is going wrong to what they are already doing or have done that has worked is all that is needed for people to be reminded of their own competence to handle things in more satisfactory ways. When people speak about what they can do differently, what resources they have, what has worked before, solutions emerge. Changing the way clients talk about their problems is what needs to be accomplished because, "as the client and the therapist talk more and more about the solutions they want to construct together, they come to believe in the truth or reality of what they are talking about. This is the way language works, naturally" (Berg & deShazer, 1993, p. 9).

Solution focused therapists ask people to describe their goals in very specific, behavioral, observable, and measurable terms so that each small step toward progress will be apparent when it occurs. They help clients establish reachable and clear goals and to think about how the future will look when those goals are achieved. They help them change the way they talk about their problems to future oriented talk—what their lives will be like *when* the problem no longer exists. Helping people think about the future and how they want it to be is a large part of what solution focused therapists do (Walter & Peller, 1996).

Even though formulaic questions and tasks offer a specific process that can be generically used, therapists are cautioned not to lose sight of the fact that each person or encounter is unique. The therapist needs to pace him or her self to the responses of the clients. Awareness of, and respect for, the uniqueness of every person and situation, along with the creation of trust and rapport within the therapeutic relationship, is essential to any successful encounter. Something powerful happens in the respectful and trusting inter-action between therapist and client.

SUMMARY

Solution focused therapy emphasizes a non-pathological view of people. It is respectful of people's innate abilities. It emphasizes people's strengths, uses a series of minimal, formulaic interventions, and is generally very brief. It is optimistic, limits problem history telling, and focuses on what is good and what has worked. Some treatments may involve only one or two sessions. The underlying belief is that people have problems largely because they become attached to trying to get to the bottom of their problems and obsess-ing about their problem's enormity. They are doing the same things over and over in their effort to change things, even though those things they are doing are not working. They have become caught in their repetitive patterns of thinking and doing things in relation to their problem and hold on to rigid beliefs that block their ability to see solutions are available to them. Solutions occur when people learn to *do* something different, think different-ly about their situation, and evoke their *inner resources*. Doing *and* thinking interact circularly to maintain change.

EXPERIENTIAL ACTIVITIES

1. Instructors may set up a class debate by dividing the class into two groups. One group is an advocate for solution focused therapy, the other for Haley's strategic problem-solving therapy. Have each group describe their techniques, how they would use them, and why their approach is the approach of choice.

2. Each student will put forth one of the formula questions used by solu-tion focused therapists and give an example of when and how they would use it. Demonstrate with a short dialogue with a role playing "family," gearing it to the anticipated goals. The instructor will ask the class to discuss which populations they see as most viable to work with through solution focused ideas.

3. The instructor will ask a small group of students to describe a presenting complaint and the people involved. Include an issue around gender in the complaint. Have one person serve as therapist, others serve as their "team behind a one-way mirror" and select people to play the complain-ing family. Have students take turns as therapist utilizing the formulaic questions.

4. The instructor will divide the class in three. One group will devise complaints. The second group will use normalizing techniques, including using anecdotes relating to those complaints. The third group is to offer their thoughts, feelings, and reactions to the normalizing processes that were demonstrated.

REFERENCES

Berg, I. K., & deShazer, S. (1993). Making numbers talk: Language in therapy. In . S. Friedman (Ed.), *The new language of change.* New York: Guilford.

deShazer, S. (1984). The death of resistance. *Family Process, 23,* 11–21.

deShazer, S. (1985). *Keys to solutions in brief therapy.* New York: Norton.

deShazer, S. (1993). Creative misunderstanding: There is no escape from language. In S. G. Gilligan and R. Price (Eds.), *Therapeutic conversations.* New York: Norton.

deShazer, S., & Berg, I. K. (1993). Constructing solutions. *Family Therapy Networker, 12,* 42–43.

O'Hanlon, B., & Wilk, J. (1987). *Shifting contexts: The generation of effective psychotherapy.* New York: Guilford.

O'Hanlon, W. H., & Weiner-Davis, M. (1989). *In search of solutions: A new direction in psychotherapy.* New York: Norton.

Walter, J., & Peller, J. (1996). Rethinking our assumptions: Assuming anew in a postmodern world. In S. Miller, M. Hubble, and B. Duncan (Eds.), *Handbook of solution-focused brief therapy.* San Francisco: Jossey-Bass.

Weiner-Davis, M. (1992). *Divorce-Busting.* New York: Guilford.

COLLABORATIVE THERAPIES

KEY THEORISTS

Harold Goolishian and **Harlene Anderson**— languaging

David Epston and **Michael White**— narrative therapy

Karl Tomm—ethical postures

Bradford Keeney— improvisational therapy

Tom Andersen— reflecting teams

TERMS TO KNOW

problem-determined systems

participant manager

languaging

coevolution

space for change

externalization

unique outcomes

cocreator

deconstructive listening

not knowing

curiosity

interpretation

deconstruction

dominating stories

relative influence questioning

subjugating dominant discourse

sparkling events

story their achievements

counter-story

dual landscape

landscapes of action

meaning questions

hypothetical stories

future focus

nurturing teams

improvisational therapy

reflecting team

HOMEOSTASIS SEEN AS LIMITING

Chapter 3 covered the beginnings of family theory. The innovators of family therapy theory described the family as a system with characteristics and organizing principles independent of the interpsychic structures of the individual family members. Family therapists see problem behaviors and symptoms as serving a function to conserve the stability or homeostasis within the family system. A family is described as a systemic entity.

In a 1987 article, Goolishian and Anderson reviewed the systems thinking and double bind theories of Gregory Bateson and his colleagues (Bateson, Jackson, Haley, & Weakland, 1956) that had energized the development of family therapy. Goolishian and Anderson questioned those foundational and central organizing principles (1987, p. 530). Along with Hoffman (1985), they expressed a need for alternatives to a homeostatically controlled systemic structure they saw as limiting possibilities for helping families. They pointed out that a person's ordinary daily experiences with the world are ever changing. Objectively defined family structures could not provide the flexibility they felt was needed to be useful to their clients.

LANGUAGE SYSTEMS AND THERAPY

Harold Goolishian and Harlene Anderson of the Galveston Family Institute were among the first to offer language systems as an alternative way of working with clients. Language system has as its core, the belief that reality is socially constructed by the way people think and speak about themselves and their place in the world. Anderson and Goolishian (1990) wrote:

> For us, psychotherapy is in a conversational domain, and the art of psychotherapy is a conversational art. The theoretical base that informs and develops the vocabulary of understanding for therapy should reflect this position. Our thesis is that a clinically responsible and effective position can evolve from a science of narrative and semantics. (p. 161)

Problem-Determined Systems

Anderson and Goolishian used the concept of **problem-determined systems** as one attempt to move therapy into the area of language, meaning, and socially created reality. This concept changed the role of therapist to that of a **participant manager** of conversations about a locally defined problem, rather than an expert who defined psychological reality and normalcy. They suggested that generating meaning through conversation defined the human community as one of evolving social action. The social system they envisioned was one that was defined by the problem and by those who are languaging, talking about the problem. These problem-determined systems exist only in language; they do not exist in social objectivity, social structure, or social roles. They are in a constant state of flux as new experiences and new meanings emerge.

Membership in a problem-determined system includes all who are **languaging**—talking about that which is seen as a problem. It is independent of any socially defined structure. It may include any number of individuals and is not necessarily limited to family. The problem-determined system is defined by the fact that there is a perceived problem. Each member of the problem-determined system brings his or her subjective definition of the problem or its solution. It is a transient system that dissolves once its membership believes there is no longer a problem. Change in this sense does not mean problem resolution or problem solving, but rather problem dissipation. Change takes place through conversation or communicative exchange. Change comes through the **coevolution** of new meaning that takes place in language.

The Therapist's Responsibility

A problem-determined system includes all those who are in active communication about, and thus create, what for them is a problem. The therapist's responsibility is to create a **space for change,** to stimulate conversation, and to loosen up ideas, meanings, or behaviors. These conversations offer participants an open dialogue through which new meaning and realities can evolve. The therapist joins as another member of the participant group, and includes him- or herself in the conversations and stories about what is going on with them.

The Therapist's Role

The distinction between therapy and other conversations is that the therapist is responsible for the *maintenance* of conversation. That is his or her primary role. The therapist must validate the other person's worldview and speak from the same point of reference. Change occurs as the therapist encourages dialogue through questions that introduce the possibility of alternative ways of thinking about the problem. Through ongoing dialogue, new meaning is always evolving (Rossfar, 1986).

The therapist takes the position that the client is the expert on what he or she is upset about. The therapist does not correct an individual's worldviews, a family's problem premise, an individual's irrational behaviors, how the group or family is organized among themselves, or the interactions among the family system's members. The therapist aims to create a conversational context that permits the evolution of new meaning, new action, and thus change (McCarthy & Byrne, 1986).

Therapy, in this view, involves the continuous generation of meaning. It does not teach or set norms. The therapist shows respect, not only for all ideas and positions, but also for the usefulness and necessity of all views. The therapist serves as an expert *only* in the management of the communicative process. He or she does not serve as an expert in diagnosing, setting standards of behavior, or of creative interventions.

Problems Exist Only in How We Think and Talk About Them

Problems and their treatment exist simply in the communicative networks through which people generate meaning. People gain an understanding of their actions through their relationship to significant others. Anderson and Goolishian (1988) acknowledged that it is not easy to shake the view that social consensus defines reality or to let go of the belief that some perceptions are more legitimate, more correct, than others. They cautioned people not to lose sight of the fact that the systems they work with exist only in language, not in social structure.

Michel Foucault

Before we move on to the work of Michael White and David Epston, we need to discuss the philosophy of Michel Foucault, a French philosopher who wrote extensively about the politics of power. His work opened the door to much of the postmodern thinking and especially to Michael White's emphasis on social justice. Foucault saw language as an instrument of power and insisted that certain stories about life, which were accepted as objective truths of the dominant culture, helped maintain the society's power structure, thereby eliminating the possibility of alternative stories about the same events (i.e., what is normal sexuality, what behavior is pathological, what is women's role in society) (Freedman & Combs, 1996).

Foucault advocated helping people get out from under the yoke of the culture's dominant stories. He urged that certain dominant-culture narratives be challenged, because following them unquestioningly eliminated the consideration of alternative knowledge or viewpoints and may be an anathema to free choice or what's best for a particular individual or family. Issues of power, privilege, oppression, control, ethics, and social justice underlie the theory and practice of Michael White's work (Goldenberg & Goldenberg, 2000, pp. 314–315).

Foucault offered new concepts that challenged people's assumptions about social institutions such as prisons, care of the mentally ill, gay rights, and welfare. He explored the sifting patterns of power within a society and the ways in which power relates to the self. He encouraged people to resist the welfare state by developing individual ethics in which one turns one's life into something that others can respect and admire (Foucault, 2001).

Foucault was much more interested in examining who people are than what people should be. He defined power as directing the conduct of others (1980, p. 11). His ethics were concerned with the relationships individuals have with themselves. He was concerned with the way in which people's experiences are controlled by others and the ways in which individuals control themselves (Coveney, 1998, p. 461). Foucault advocated having choices, making choices, and being able to make the right choice—always against an index of morality. He offered a particular understanding of freedom (Coveney, 1998, p. 462). He encouraged the fostering of means by which individuals become self-reflective as either individual agents of scientific contemplation, or by becoming members of competent communities (Coveney, p. 466). Foucault interpreted the accepted "knowledges" in many fields that were presented as objective reality, as stories perpetuated to maintain power structures and marginalize alternative stories (Nichols & Schwartz, 1998, p. 318).

NARRATIVE THERAPY

David Epston and Michael White are primary developers of narrative therapy. They have been colleagues and cocreators of many innovative ideas. Based in Australia, White and Epston travel the world demonstrating their ideas. The foundation for many of their ideas evolved from the work of Michel Foucault.

Externalizing the Problem

White and Epston developed the concepts of **externalization** and **unique outcomes.** They expanded consideration of the universe of influence in each person's life. According to O'Hanlon (1994), "when people found themselves in a corner, Epston and White could paint a door on the wall where it was needed, and then like Bugs Bunny in the cartoons, open it and help them walk through it" (p. 21). For example, in a workshop in Omaha, Nebraska, that Bill O'Hanlon had sponsored, David Epston presented a videotape of a third interview with a 15-year-old girl who was close to dying from anorexia. Epston saw her struggle as a need to be freed from the trap she had internalized through cultural messages about thinness. In that video, Epston was demonstrating a primary effective narrative tool—externalization. It's the conscious collaborative use of words to deconstruct and reconstruct meanings in ways that allow a more preferred story to be told and lived:

> The girl was a skeleton lost in a large sweater, trying to make herself invisible, curling her arms around herself and slumping down in her chair. In response to David's persistent questions she said she felt fine and had lots of energy. He leaned forward in his chair, spoke with intense interest, and asked question after question: "Can I just ask you why you think it is that Anorexia tricks people into going to their deaths thinking they are feeling fine? What purpose would it have, getting you to go to your death smiling?" The girl would not engage. He persisted: "Okay, okay, okay. If that's how you're feeling, how's it fooling you? Most people, when they're near death, know they're being murdered, right? How's Anorexia doing this to you? Because if it's making you feel good, or telling you you're feeling good, then I'd like for you to ask this question of yourself: Why does it say to you you're feeling good? Why would it do this? Why does it want to murder you? Why doesn't it want you to protest? Why doesn't it want you to resist?"
>
> Then suddenly and inexplicably, the girl responded. Anorexia, she said, fooled her by telling her she was fat when she was thin. "Is it telling you that right now?" David asked. "No," she said, "I am too thin." She sat up in her chair. David asked her, "Do you think Anorexia loves you?" "No," she said. "It's killing me."
>
> Her voice grew stronger. Her body language changed. She began to make plans for standing up to Anorexia and not letting it fool her into starving herself any more. David *enlarged the new doorway,* asking her how, in the past, she had shown herself to be the kind of person who could stand up to something like Anorexia. By the end of the session, no one in the room was talking about her hospitalization anymore. She had become an ally in her treatment, rather than a reluctant bystander. (O'Hanlon, 1994, pp. 21, 22)

The Narrative Approach

"What we know about ourselves is defined for the most part by the linguistic cultural practices of describing, labeling, classifying, evaluating, segregating, excluding, etc., in which we are embedded"(White & Epston, 1990, p. *viii*). When a problem-saturated story predominates, people are repeatedly invited into disappointment and misery. It becomes increasingly difficult to liberate themselves from habitually performing the same old problematic story. The hallmark of the narrative approach is "The person is never the problem; the problem is the problem" (White & Epston, 1990).

With narrative therapy, the therapist's thinking changes from seeking information or patterns, to hearing and telling stories. His or her role changes to **cocreator** of a new and more freeing reality—to be interested in people, to listen and join with them, and to be skilled at asking questions that draw out people's knowledge and experience as carried in their stories. Therapists collaborate on the construction of new realities together with the other participants. They ask questions designed to awaken the other participants' awareness of the influence of the restrictive cultural stories on which they have based their lives. The goal is to help people expand their own stories to be more self-empowering ones.

When the problem has been externalized, as was demonstrated in the previous example of Epston's session with the girl under the influence of anorexia, and given an entity separate from the person, the question can be asked: Is the problem gaining more influence over the person or is the person gaining more influence over the problem?

Externalization offers a way of viewing clients as having parts of themselves that are not contaminated by the symptom. This idea creates a view of the person as *not* predetermined to be as they are, but as *accountable,* responsible for the *choices* he or she makes in relationship to the problem (O'Hanlon, 1994). Participants co-construct alternative stories a bit at a time from experiences that do not fit with dominant, problematic stories. The therapist frequently checks, during the session, to be sure that the direction or meaning of these experiences is preferred by participants to those of the problematic stories (Freedman & Combs, 1996, p. 129).

Karl Tomm (1989), an influential Canadian family researcher and therapist, said:

> The technique of externalization is both simple and extremely complicated. It is simple in the sense that what it basically entails is *a linguistic separation of the problem from the personal identity of the patient.* What is complicated and difficult is the delicate means by which it is achieved. It is through the therapist's careful use of language in the therapeutic conversation that the person's healing initiatives are achieved. . . . What is new about the narrative approach is that it provides a purposeful *sequence* of questions that consistently produce a freeing effect for people. (pp. 54–59)

People construct their realities (stories) as they live them through essentially four processes:

1. Typification—the process through which people sort their perceptions.
2. Institutionalization—the process through which institutions arise around sets of typifications. It helps families bond around and maintain and disseminate knowledge gained over time.
3. Legitimization—the process that legitimizes institutions in a particular society. Institutions become experienced in honing a reality of their own.
4. Reification (internalization)—implies man is capable of forgetting his own authorship of the human world (Berger & Luckmann, 1966).

Therapeutic Conversations

In any life there are always more events that don't get *storied* than there are ones that do. This idea means that life narratives that carry hurtful meanings or seem to offer only unpleasant choices can be changed by constructing new narratives that highlight previously un-storied events, or by taking new meaning from already storied events. Narrative therapy is about the retelling, questioning, revising, reliving, and creating new meanings for life stories. As people free more and more of their pasts from the grip of problem dominated stories, they are able to envision, to make choices, and to expect and plan less problematic futures.

The Narrative Therapy Process

Deconstructive listening: This is the kind of listening required for accepting and understanding people's stories. It is the therapist's job not to internalize or intensify the powerless, painful aspects of the stories told by their clients. People are encouraged to relate to their life narratives as actively constructed stories, open to change. Therapists help them see those stories as something they have shaped over time, and can therefore reshape. The meaning a listener makes of the story he or she tells is, more often than not, different from the meaning the speaker intended. Therapists capitalize on this by exploring gaps in understanding and asking people to fill in the details. They listen for vagueness, uncertainties, and ask people to clarify, provide more specific details, and to express their ideas of ways to resolve those uncertainties (Freedman & Combs, 1996, p. 47).

Not knowing: Therapy is a process in which "We are always moving toward what is not yet known" (Anderson & Goolishian, 1990, p. 159). The therapist's knowledge is about the *process* of therapy, *not* about the content and meaning of people's lives. The content is the domain of the participants. Each person is an expert informant on his or her life experiences as they are perceived at that time.

Curiosity: Narrative therapists ask lots of questions. They want to know more. They encourage people to develop their thoughts more completely.

They ask for specific details. When a conversation turns in an unexpected direction, they ask even more questions (Freedman & Combs, 1996).

Interpretation: Narrative therapists are aware that all people (including themselves) are interpreting their life events from the worldview they have developed over time from their life experiences. Each person is respected as an expert on his or her own life.

Deconstruction of Subjugating Stories

White (1991) suggested that **deconstruction** could help unmask the so-called truths that hide the biases and prejudices that give an air of legitimacy to restrictive and subjugating stories. He explained it was the responsibility of the therapist to cultivate a growing awareness of the **dominating stories** in society and to examine collaboratively the effects of those stories. Almost all deconstructive questioning takes place within externalizing conversations. Questions address things that are part of a problem-saturated story or that seem to be maintaining a problematic narrative. Therapists must remain aware of their own perceptions and biases and openly explore personally held beliefs and practices *with* clients. When the therapist asks questions like the following, the therapist's own responses need to be included in the conversations:

> What attitudes do you think you or others have that justify the behaviors you have described?
>
> What do you think gets in the way of developing the kinds of relationships you would like to have?
>
> How do you think that (belief, feeling, attitude) you talked about is influenced by the kind of family (culture) you grew up in?

Externalizing Conversations

People can most easily examine the effects of problem-saturated stories on their lives when they do it in the context of an externalizing conversation. The first step in this process is building trust. The therapist must acquaint him- or herself with the individual participants and their group values, customs, and preferred ways of relating. The therapist should have some knowledge of the stories emanating from the participants cultural backgrounds. They use the language style used by participants in their description of their problems. Therapists then externalize a problem, and ask questions about it. Tomm (1993) suggested pathologizing the pattern itself, rather than the person enacting it. For example, if a person talks about "flying off the handle," the therapist could begin asking for details about how "anger" was controlling his other actions.

Relative Influence Questioning

Michael White (1991) introduced **relative influence questioning** as a way to structure externalizing conversations. People are asked to first map the influence of the problem in their lives *and* relationships, and then to map *their* influence on the life of the problem. The idea is to establish that the person has *a relationship with the problem,* rather than the person *being* the problem. Since this process addresses the way others in the relationship group are affected by the problem, it helps to demonstrate that others in the problem-determined system also have a relationship with the problem. Knowing that about the others helps keep the problem separate from the identity of any person. Each person in the therapy meeting is asked how he or she has been influenced by, or influences the problem.

White writes of the **subjugating dominant discourse** as the cultural messages that influence people's self-perceptions. He exposes the role of those subjugating messages by asking questions like: "How were you recruited into this way of thinking?" "What feeds the problem?" "What starves it?" "Who benefits from it?" "How might it be useful?" "What sort of people would definitely oppose it?" (White & Epston, 1990).

When people see their local problems as particular reflections of political problems in the larger society, they can become motivated to deal with them differently. When they stop living their lives through the dictates of a political problem (i.e., prejudice), they often go on to help deconstruct the problem at a societal level. For example, a woman came into my office with a story of being depressed. Her story was deconstructed to where she understood that her depression had been influenced by societal messages about the expected role of women. She recognized how those messages had limited her view of herself as able to pursue a new career. When she realized the problem was not within her, but related to an external message, she was able to change her perception of her own abilities and separate them from the messages imposed by societal limits. With new courage, she pursued a career she had not seen as possible before. In turn, her actions may have an effect on larger societal attitudes and chip away at the hold those dominant cultural messages have on other women.

Dominant discourses can also be exposed by asking people about the history of their relationship with the problem. Therapists ask: "Where did you learn this way of thinking?" "What did you experience that supported these kinds of attitudes?" "How did (fear, for instance) coach you so easily to believe that?"

Story Development   Anderson and Goolishian wrote that the purpose is to co-construct stories in which people can live in preferred ways (1992). Stories are cocreated through conversation. People tell of their experiences and the ways they are interpreting them. Neither therapist nor client knows where the stories will eventually take them. They are coauthored one piece at a time. This method is different from setting goals and finding experiences to support those goals. It calls for curiosity and involvement in each bit of the story as it emerges. It involves asking numerous questions which may lead to a new direction. The therapist must remain alert to verbal and nonverbal responses. The therapist may offer some tentative possibilities by using terms like "Could it be . . . ?" or "What if . . ." to encourage participation and invention.

The Construction of Preferred Stories The construction of preferred stories occurs concurrently with the deconstruction of old ones. Unique outcomes or **sparkling events** arise from openings that, through questions and reflective discussion, can be developed into new stories. This process begins as the therapists invite people to **story their achievements,** talk about their successes. For example, if a client tells of a reduction in a reaction like anger, the therapist asks him or her for specifics, "How you did you do that?" "How did you resist (anger) when it tried to get the upper hand?" Or, "Have you ever escaped from (depression) for just a few minutes?" "How did you do that?" These questions invite a change of one's personal story to a more optimistic one. If a person is having difficulty coming up with a hopeful or successful experience, the therapist asks something like, "What do you think there is about you that could have developed more in better circumstances?" When people do notice a sparkling moment or unique outcome, the therapist asks: "Is that a good or bad thing?" "Do you want more of that in your life?"

Narrative therapists help people identify resources from nonproblematic life contexts (what has worked in the past) and put those resources to work for them in problematic contexts in the present. Tapping into awareness of existing strengths can alter problematic narratives in a satisfying way. People are encouraged to review, reexperience, and link together what came before that led to present unique outcomes.

A unique outcome does not have to be a triumph over the problem. It can be a thought that differs from the problematic story, or doing something differently in response to the problematic story, or making preparations to have a different relationship with the problem. When asking questions in relation to unique outcomes, therapists acknowledge the power of the problem. That helps people feel understood. Participants are recognized for any small differences they make and told that small differences are the pathways to bigger differences.

Narrative therapists ask questions like:

I hear that this has been a lifelong problem, but when you compare different times in your life, were there times when ____ played less of a role?

I understand the fear is still keeping you somewhat confined, but do you sense that you are working up to changing that? Can you tell me specifically what's giving you that sense?

Think like a Novelist The cocreated story is called a **counter-story.** It is important to develop as rich, detailed, and meaningful a counter-story as possible. The narrative therapist asks questions that elicit specific, detailed responses that help the participants experience the new images through all their senses. People are asked to express their thoughts and feelings, what they see, hear, and sense. They are asked about other significant people and how they think those people would respond to changes. They are asked questions like, "How would your mother see and tell about this?" or "What would a friend say about how the problem is affecting you or is affecting him or her?" or "What would ____ appreciate most about you?" Questions are asked that help clarify, build, and support their counter-story.

Landscapes of Action   Michael White wrote about "**dual landscapes** of action and consciousness" (White & Epston, 1990). **Landscapes of action** relate to "who, what, when, where, and how." Once the landscape (context) of the problem has been broadened through deconstruction questions, the therapist looks for those experiences that lie outside the problem-saturated narrative and would not be predicted by it. These different experiences are what White and Epston describe as unique outcomes and sparkling events.

Therapists ask questions that support a person's inherent strengths discovered in the emerging stories (Adams-Westcott, Dafforn, & Sterne, 1993) (questions like "How did you do that?" "How did you notice ____?"). Therapists look for a turning point and then focus special attention on it, to strengthen it.

Meaning Questions   To help make the meaning of a new story part of a person's conscious awareness, therapists ask **meaning questions** that invite participants to tune into their values and feelings about what they are experiencing. This process helps people to add new ideas and actions as they become aware of their strengths and aptitudes and create a new image of self. White suggested the weaving of these dual landscapes—action and consciousness—continuously back and forth to bond and support the process of co-constructing improved self-perceptions. Through meaning questions, people are invited to reflect on different aspects of their stories, themselves, and their relationships. People are encouraged to experience the implications of unique outcomes arising from their newly storied experiences. Participants are asked questions like:

> If you were to apply this knowledge to your life now, in what context would it make the most difference? What difference would it make?
>
> What is the importance for you as a family that you are talking together about this new development? (Freedman & Combs, 1996, pp. 136, 137).

Hypothetical Stories   Narrative therapists elicit **hypothetical stories** from the realm of one's imagination that become the basis for both present and future events. They ask questions like, "How would you be different if you were brought up in a more loving household?" Therapists extend the emerging story into the future by asking, "How will these new ideas help you get ready for future events?" "Three months from now, who do you think will be most pleased by the consequences of this new understanding?" "What do you think those consequences will be?" "How is this different from what you would have done before?" "You seem pretty pleased about ____. How will you use that experience in the future?" "What do you think your next step could be?" (Freedman & Combs, 1996, pp. 134, 135). Asking future-focused questions extends alternative stories into the future and encourages people to change their expectations about what is ahead for them.

Respectful Requests   Narrative therapists may ask permission to take notes and then make a point of writing when people express new, helpful ideas. The act of writing down a specific point when it is made conveys a message to the participants that what they said was perceived as especially important. Therapists may also ask if they may tape a meeting so everyone may refer back to it together, and build on some of the ideas they each find useful when they play it back.

Letter Writing   David Epston originated the idea of letter writing to clients. In a survey he did, he found that on average, people who had received letters as part of their therapy process, thought a letter was worth four or five sessions (White, 1995). Letters were seen to serve at least four purposes:

1.   To summarize and recap the meeting.
2.   To extend ideas and stories initiated in therapy.
3.   To include people who had not been there.
4.   To share post-session thoughts.

Often participants in therapy meetings are encouraged to write letters to specific people relevant to their story and to cocreate signs, certificates of accomplishments, or affirmations to themselves and others, as tools toward self-empowerment.

For example, after a session with a woman who had been sexually abused by her sister's husband, Epston wrote her a letter. A few excerpts are included here:

> I take it that telling me, a virtual stranger, your life story, which turned out to be history of exploitation, frees you to some extent from it. To tell a story about your life turns it into a history, one that can be left behind, and makes it easier for you to create a future of your own design.

(This tells her he has heard her pain and sees it as a strength that she could talk about it.)

> Also, your story needs to be documented so it isn't lost to you and is in a form available to others whom you might choose to inspire. They will come to understand, as I have, how you were, over time, strengthened by your adverse circumstances. Everyone's attempt to weaken you by turning you into a slave paradoxically strengthened your resolve to be your own person.

(Telling her she is not alone, her situation was allowed to go on because of the dominating cultural discourse, and now she can help others in similar situations as part of helping herself.)

This, of course, is not to imply that you haven't paid dearly for this and haven't suffered. You almost accepted your family's attitude towards you and this accounted for the doormat lifestyle you lived for some time.

In your thirties, your own power surfaced and was accepted by you. And no one could submerge it any longer. You had so much courage, in fact, that you have decided to seek justice and put things right. By doing so, you drew a distinction between your history and your future. . . . No wonder you feel dizzy with possibilities.

(Points to a **future focus,** concerns she might feel overwhelmed, and reinforces her newly surfaced personal courage.)

Epston reported that the woman returned several weeks later with her husband. She had reread the letter many times. Seeing it all "in black and white" she said she could not deny it. Now she saw herself as a person who had been in a terrible life but had always been strong and never submitted completely to a devalued view of herself. She told Epston she didn't feel a need to see him anymore at that time. She did contact him five years later, spoke of a successful business she had developed and reported she kept her resolve strong by reading and rereading that letter (O'Hanlon, 1994, p. 20).

Nurturing Teams   Michael White (1995) introduced the idea of **nurturing teams.** He saw these teams as counterweights for abuse teams that may have been working in people's lives. White asks if there has been an abuse team, who is in it, for how long and with what intensity has it operated in the person's life. He then calculates the weightiness of the abuse by multiplying the number of abuse team members by the number of years per member and by the level of intensity per year. Then he wonders out loud, "What may serve as a counterweight?" and proposes the idea of a nurturing team. Along with the person who described the abuse team, he explores how big the nurturing team needs to be. He asks people who they think should be included and asks if they would like to invite them in for a meeting.

When a nurturing team meeting is set up, the inviter (protagonist) tells them about the abuse team members, their activities, its duration, and how it has affected him or her. People are then told how they can help as a nurturing team to undo the work of the abuse team. Prospective team members are invited to talk about the sort of ongoing contribution they might be willing to make. A discussion ensues between the protagonist and invited guests and plans are made for their work to begin. This planning is all done with great specificity. White suggests the therapist attend the first few meetings to be available to support and clarify the process (White, 1995, p. 106).

Maintain a Narrative/Social Constructionist Stance   In order to evaluate their contribution to maintaining the conversation, narrative therapists are encouraged to ask themselves these kinds of questions from time to time:

Am I listening so as to understand how this person's experiential reality has been socially constructed?

What are the stories that support this person's problems?

Are there dominant stories that are oppressing or limiting this person's life?

Am I focusing on *meaning* instead of on "facts"?

Am I evaluating the person or am I inviting him or her to evaluate a wide range of things, how the therapy is going, and the directions he or she would prefer life to be going?

Am I situating my opinions in my personal experience?

Am I being open about my context, values, and intentions?

Am I getting caught up in pathologizing or normative thinking?

Narrative Therapy Is Not a Panacea for Every Situation   White does not propose that these narrative practices are the only way of therapy for all persons, in all situations, and at all times (White & Epston, 1990, p. 75). Any existing family therapy model can be applied in a way that is or is not consistent with the implications of second-order cybernetics. Therapists may continue to draw on the more pragmatic, first-order models as long as they do not become too attached to the client's acceptance of their suggestions and interventions (Atkinson & Heath, 1990, p. 154). In other words, they don't present themselves as experts who know what is the best way for the client to live his or her life.

KEENEY'S IMPROVISATIONAL THERAPY

The social constructionist underpinning of narrative therapy opens the field as wide as the imaginations of the professionals and the people they work with care to take it, so long as the theme of developing a more empowering way of living prevails for all participants. Bradford Keeney's **improvisational therapy** offers an example of another way to meet the ethical criteria of social constructivism. As do all postmodern theories, it challenges the concept of the therapist as a professional with a privileged kind of knowledge. Keeney promotes the concept of therapy as a performing art. Therapy becomes a conversation without a predetermined narrative. It is not encumbered by theoretical subject matter as learned by most mental health professionals. Each meeting of participants is viewed as a new scene for a conversation that is not formally guided toward some theoretically predetermined end. Keeney's model encourages the therapist as participant to "share the creative inventions of one's own imagination" (Keeney, 1990, p. 5).

Keeney (1990) suggests therapists do the following:

1. Cultivate a healthy irreverence for all teachers and teachings.
2. Do what they want with any therapeutic model, school, or orientation—utilize it, ignore it, kick it, invert it, reverse it, distort it, misunderstand it, play with it.
3. Be cautious when therapy doesn't feel like play, never forgetting that play is serious work.

4. Experience psychotherapy as theatre: When it's boring, change anything—the script, the actors, the director, the audience.

5. With every new understanding one gains, a new dimension is added. The new understanding is added to the person's worldview. With this new understanding, he or she cannot continue to think, feel, or do things exactly the way he or she had done them before. This leads to learning to do some things differently. Doing things differently leads to yet a new experience, which in turn can be the source of even more new understandings. (pp. 5, 6)

THE REFLECTING TEAM

Tom Andersen, a Norwegian psychiatrist who began his career as a family physician, became interested in the social context of illness. He and his colleagues developed a model of therapy that is clearly consistent with postmodern, second-order cybernetics, social constructionist/narrative traditions. In Finland, in the 1980s he and his colleagues arranged for a group of 20 families of hospitalized patients to live and work in therapy together. All family members, including the patients, were involved as active participants in the planning and implementation of treatment. In 1984, he began inviting everyone referred to him to a discussion with all the professionals who were to be working with the family, before any treatment plan was made. Two rules were established:

1. Confidential talks with the identified patient, without the family present, were kept to a minimum.

2. They spoke of issues related to the identified patient only when he or she was present. Decisions were made related to the family only when the family was present.

This open, democratic approach provided the structure for communication that enabled dialogue even when the participants had previously felt embattled, humiliated, unheard, or devalued. This clinical work suggested that a reflecting team consultation can open fruitful dialogue between clinicians, identified patients, and family members. Two aspects of the reflecting process are considered critical to its usefulness:

1. The reflecting process creates a physiological readiness to perceive the world in a different way.

2. The reflecting process deconstructs professional knowledge in a way that rebalances power relations between clinicians, patients, and families (Griffith & Griffith, 1994, p. 161).

Andersen was looking for answers to questions like these:

Could there be alternatives to the beliefs that "mentally ill patients" can be steered into health? Could there be alternatives to separating the "mentally ill" from their family, friends, jobs, and so forth? Could patients be called something other than "patients"? Could alternatives to standard treatment (namely being locked behind closed doors, given medication against one's will, behavior modification, and so on) be more coherent with the context of the patient-family-friends-job-neighborhood? (Andersen, 1992, p. 56)

Initially, these questions led Andersen and his associates to study and attempt to apply principles from the work of Minuchin, Haley, and MRI. They had less success than they had hoped for. They studied Bateson's ideas as well as those of Boscolo and Cecchin of the Milan team, and of Hoffman and Penn from the Ackerman Institute. The perspective of therapist as "expert" just did not feel right to them. This discomfort with the "expert" role prompted Andersen to ask, "Why did we hide away our deliberations about the families?"(1992, p. 57).

These and other questions, shared among his staff, fostered the development of the **reflecting team.** They arranged for a team of therapists to observe the family interviews. It was suggested that the family and interviewer (primary therapist) together, listen to the thinking of the team that had been watching the family and the interviewer. Andersen explained that talking *to* others was *outer talk.* When we listen to others talk, we talk with ourselves. That is our *inner talk.* As particular issues are passed from outer talk to inner talk and back to outer talk among us, issues are passed through multiple perspectives. Participants are not only collaborators, but also co-researchers. They are recursively responsive to one another. One participant might understand the same issue differently from the various perspectives they hear, and when these different ways to understand are put together (as in this reflecting process), they can create new ideas about the issues in focus. As in narrative therapy, the reflecting team process invites people to be the experts on their own lives and empowers them to make choices from among the reflections of others, as they see fit.

Family members who want to speak may talk as long as necessary. All participants are given the time they need in order to tell what they want others to know. As listeners, the therapist and the team must be cautious not to interrupt. They are coached to listen beyond what is spoken, to notice *how* it is said. It is not taken for granted that everyone can or wants to talk about everything every time. The therapist might raise the question, "Who might/can/ought to talk with whom about which issue, in which way, and when should they do this?" This type of question will ensure that those who want to talk will have a chance to do so, and those who are not prepared to talk will be excused from talking.

Andersen acknowledged, "What I myself found important, but extremely difficult to do, was to try to listen to what clients say instead of making up meanings about what they say. Just listen to what they say" (1993, p. 321).

Many Contexts for the Reflecting Team Process

The ways the reflecting team process can be set up are infinite, limited only by one's own imagination, and by time. All participants are always hearing what is being said. Nothing is hidden from client, therapist, or team members. Here are a few suggestions for ways to set up reflecting teams:

A team can sit behind a one-way mirror. If there is no one-way mirror, everyone can be in the same room, with the team keeping themselves out of the line of vision of the therapist and family. The team is listening to what is being said. When it is their turn, the team reflects on what they have heard, talking from another side of the room, and discussing their reflections with one another as the family and primary therapist listen. The family will then have the opportunity to reflect and comment on what they have heard from the team. A therapist without a team could have one colleague present to talk with during reflecting intervals.

If the therapist is alone, without a team, he or she could speak with one member of the family while the others in the family listen. Then the therapist speaks with another family member and the first person listens. Later the therapist could ask that first person to talk about, reflect on, what he or she heard. The family and the therapist become a reflecting team.

If the therapist is alone with one participant, they might talk about an issue from the perspective of one who is not present. For example, the participant may be asked to talk about what she thought her husband would think and say about whatever was being talked about. She might then be asked, "What are your thoughts about your husband's thoughts?"

In a conference consultation with an audience, the whole audience might serve as a reflecting team. (Madigan & Epston, 1995, p. 19)

Reflecting teams can also be used in other settings, such as supervision groups, at staff meetings, management workshops, and in qualitative research. The less the process is planned, the greater the possibilities of letting the situation determine its form.

Introducing New Ideas to Clients

The reflecting team process may be foreign to people coming into a therapist's office. In addition to their discussion with their therapist, participants will be talked *about* rather than talked *to* by the reflecting team and this may be initially uncomfortable, or even seem intimidating. Always inform the family (or group) about the process at the start of the meeting. There needs to be a joining phase. Team members are introduced to the participants before the meeting begins.

The primary therapist may tell participants, "These team members will be listening to our talk. After a while we will pause so that those listeners can share their thoughts with us about what they have been hearing. Then you will have the opportunity to share your own thoughts about what the listeners have said."

How Team Reflections Are Framed

Reflections by team members follow a language pattern similar to the style that language participants use to tell their stories. Andersen (1991) suggested that reflecting conversations could include interventions as tentative "what if" ideas offered to the clients that they *may* want to examine for themselves. In that way, the therapist can maintain a position of collaboration with the client, offering his or her experience and expertise, while calling on the expertise and experience of the participants to decide whether and how to use the suggested intervention.

When Clients Give No Response to Reflecting Team Comments

There are times when reflecting comments are completely ignored by the client. It could be because of any number of reasons. Perhaps the team did not connect or missed the point of the therapy conversation, or it could be the participants (or therapist) are just not ready or able to let go of their stated positions. It is the role of the therapist to explore the responses, or lack of responses to the reflections. The therapist might ask questions like: "What would you have liked team members to have said?" "Were there parts of their conversation you did not understand?" The therapist's curiosity may facilitate the transition from ignored comments to new understandings.

The only limit to the number of reflections given within a session is time. After the team and the participants have completed their reflections on each other's reflections, the participants are able to take with them what they find useful from what they have heard, think about them some more, and decide on actions that will make a difference in their lives.

TYPES OF REFLECTION AND RULES OF PROCEDURE

1. Speculations are restricted to the conversations that have taken place in the room. Nothing that has not been talked about in the interview may be introduced by the team.
2. Ideas are presented tentatively, with qualifiers such as "I was wondering," "Perhaps," or "It's just an idea. . . ."
3. Comments and reflections are given positive connotations.
4. Team members, who are sitting in the same room with the family and the therapist, maintain eye contact with one another (other reflecting team members) while talking with one another. This procedure helps to maintain the separation between the listening and talking positions.
5. Perceptions are shared and consultants' thoughts, images, or imaginings do not judge or evaluate what was observed or heard.
6. Reflections attempt to present both sides of a dilemma, moving from an either/or position to a both/and position.*

Reflections should not be too usual *or* unusual from the pacing, style, or wording of the conversation preceding them. Use the language and metaphors of the people in the therapy room. The task of the reflecting therapist is to balance the tension between levels of difference. If two members of a reflecting team come up with the same idea, it is the responsibility of one of them to present a different idea. Not permitting private talking among

*From *The Body Speaks: Therapeutic Dialogues for Mind-body Problems*, by Jane L. Griffith and Melissa Elliott Griffith. Copyright © 1994 by Basic Books, Inc. Reprinted by permission of Basic Books, a member of Perseus Books, L.L.C.

reflectors makes it more possible for each reflector to formulate his or her unique responses.

Modeling

Therapists and reflecting teams provide participants with a different experience in the world. The team models the acceptance of many ideas, demonstrating the inclusion of active agreement and disagreement within a conversation and listening carefully and respectfully to one another's views. Participants are encouraged to ask questions of both the therapist and the reflectors during and after the interview. The therapy meeting may be the only experience people have ever had where they are not being judged or cut off for disagreeing.

Andersen (1987) suggested reflections should be brief, not taking more than 5 or 10 minutes. Reflecting team members need to be aware of not providing more information than the clients can absorb. They need to be sure to include all members of the group in their comments. It is just as powerful to be omitted from commentary as it is to be addressed. Reflections should include the therapist, who is often left out of the reflecting comments yet is very much a part of the system.

Timing of Reflections

After the therapist meets with the family about 30 minutes, the therapist and the family trade places with the team and listen as the team shares their reflections with one another. The team talks about what they had been hearing the family members and the therapist talk about. In addition to offering personal reactions to what they have heard, team members express ideas that help to externalize the problem. They offer hopefulness. The team uses phrases like:

"I'm interested to know when (e.g., fear) was less troublesome."

"So many stories are being told about (e.g., anger) it leaves no room to tell other stories about strengths. I'd like to hear about those."

After their reflections are heard, team members could ask each other:

"What in the interview triggered your ideas?"

"Are there any ideas or values you hold that influenced your comments?"

"Were there any experiences in your life that may have led you to have those thoughts and would you be willing to speak about them?" (Lax, 1992, pp. 69–85).

A Liberating Force

Reflecting teams serve as a liberating force that enables therapists, team, and family alike to share their thoughts and feelings in an open, nearly mutual arena. Points of view are seen "not as rigid explanations but as tentative thoughts" (Lax, 1992, p. 133). Participants are given the opportunity to talk back, question, and reflect about their thoughts and about what others have said. As they do, they are co-constructing the language of their own change (Epston & White, 1990). They are speaking differently about the situation they brought into therapy, and about their responsibility and ability to change.

SUMMARY

Language systems were introduced by Anderson and Goolishian (1988) who described psychotherapy as a conversational art. They suggested a changed role for the therapist that they called "participant manager." The therapist's job is to keep the conversation going, and to coauthor, with the client, new meanings around the client's dilemmas. The clients were seen as experts on their own lives. Their problems were recognized as influenced by the larger, problem-determined systems whose messages they had internalized.

White and Epston created narrative therapy and developed the techniques of externalization and unique outcomes. They built on the concerns about the influence of problem-saturated stories from the dominant culture. Narrative therapists collaborate on the construction of new realities and ask questions designed to encourage clients to rethink the messages they have internalized that are giving them a sense of powerlessness or hopelessness. People are helped to see new possibilities and to recognize their own strengths. White developed a number of techniques to deconstruct problem-saturated stories and separate the problem from the person. To assist in expanding the global effect of client change, White developed nurturing teams. These teams consist of groups of people, identified by a person in therapy, that were seen as potential support systems.

Karl Tomm advanced the narrative approach by offering a purposeful sequence of questions designed to externalize the problem. Keeney demonstrated the social constructionist stance for being open to new ideas when he introduced improvisational therapy.

Tom Andersen originated the idea of reflecting teams. The reflecting team affords the family the opportunity to hear diverse responses to their dilemmas and strengths, and to select those ideas that fit best with their perceptions.

All postmodern therapies emphasize the importance of building trust through open and honest information and dialogue. Narrative therapy is about telling and retelling, questioning, revising, reliving, and creating new meanings for life stories as a means of encouraging people to become aware of, and experience their own competence.

EXPERIENTIAL ACTIVITIES

1. The instructor will ask students to select some of the questions offered in this chapter and set up small group demonstrations of how they could use them in a dialogue with a participant family.

2. Students may bring in articles from current newspapers and magazines that describe social issues that may impact people's self-perceptions and exacerbate their problems. Discuss in class.

3. The instructor may set up groups of students to act as therapist and participants with a presenting problem and a reflecting team to discuss what the therapist and participants have talked about. Allow time for the therapist/participant group to reflect on the reflections.

REFERENCES

Adams-Westcott, H., Dafforn, T., & Sterne, P. (1993). Escaping victim life stories and co-constructing personal agency. In S. Gilligan & R. Price (Eds.), *Therapeutic conversations* (pp. 228–271). New York: Norton.

Andersen, T. (1987). The reflecting team: Dialogues and meta-dialogues in clinical work. *Family Process, 26* (4), 415–428.

Andersen, T. (1991). *The reflecting team. Dialogues and dialogues about dialogues.* New York: Norton.

Andersen, T. (1992). Reflections on reflecting with families. In S. McNamee & K. J. Gergen (Eds.), *Therapy as social construction* (pp. 54–58). London: Sage.

Andersen, T. (1993). See and hear: And be seen and heard. In *The new language of change* (pp. 54–68). New York: Guilford.

Anderson, H., & Goolishian, H. (1988). Human systems as linguistic systems: Preliminary and evolving ideas about the implications for clinical theory. *Family Process, 27,* 371–393.

Anderson, H., & Goolishian, H. (1990). Beyond cybernetics: Comments on Atkinson and Heath's "Further thoughts on second order family therapy." *Family Process, 229,* 157–163.

Anderson, H., & Goolishian, H. (1992). The client is the expert: A not-knowing approach to therapy. In S. McNamee & K. J. Gergen (Eds.), *Therapy as social construction.* Newbury Park, CA: Sage.

Atkinson, B., & Heath, A. (1990). The limits of explanation and evaluation. *Family Process, 229,* 154.

Bateson, G., Jackson, D., Haley, J., & Weakland, J. (1956). Toward a theory of schizophrenia. *Behavioral Science, 41,* 251–264.

Berger, P., & Luckmann, T. (1966). *The social construction of reality.* New York: Doubleday.

Coveney, J. (1998). The government and ethics of health promotion: The importance of Michel Foucault. *Health Education Research 13,* 3, 459–468.

Epston, D., & White, M. (1990). Consulting your consultants: The documentation of alternative knowledges. *Dulwich Center Newsletter,* p. 4.

"Foucault, Michel," Microsoft Encarta Online Encyclopedia, 2001.

Foucault, M. (1980). The eye of power. In C. Gordon (Ed.), *Power/knowledge: Selected interviews and other writings, 1972–1977* (pp. 146–165). New York: Pantheon.

Freedman, J., & Combs, G. (1996). *Narrative therapy: The social construction of preferred realities.* New York: Norton.

Goldenberg, I., & Goldenberg, H. (2000). *Family therapy: An overview* (5th ed.). Pacific Grove, CA: Brooks/Cole.

Goolishian, H., & Anderson, H. (1990). Understanding the therapeutic process: From individuals and families to systems in language. In F. Kaslow (Ed.), *Voices in family psychology.* Newbury Park, CA: Sage.

Griffith, J. L., & Griffith, M. E. (1992). Speaking the unspeakable: Use of reflecting positions in therapies for somatic symptoms. *Family Systems Medicine, 10,* 41–51.

Griffith, J. L., & Griffith, M. E. (1994). *The body speaks: Therapeutic dialogues for mind-body problems.* New York: Basic Books.

Hoffman, L. (1985). Beyond power and control: Toward a "second order" family systems therapy. *Family Systems Medicine, 3,* 381–396.

Keeney, B. (1990). *Improvisational therapy.* St. Paul, MN: Systems Therapy Press.

Lax, W. P. (1992). Post-modern thinking in clinical practice. In S. McNamara & K. J. Gergen (Eds.), *Therapy as social construction.* Newbury Park, CA: Sage.

Madigan, S., & Epston, D. (1995). From 'Spy-chiatric gaze' to communities of concern: From professional monologue to dialogue. In S. Friedman (Ed.), *The reflecting team in action: Collaborative practices in family therapy.* New York: Guilford.

McCarthy, I., & Byrne, N. (1986). Mistaken love: Conversations on the problem of incest in an Irish context. *Manuscript submitted for publication.*

Nichols, M. P., & Schwartz, R. C. (1998). *Family therapy: Concepts and methods* (4th ed.). Boston: Allyn & Bacon.

O'Hanlon, B. (1994). The promise of narrative: The third wave. *Family Networker* Nov./Dec. pp. 1–29.

Rossfar, V. (1986). Wittgenstein and therapy. Lecture given at the Galveston Family Institute, Galveston, TX.

Tomm, K. (1989). Externalizing the problem and internalizing personal agency. *Journal of Strategic and Systemic Therapy, 8* (1), 54–59.

Tomm, K. (1993). The courage to protest: A commentary on Michael White's work. In S. Gilligan & R. Price (Eds.), *Therapeutic conversations* (pp. 62–80). New York: Norton.

White, M. (1991). Deconstruction therapy. *Dulwich Centre Newsletter,* pp. 21–40.

White, M. (1995). *Re-authoring lives: Interviews and essays.* Adelaide, Australia: Dulwich Centre Publications.

White, M., & Epston, D. (1990). *Narrative means to therapeutic ends.* New York: Norton.

RESEARCH PERSPECTIVES

PART V

HOW EFFECTIVE IS COUPLE AND FAMILY THERAPY?

TERMS TO KNOW

quantitative	efficacy	meta-analysis
qualitative	effectiveness	

The questions about the efficacy of psychotherapy being asked in 1967 were: "What therapy is most effective for what problems, treated by what therapists according to what criteria in what setting?" (Paul, p. 11). Which therapy is most cost-effective, least dangerous, more long-lasting than others? How different would the outcome be if the family had no psychotherapy? How does the background of the family, its psychosocial demographics, affect the choice of the kind of therapy to be used? Do specific problems require specific therapeutic treatments (i.e., delinquent children, domestic violence, substance abuse, or depression)?

To further pin down what specifically works and what doesn't, researchers are now asking: "What are the *specific* effects of *specific* interventions by *specified* therapists at *specific* points in time, with *particular patients* with *particular presenting problems*?" (Gurman, Kniskern, & Pinsof, 1986, p. 601). Relying on cold statistical figures alone is not enough. It is important to look at how much each client family has improved. Researchers are considering subjectively evaluated criteria such as these: Could the clients be described as: Happily married, unchanged, deteriorated, separated, or divorced, relapsed? (Jacobson, Schmaling, & Holtzworth-Munroe, 1987).

WHERE IS THE FIELD OF FAMILY THERAPY GOING TODAY?

In an interview with Christopher Burnett, the director of the doctoral program for Graduate Studies in the Humanities and Social Sciences at Nova Southeastern University, he suggested there are two answers to the question of "Where is the field of family therapy going today?" He said there was "more and more emphasis for clinicians to work from an evidence-based model with no specific theory." This statement means therapists need to be client-centered. Do what works and be able to demonstrate outcome.

Burnett continued, "Systemic theories provide the foundation for understanding relationships and provide the grounding from which students and therapists can develop their own ways of being effective. Yet the systemic perspective is now given less importance than being able to demonstrate effectiveness. With competition from psychology, social work, and mental health counseling, specific family theory is being squeezed out. At the master's level, students want techniques they can use quickly and effectively. However, the doctoral programs continue to be interested in theory. Instructors need to pay attention to larger systems that promote understanding of relationships" (personal interview, Nov. 16, 2001).

SEEKING COMMON FACTORS THAT PROMOTE CHANGE

Studies over 40 years clearly support the idea that people who undergo most established psychotherapy treatments are better off than those who do not (Lambert & Bergin, 1994; Smith, Glass, & Miller, 1980). Hubble et al. (1999, p. 2) reported that psychotherapy has been shown to work and that "regarding at least its general efficacy, few believe that therapy needs to be put to the test any longer."

However, there is no clear indication as to exactly which therapy approach is most effective (Miller, Duncan, & Hubble, 1997). A meta-analysis of the MFT field confirmed that no theory of MFT was superior to any other theory of MFT (Shadish, Ragsdale, Glaser, & Montgomery, 1995).

COMMON FACTORS IN PSYCHOTHERAPY

Lambert (1992) followed by Miller et al. (1997) researched four common factors affecting the outcome of psychotherapy in general: Client/extratherapeutic factors (what happens outside of therapy or by virtue of characteristics of the client); relationship factors (relationship between client and therapist such as warmth, respect, genuineness, and empathy); technique/model factors (theory-specific processes); and expectancy, placebo, and hope factors (expectations of client and/or therapist, feelings of hope by either client and/or therapist). Sprenkle, Blow, and Dickey (1999) suggest five common factors that are specific to marriage and family therapy: Relational conceptualization; the expanded direct treatment system; the expanded therapeutic alliance; behavioral, cognitive, and affective common factors; and the privileging of client's experiences (building on the strengths growing from the client's experiences). The first three are unique to marriage and family therapy in that they are not emphasized in individual therapies. Behavioral, cognitive, and affective factors are only unique to marriage and family therapy to the extent they operate through relational conceptualization, the expanded direct treatment system, and the expanded therapeutic alliance.

A variation of the Delphi method of research was used by Sprenkle et al. (1999) to obtain expert group consensus on a variety of topics. In the Delphi method, data are collected by a series of questionnaires that are sent to a group of experts, referred to as panelists, until there is a consensus of opinion about the topic (Fish & Busby, 1996). The factors identified in these questionnaires are given numerical significance. However in a modification of procedures named "Delphi II," in place of a third round of questionnaires, qualitative interviews were conducted with six panelists (Linstone & Turoff, 1975). The Delphi II process was used in the study reported below.

In this study, Sprenkle and his colleagues considered the following criteria in selecting the panelists: They chose panelists from a wide variety of family therapy theories, depth of clinical experience, experience in the field of marriage and family therapy specifically, who held advanced degrees in marriage and family therapy or a closely related field. They made selections from the member lists of the American Family Therapy Academy (AFTA), a list of faculty members of the Commission on Accreditation for Marriage and Family Therapy Education (COAMFTE), training programs, and a pool of candidates thought to be suitable by the research team because of the extensive clinical experience, theoretical knowledge, or recommendation by another panelist. Of 95 surveys sent out, 40 panelists responded and 35 panelists completed both rounds of questionnaires. Six of the panelists participated in the qualitative interviews (Blow & Sprenkle, 2001, pp. 385–401).

A weakness of this study is that the panelists were predominantly Caucasian, and it may reflect the viewpoints of the white middle class. Two-thirds of the sample were men. Sixty-four percent of the panelists were involved in an academic setting. The sample was also skewed in the direction of integrative theory as a first choice of panelists, and away from more traditional approaches to marriage and family therapy. The results of this study represent the subjective viewpoints of this particular group of panelists regarding the common factors that may be operative in marriage and family therapy (Blow & Sprenkle, 2001).

Some Results of This Study

Client/extratherapeutic factors—respondents paid less attention to the role of clients in the change process than they did the role of therapists. This outcome may suggest that the field may not be paying sufficient attention to the client's role in the change process.

Relationship factors—respondents considered them to be important from both the perspective of the client and of the therapist. The respondents rated working collaboratively with clients more highly from a personal perspective than from their view of the marriage and family therapy theories as a whole. Client belief and trust in the therapist was seen as important. The respondents seem to believe they have a more important role in establishing strong therapeutic relationships than they believe is emphasized in marriage and family therapy theories as a whole. Ethical integrity made it into the final profile as an important characteristic for the therapist.

Models/technique factors—these were given a great deal of importance. Therapist activity, the importance of joining, and the value of cognitive and behavioral strategies were all seen as having great value to the therapy process. Techniques related to history did not make it into the final profile of what was important to the efficacy of family therapy.

Hope, placebo effect, expectancy factors—panelists reported that it is important that therapists and clients believe that change is possible and that clients believe the therapist is competent. No variables made it into the final profile from the perspective of marriage and family therapy theories as a whole (Blow & Sprenkle, 2001).

Implications and Recommendations from This Study

The authors of this study suggested the marriage and family therapy culture needs to move away from "the worship of cherished theory-specific models and the belief that it is the unique aspect of these theories that brings about change. . . . Common factors should be given much more attention in the training of MFTs. Common factors such as helping to instill hope in clients are rarely taught. Other common factors such as those that reside within the client and extratherapeutic factors, tend to be underemphasized, whereas the therapist's role in the change process is given too much weight" (Blow & Sprenkle, 2001, p. 399).

In conclusion, this study reported that much of the work that marriage and family therapists do overlaps with psychotherapy generally. It said that the general psychotherapy field has paid much more attention to common factors. They asserted that "this study helps move the field in the direction of lesser marginalization by emphasizing that which unites us internally as well as with our sister disciplines. The study is supportive of the integrative movement within psychotherapy in general, and marital and couple therapy in particular. . . . It suggested it was time for the field of MFT to establish a more ecumenical view concerning what really brings about change" (Blow & Sprenkle, 2001, p. 399).

THE FUTURE OF PSYCHOTHERAPY

Barry Duncan wrote he was moved to write an article on "the future of psychotherapy . . . after coming to grips with the predictions that many leading luminaries were making. The more I read about the future—integrated databases and mandated protocols for client problems (the so-called evidence-based practices)—the more uncomfortable I felt." Excerpts from Duncan's article follow*:

> The American health-care industry sees another sweeping change in the offing. Soon, they say, behavioral care, like most other medical specialties will be "carved in"—that is, mental health services will be treated as an integral part of medical patient care and administered accordingly, with all the advantages and liabilities that entails.

---

*From "The Future of Psychotherapy: Beware the Siren Call of Integrated Care," by B. Duncan, *Psychotherapy Networker*, July/August, 2001, 24–33, 52, 53. Reprinted by permission of the authors.

The reason for this coming change, of course, is the tremendous pressure on health-care administrators to reduce spiraling costs, especially those that are racked up by patients who repeatedly seek medical treatment—often expensive specialty consultations—for complaints that are at least partly due to undiagnosed psychological issues. . . . Over the last four decades, studies have repeatedly shown that as many as 60 to 70% of physician visits actually stem from psychological distress that finds somatic expression. Advocates of carving in behavioral care say it will not only save money, but will bring real advantages to therapists and patients alike.

And here is another apparent advantage of bringing together the medical and psychological disciplines: it becomes easier to provide care for people with disorders like chronic pain and insomnia that don't clearly fit into DSM categories; for people whose disorders are medical but clearly have a psychological or relational component, such as irritable bowel syndrome and high blood pressure, and for people who fit into multiple categories, such as alcoholics with renal system problems.

The beauty of an integrated system, its supporters say, is that patients get a reliable diagnosis from a properly trained professional and no longer need to diagnose themselves. They get the medical and therapeutic care they need quickly and cost effectively. The system becomes more coherent—with mental health services easily available—but only through the primary care physician. The bottom line: Carve-ins—done right—increase collaboration, improve care, and make psychotherapy more central to health care. And it saves insurance companies a lot of money.

So if carving in offers all this, why do many therapists fear it could undermine our relationship with our clients, rob us of our creativity, and challenge the fundamental values that underlie good psychotherapy? . . . What is obscured is the very real danger that in the name of "integration," psychotherapy will become ever more dominated by the assumptions of the medical model. At issue here is not the theoretical advantages of greater collaboration among health-care professionals or bringing more of a therapeutic perspective to bear on medical conditions, but whether we will lose our bearings—and our autonomy—as a profession by becoming immersed in the powerful professional culture of biomedicine today.

Integrated care, in and of itself, does not provide safeguards. . . . Of particular concern should be an element that its proponents consider a cornerstone of the health care of tomorrow—the integrated database. . . . treatment would permanently follow (the patients), available to anyone with access to the system. . . . In fact, background checks for any reason would take on ominous overtones in a system that would document "mental illness" as part of the medical record.

Duncan's article continues to explain how the American Psychiatric Association and American Psychological Association both set out to establish guidelines for specific disorders in the mid 1990s. They each defined particular treatments for particular diagnoses in line with their professional biases.

To continue to quote Duncan:

There is a certain seductive appeal to the idea of having a specific psychological intervention for any given type of problem—the psychological equivalent of a pill for emotional distress. But, in fact, a closer look at the research literature on therapy clearly reveals that the whole idea of empirically supported treatments is critically flawed, especially as any kind of mandate for what should be done in therapy . . . the approaches studied are all required to follow a script so that the "variable" presumably being examined—a precisely defined and structured form to treatment—can be strictly controlled.

But while certain kinds of therapy can be scripted—cognitive-behavioral therapy being the most prominent—most cannot. . . . There is no solid evidence demonstrating that specific treatment models have unique effects, or that any single therapeutic approach is superior to another. . . . No approach can reliably make a greater claim to effectiveness than any other.

So, if empirically supported treatments aren't what makes psychotherapy beneficial to clients, what is? . . . The real key to the success or failure of therapy, is the resources a client brings into the room. . . . Clients who are, for example, persistent, open, and optimistic, who, for that matter, have a supportive grandmother or are members of a religious community are more likely to make gains. . . . The client's perception of the therapeutic connection is the second most important ingredient of successful therapy. . . . Therapy is much less about method than about the quality of the bond established between therapists and clients. To many clinicians, this may seem obvious, but partisans of models and manuals too easily ignore this basic truth: The nature of a client's relationship with a therapist is more important than our cherished theoretical schools, our favorite techniques, or our most worshipped gurus.

Duncan's article concluded:

Today we may stand on the brink of a misguided system of "integrated care" in which manualized therapy will reduce clinicians to mere technicians. And, to make matters worse, integrated databases will make it easier than ever for managed-care organizations to keep track of whether our clients are adhering to the standardized regimens prescribed for them. Lists of approved treatments will give health-care bureaucrats a potent weapon to use against those of us who don't order off the menu. This could even leave us in the ethically dubious position of enforcing compliance with treatments we don't endorse, and reporting our clients' lapses to the HMOs.

When our services are provided without a partnership with those receiving them, the client can easily become a cardboard cutout. . . . So before carved in care becomes the only game in town, those of us who envision a different future of psychotherapy must step forward to make the case for therapeutic multiplicity.

No matter how invested we are in our own particular clinical methods, we first need to acknowledge that there are many ways to respect our client's values and perceptions, many ways to be effective, and many ways to maintain our clinical integrity. This isn't as easy as it sounds. We have all worked hard to establish our own distinct identity as therapists. We have invested heavily in our own methods. But if we do not unite behind methodological pluralism, we will be easy targets for medical-model ideologues, the proponents of empirically supported treatment, and the bean counters of the HMOs. (Duncan, 2001, pp. 24–33, 52, 53)

IMPLICATIONS FOR THE PROFESSION
OF COUPLE AND FAMILY THERAPY

This book has described a variety of distinct, competing theories, each built largely around the ideas and personality of charismatic theoreticians and gifted clinicians. The multiplicity of theoretical ideas leaves the clinician a wealth of options to choose from in working with clients. This wealth may be confusing to the novice clinician. Identifying common factors found in most theories and practices can be helpful as clinicians weave their way through the myriad of therapeutic possibilities. More studies are suggested to reinforce the existence of commonalities among theories. Recognizing those commonalities may help the therapist gain confidence in integrating theories and practices to meet specific client needs (Sprenkle et al., 1999).

QUANTITATIVE AND QUALITATIVE RESEARCH—
A BOTH/AND PROCESS

Researchers may use both quantitative and qualitative approaches. The following information explains some of the rationale and methods researchers use to determine the way they organize their studies. The process of researching family therapy is fraught with challenging complexities. Events that occur during sessions usually result from many factors, making it difficult to identify and control variables. The family unit is in constant flux. The treatment structure includes the therapist as part of the client system. He or she may change as the system changes. The researcher needs to consider intrapsychic issues, relationships within the group and between subsystems, group interactions, as well as contextual influences such as community, cultural backgrounds, and social pressures (Fox, 1976).

In the 1980s, critics of the appropriateness of the use of conventional methods of research argued that most family therapy research designs reflected the assumptions of logical positivism—linear cause-and-effect measurements—and attempted to emulate the traditional scientific methods of the natural sciences based on objective observation (Tomm, 1983). In the view of some family therapists, traditional research methodologies are of little use in untangling the complexities of systemic phenomena or in helping establish a causal relationship between a method of treatment and its effect on the family (Keeney & Sprenkle, 1982; Tomm, 1983). Most social science researchers have stayed with a methodology that tests hypotheses and seeks to generalize *to* populations *from* data gathered on individuals—a linear process. This is **quantitative** research. Some modifications have occurred in the way quantitative research is done, but the basic assumptions have remained the same. Subjectivity itself, in the form of cognition and beliefs, is now a legitimate topic for systematic, controlled observation. Efforts have been made to minimize and allow for the biases and values of the researcher through controls in the research design. Quantitative research involves hypotheses testing of theories that purport to be accurate maps of the world. Further, their research design seeks to disconfirm, and only disconfirm, the theoretically predicted outcome as stated in the alternative hypotheses. While the theory being tested may be the target of the specific investigation, it is recognized that other theories are operating at the same time. Quantitative research emphasizes experimentation, large samples, data collection and statistical analysis, objectivity, and verification. The researcher is seen as an outside observer who manipulates variables and measures resulting changes (Goldenberg & Goldenberg, 2000, p. 347).

Funding is more readily available for quantitative research that studies the deviant behavior of the person or group described than for studies of the deviant behaviors *within the society* that produces those behaviors. Not surprisingly, many of the models that have been developed for studying the family utilize the traditional research paradigm (Becvar & Becvar, 1982).

However, this process of focusing on individually defined deviance puts researchers and practitioners of systemic therapy in a double bind: If they don't comply with the rules of the quantitative research protocols, they may disqualify themselves from funding for family research, as well as from reimbursements from third-party payers. If family therapy researchers comply with the rules of quantitative research *exclusively,* they risk being inconsistent with their systemic perspective. It creates a reality, both for clients, and for therapists, that is antithetical to postmodern concepts.

Traditional quantitative research is consistent with the simple cybernetics, modernist tradition. Indeed, traditional, normative, medical-model mental health practice, to be consistent with itself, needs traditional quantitative research. Quantitative outcome studies may be more appropriate for evaluating pragmatic approaches concerned with measurable behavioral changes, such as cognitive/behavioral family therapy or behavioral marriage/couples therapy.

Issues such as these open up a consideration of **qualitative** research. The two methodologies, quantitative and qualitative, can be seen as logical complements, each of which may be understood as having utility relative to context. Traditional quantitative research is consistent with the simple cybernetic, modernist tradition. As stated above, traditional, normative, medical-model mental health practice needs traditional quantitative research to be consistent with itself. However, a cybernetics of cybernetics, postmodern, social constructionist approach to research requires something different. It rejects the idea of one truth or that science is objective. Approaches based on social constructionist ideas are more inclined to turn to qualitative research methods.

Qualitative Research

The spirit and underlying philosophy of qualitative research is more consistent with therapeutic practices based on postmodern, social constructionist thinking. Qualitative research has a perspective that emancipates people from the tight boxes of normative social science and mental health practice. Postmodern researchers know that they are part of the system being researched. Qualitative research, like quantitative research, also seeks commonalities across human experience, just as an anthropologist seeks to understand the worldview of different cultures. However, it does not see commonalities among participants as setting normative standards by which people are compared with one another. Qualitative research tends to be exploratory, open-ended, directed more at discovery than evaluation. It recognizes subjectivity as inherent to any social interaction and that research is grounded on the researcher's representation of the world. It does not depend on any formal theory for understanding. Data is seen as valid only under the unique conditions of a particular project at a particular time and place (Becvar & Becvar, 1982). Its methods are intended to expand and enhance quantitative research techniques, and to provide a context for better understanding of the meaning of the quantitative data collected. It is useful for describing complex phenomena, defining new constructs and relationships among variables, and to help answer "why" questions (Moon, Dillon, & Sprenkle, 1990; Sprenkle, 1994). Qualitative research is most consistent with the postmodern, social constructivist developments in the field.

Qualitative research is accomplished through ethnographic interviews within which the researcher is a participant, aware of how his or her presence influences the people being interviewed, and how all participants influence the researcher's process.

Beginning with the 1990s, researchers demonstrated a greater willingness to engage in qualitative research in addition to quantitative research (Piercy & Sprenkle, 1990). To be more consistent with systemic and postmodern thinking, researchers need to consider the use of qualitative research. The two methodologies, quantitative *and* qualitative can be seen as logical complements, each of which may be understood as having utility relative to context. As researchers recognized that traditional experimental designs were not readily applicable to family therapy settings in which a multitude of interactions and circular systemic processes were occurring, they began using qualitative, quantitative, and mixed research methods in tandem with each other (Goldenberg & Goldenberg, 2000, p. 348).

Benefits for Clinicians and Researchers

Many clinicians and researchers have not eagerly integrated each other's expertise into their work. However, both researchers and therapists do benefit from the cross-fertilization of ideas, particularly since they share a common quest for the underlying issues that determine family functioning. Therapists benefit when they examine the premises, circumstances, and ingredients of their clinical interventions, and researchers profit from moving beyond systematic data collection to become more responsive to the more informal conceptual inquiries carried out in the daily practices of their clinical colleagues (Wynne, 1988).

What's at Stake?

Pinsof and Wynne (1995) wrote:

> Now, for the first time, family clinicians, training directors, clinic administrators, and family organizations have anxiously begun to clamor for "hard evidence" about the effectiveness of marital and family therapy that they can present to students, third-party payers, legislative bodies, and fellow professionals. (p. 341)

William J. Doherty, a Professor of Family Social Science and Director of the Marriage and Family Therapy program at the University of Minnesota made the following points in a talk at the Inaugural AAMFT Research Conference in Santa Fe, New Mexico, about who the beneficiaries were of marriage and family research (July 31, 1997).

He spoke about the individuals or groups who have an interest—something to gain or lose—in the kind of research being done. The point of his talk was that family therapy researchers needed to take into account all of the parties affected by the outcome of their studies when planning, conducting, and disseminating their research.

Doherty identified twelve "stakeholders" whose work and/or experiences were touched by family therapy research. They are listed in Table 13.1.

All of these stakeholders have important and legitimate interests in the way research is done, the information that is described, and how it is utilized. All stakeholders have biases. For example, someone who is primarily a clinician may have biases around what should be involved in conducting sound, credible research and those biases may differ from those of the researcher or the third-party payer.

Doherty concluded his talk describing four implications for marriage and family therapist researchers:

> *First*, consider multiple stakeholders at every stage of a study. *Second*, align with stakeholders' interests that are not traditional with researchers, especially cost savings and generalizability to community settings. Co-identify research problems along with members of the communities we are working with. *Third*, use our systems knowledge to negotiate how a number of stakeholders can get their needs met through a particular study. *Fourth*, do more research in "real world" settings. This is a most challenging endeavor, especially when you are doing a study with several hundred community based therapists who are not using a manual, without a predetermined number of sessions, and where the outcomes are based on reports from the therapist and reports from the clients, with a variety of problems being treated. (1997, pp. 5–13)

According to Doherty, this is exactly the kind of research that responds to the legitimate interests of all the stakeholders in marriage and family therapy research. There are multiple components to be considered in the design of marriage and family therapy research related to the type of therapy, the processes to be measured, what the researchers are looking for and who will benefit from the information.

TABLE 13.1 | DOHERTY'S 12 "STAKEHOLDERS"

Stakeholder	Stake/Interest in Family Therapy Research
Researcher	Generate knowledge, help families, assist practitioners, promote the profession, gain professional status, obtain funding.
Graduate Students and Fellows	Learn research, obtain financial support, generate theses, advance opportunity for academic careers.
University	Generate knowledge, obtain funding for infrastructure, promote peer and public recognition, train students.
Research Community	Generate knowledge, promote funding, enhance status of the field, advance career opportunities.
Profession	Generate unique knowledge, enhance status and legitimacy of the profession, promote employment and financial opportunities.
Practitioners	Receive useful knowledge, enhance professional status and legitimacy, gain access to reimbursement for services.
Foundations	Fulfill mission, enhance family life and social conditions, satisfy agendas of board and source of funding, obtain public recognition.
Government	Generate basic and applied knowledge, promote agency's mission and status, emphasize generalizability and dissemination of clinical findings to diverse settings and populations, control health-care costs, satisfy constituents and campaign supporters, gain political leverage.
Health-care Organizations	Generate knowledge relevant to health services, promote cost-effective services, emphasize generalizability to settings and populations served, prevent health problems, increase competitive advantage and market share.
Business	Promote healthy workforce, control costs, satisfy employees, maintain competitiveness and please owners/stockholders.
Media	Inform consumers, emphasize what is new and different, unearth scandals, promote market share and profitability.
Consumers	Gain helpful knowledge to promote personal and family well-being, obtain effective and accessible services, hold down personal costs, preserve choice of providers.

REVIEWING AND ASSESSING RESEARCH ON COUPLE AND FAMILY THERAPY

Couple and family therapy has received considerable attention both in professional circles and in the popular culture. It is now one of the most common forms of mental health treatment and is used to treat a variety of difficulties. Society, including government and business groups, has come to recognize the importance of family life and the risks to individuals within dysfunctional families (Lebow, 1995).

There has been a great deal of probing discussion of the theories underlying a family systems viewpoint, resulting in considerable elaboration and revision in recent years. New theoretical perspectives have moved away from earlier notions of family as the exclusive etiologic agent in the development of emotional difficulties, and as the only preferred target for intervention across all difficulties. The *social context* is an integral part of the treatment system. Recently a movement toward an integrative viewpoint has emerged that includes concepts from various family methods of intervention, as well as interventions with an individual focus (Lebow, 1984, 1987) and with larger systems (Breunlin, Schwartz, & Karrer, 1992). Lebow & Gurman (1995) wrote:

> The field has been boiling over with ideas and concepts and ways of examining the family and how to have an impact on it. Treatments have emerged and been refined, theories have undergone considerable revision, and assumptions have been continually examined within the emerging perspectives about family within the broader society. (p. 29)

Relevant Trends

Despite the fact that family therapy serves up a vast amount of complex challenges for researchers, the research in couple and family therapy that has emerged is quite remarkable. Today's methodology is vastly improved over the research that was produced a decade ago. In the past, most of the research on couple and family therapy had studied behavioral couple and family therapies. It is easier to set up studies on those particular methods because of their adherence to specific and measurable techniques and objectives. The other methods of couple and family therapy have not produced as many research studies.

Things are changing: There are more and better studies being done on nonbehavioral methods, more sophisticated questions are being asked, and there is a much greater overlap in the practice of behavioral and nonbehavioral therapies. These trends make research on couple and family therapy more relevant to the everyday practice of couple and family therapy. In fact, looking at the actual practice of structural, strategic, experiential, solution focused, and other brief therapies, one can observe an extensive use of behavioral interventions and tasks (Lebow, 1995).

Defining Family Therapy

Initially it may have been understood that the common ground for family therapies was that multiple family members were treated together. Any student of family theories will realize this is not so. For example, Bowen geared his therapy to the treatment of one person. He stressed that one family member, who was motivated to change, could affect changes in the entire family. Gurman et al. (1986) offered a classic definition for family therapy:

> Family therapy may be defined as any psychotherapeutic endeavor that explicitly focuses on altering the interactions between or among family members and seeks to improve the functioning of the family as a unit, or of its subsystems, and/or the functioning of individual members of the family. (p. 565)
>
> Most family therapists do see more than one family member in a session, but the number of people in a session does not define family therapy. The essence of family therapy is its focus on the importance of altering ongoing interactions. In couples and family therapy, change in family process is always both a mediating and an ultimate goal, as well as a change in an individual and in a broader dimension of relational life, such as marital satisfaction. These are among the factors that need to be considered in the research. (Lebow, 1995)
>
> The reader may have noticed the change in this portion of the text, from "marital and family therapy" to "couple and family therapy" following the wording in the above referenced Lebow article. It is a change in terminology made out of respect for the diverse forms of family in our society (Walsh, 1993). In reality, couples, regardless of their marital status, are a unit seen in therapist's offices. Families are also redefined as a variety of affiliative groups that have come to be recognized as "family."

EFFICACY OF COUPLE AND FAMILY THERAPY

Two definitions are in order before we go on. **Efficacy** is defined as the *capacity* for serving to produce change. It speaks to the question of whether or not the methods being researched are *capable* of influencing change. **Effectiveness** looks at whether the *method is* accomplishing its intended purpose and producing the intended results.

Over the past 30 years, the research literature has concluded, almost without exception, that the outcomes achieved by treatment groups have exceeded those of control groups. This result holds true for reviews considering the full range of couple and family therapy (Alexander, Holtzworth-Monroe, & Jameson, 1994; Gurman & Kniskern, 1981; Gurman et al., 1986). There have been dissenting views about the effectiveness of nonbehavioral treatments (Beach & Leary, 1985; Bednar, Burlingame, & Masters, 1988), but with more and better recent research emerging in the last few years, the evidence for overall effectiveness has become unequivocal (Jacobson, Dobson, Fruzzetti, Schmaling, & Salusky, 1991; Lebow, 1995; Snyder & Wills, 1989). In general, the literature suggests:

- Couples therapy is more effective than individual therapy for relationship problems, particularly for depressed women.
- Younger children tend to do better in the context of family therapy than adolescents do.
- Family therapy tends to be less effective for families that are disorganized, socially isolated, and disadvantaged.
- Family treatment that is responsive to the cultural context of the problem can be effective for high-risk individuals and families.

META-ANALYSIS OF EXISTING RESEARCH

Another definition is in order: **Meta-analysis** is a statistical analysis of a *group of studies* in which each study is considered to be one subject. It involves the collective evaluation of existing studies. The effect size refers to the standard difference between the treatment and comparison (untreated) groups (Shadish et al., 1995).

Shadish et al. (1993) examined 63 studies conducted before 1988, all of which involved random assignment of a clinically distressed population with a mean treatment duration of eight sessions. His meta-analysis of these studies suggested that therapy clients were better off than 70% of the control clients. Couple and family therapies appear to produce statistically significant results and considerable effect sizes within traditional comparative designs. These effect sizes are not unlike those emerging for other successful psychosocial treatments (Lebow, 1995).

DIRECTIONS IN FAMILY THERAPY RESEARCH AND FAMILY THERAPY

According to Lebow (1995), the movement is clearly toward a rapprochement between research and practice. He wrote, "Researchers make more effort to translate their findings for clinicians and clinicians increasingly consider the ramifications of research and suggest questions that are of interest"(p. 45). Many family therapies no longer exclusively focus on interpersonal process or assess change exclusively in terms of circular causality and homeostasis. They have begun to integrate other paradigms and processes into their therapy sessions. This shift has led to greater focus by clinicians on the kinds of questions about efficacy that are more amenable to research (e.g., "With whom does a particular treatment approach work") (p. 46).

Researchers are now studying the more typical approaches of therapists' interventions, and are looking at the more complex assessments of the kinds of circular processes that have been central within the systemic viewpoint (Lebow, 1995, p. 46).

Lebow's 1995 article concluded that there is sufficient demonstration of effectiveness to serve as the cornerstone in any public policy discussion of couple and family therapy. Much more important for future investigations are questions at greater levels of specifity such as when, and under what conditions, are particular types of couple and family therapy effective? More work is emerging that links process to both short-term and long-term outcome. Lebow suggested that *both* clinical trials *and* process and outcome analysis should be conducted, each supplementing the other.

Although there is substantial data verifying the effectiveness of couple and family therapy, follow-up research on long-term gains indicates that the benefits of therapy diminish over time. Research has begun to assess whether there are methods for increasing the maintenance of change over time. "More clinicians are moving to open-ended views of treatment that may fit better with the realities of family life over the life cycle than the notion of treatment as ending all difficulties forever" (Lebow, 1995, p. 47). Research studies are moving toward defining a set of generic interventions, to construct methods that meet the needs of specific populations. These studies run parallel to the way family therapy is integrating various forms of treatment (Lebow, 1984, 1987).

The substantial question remains: "Under what conditions do family, couple, or individual sessions maximize impact?" (Lebow, 1995, p. 48). Researchers need also to assess which diagnosis, in which contexts, are most responsive to couple, family, or individual therapies. They need to consider the influence of gender, ethnic and racial backgrounds, and other cultural and social pressures.

"An outstanding body of research is now available on family process and family development" (Lebow, 1995, p. 49). For example, Gottman and associates' much publicized studies of patterns and sequences of dysfunction in marriage point out certain patterns around conflict that lead directly to decreasing levels of marital satisfaction and ultimately to divorce (Buehlman, Gottman, & Katz, 1992; Gottman, 1991, 1992, 1993; Gottman & Krokoff, 1989). Emphasis in family therapy on life-cycle perspectives is increasing (Carter & McGoldrick, 1988).

Not enough attention has been paid to issues of treatment and consumer acceptance and satisfaction (Lebow, 1995, p. 49). Because research has pointed out the frequency of violence in the general population and in clinical samples, family therapists are looking for ways to become more effective in treating families with violent behaviors (Babcock, Waltz, Jacobson, & Gottman, 1993; Burman, Margolin, & John, 1993; Murphy & O'Leary, 1989). More research is needed on the impact of health crisis in families, on aging parents and care-giving needs. The whole field of family systems medicine needs to be explored.

Systemic thinking suggests that the range of assessment should always extend beyond the individual to those who have intimate connections to the patient (Gurman & Kniskern, 1981). This thinking is reinforced by findings in research comparing individual and couple or family treatments that use both types of measures—quantitative and qualitative—and that show a variety of effects extending beyond the patient (Jacobson et al., 1991). Studies also are needed to assess the effectiveness of the training and supervision of couples and family therapists.

Lebow (1995) states:

> Replication may represent the greatest single need in this body of work. Studies are difficult to execute, time-consuming and costly. . . . Despite these obstacles, we can now see the kind of replication and further inquiry that characterizes good science in a number of areas including behavioral couple therapy, parent training, and family therapy for adolescent substance abuse. . . . The stage appears to be set for a fruitful and "clinically significant" next decade of research on couple and family therapy. (pp. 50, 51)

CLINICIANS AS RESEARCHERS

In a 1996 article in *The Family Therapy Networker,* Lebow wrote that it was ever more important to have a substantial body of precise data about the typical duration of treatment, and the level of patient satisfaction, not only to identify what works best for our clients, but also in the interest of credibility for managed-care organizations, employers, and government policy. He built a case for clinicians to do their own research on their own caseload. As a starting point, he suggested clinicians ask themselves what they really want to know. Just as in any good therapy plan, the research plan should focus on a few key items and should be kept simple. He went on to suggest research methods for clinicians that would enhance this data collection:

1. Begin by gathering statistics about who you see and for how long.
2. Note the most frequently encountered problems.
3. List how many couples, individuals, and families that you see.
4. Note the ages, gender, and ethnicity of your clients.
5. Note how many sessions are typical for each problem area.
6. List which clients account for what percentage of your income.
7. Keep a running tally and summarize your data on a regular basis. (pp. 61, 62)

Other ideas for clinicians to do their own research, included devising questionnaires for clients that ask about their treatment experience, or making scheduled follow-up calls at set time periods, asking clients what they feel they achieved in therapy. Therapists could use goal attainment scaling through which the therapist and client agree on a set of problems and their related goals and then project a range of potential outcomes. Goal attainment in each identified problem area would then be rated by client and therapist as the treatment progresses. Lebow reported that when he and his colleagues used this last process, it helped to sharpen their clinical focus about where the treatment was aimed and to evaluate the success in reaching treatment goals. The data obtained helped to validate that progress was being made on core goals (Lebow, 1996, p. 62).

Therapists should pay attention to information that is readily available, like which clients come back for more treatment, which ones refer other clients, which couples ultimately divorce. Clinicians should observe, follow up, and record behaviors that interest them. This process provides information that may help clinicians refine the way they do therapy. It may be useful to ask for some help in organizing research plans from someone experienced in doing research (Lebow, 1996, pp. 62, 63).

Reverberating from the Terrorist Threat

Barbara Buzzi, Professor of Marriage and Family Therapy in the social science and counseling department at St. Thomas University, pointed to issues exacerbated by the 9/11 terrorist threat:

> Family therapists are doing more trauma work as families struggle with everyday violence in their lives. After September 11, 2001, we, and our clients, are feeling violated and vulnerable. We will all be reverberating from these terrorist threats and the losses they bring for a long time to come. This is a new dimension that impacts all of our life-cycle challenges. Marriage and family counselors need to treat the effects of trauma first, providing a safe place for families to tell their survival stories, and then move on to family systems work.
>
> We need to continue to expand our practices. For example, there is a relatively new trend toward working within medical settings, and within school-based systems. In the juvenile justice system we need to give more attention to families in pre-trial, detention, and release programs.

Buzzi spoke about the current emphasis on evidence-based evaluation of psychotherapies:

> It is difficult to say when the evidence is in on the outcome of a therapeutic experience. So often, so much of the outcome, the evidence, doesn't show up for weeks, months, even years later. This could make the efficient determination and judging of outcome, very difficult. Over the years, as teachers, we have followed our charismatic pioneers, focused on their theories and methods. Now, we need to expand our interpretations of "what works" by integrating what fits with our clients' situation and our own abilities and propensities. We need to pay attention to, and build upon, common factors such as client/therapist relationships, the strengths inherent in our clients, and the family and community supports available for our clients. (phone interview, November 26, 2001)

SUMMARY

Research on the efficacy and effectiveness of couples and family therapy is not only important to improve the quality of treatment services offered to clients, but also becoming more and more necessary to demonstrate its value to third-party payers, government policy makers, businesses, and society in general. The analysis of existing research offers convincing data that couples and families who have treatment for specific problems improve significantly more than those persons with like problems who do not undergo treatment. Questions remain as to specifically which problems, from which populations and cultural backgrounds respond best to which specific treatment methods. Clinicians and researchers alike need to continue to look for common factors that can be identified as being present in studies of the successful outcome of marriage and family therapy experiences.

Ideas that may be helpful for clinicians and researchers, and all interested parties include increasing dialogue between researchers, clinicians, and a full component of stakeholders to learn more about the benefits each is looking for. Clinicians are encouraged to research their own practices for information that will help them assess what works best for their clients, and to set measurable goals, along with their clients, and to engage in periodic reviews of how effective the process is toward achieving those goals. Client satisfaction can be researched through questionnaires and follow-up phone calls.

The news on research seems encouraging as both clinicians and researchers find more common ground with which to help one another improve the effectiveness and satisfaction of couples and family therapy. Family therapists have long emphasized the importance of relationships to mental health. It seems a short leap to recognizing the relationship between client and therapist as a natural component of all effective therapies. As family therapists become more integrative in their practices, the possibility for more useful research increases. As research designs expand to utilize the best of both quantitative and qualitative research, clinicians will be better able to provide treatment with more effective long-term benefits to client families.

REFERENCES

Alexander, J. F., Holtzworth-Munroe, A., & Jameson, P. (1994). The process and outcome of marital and family therapy: Research review and evaluation. In A.E. Bergin & S. L. Garfield (Eds.), *Handbook of psychotherapy and behavior change* (4th ed.), pp. 595–630. New York: Wiley.

Babcock, J. C., Waltz, J., Jacobson, N. S., & Gottman, J. M. (1993). Power and violence: The relation between communication patterns, power discrepancies, and domestic violence. *Journal of Consulting and Clinical Psychology 61*, 40–50.

Beach, S. R. H., & O'Leary, K. D. (1985). Current status of outcome research in marital therapy. In L. L. Abate (Ed.), *The handbook of family psychology and therapy* (pp. 1035–1072). Homewood, IL: Dorsey.

Becvar, R. J., & Becvar, D. S. (1982). *Systems theory and family therapy: A primer.* Washington, DC: University Press of America.

Bednar, R. L., Burlingame, G. M., & Masters, K. S. (1988). Systems of family treatment: Substance or semantics? *Annual Review Psychology, 39*, 401–434.

Blow, A. J., & Sprenkle, D. H. (2001). Common factors across theories of marriage and family therapy: A modified Delphi study. *Journal of Marital and Family Therapy, July 2001, 27, 3,* 385–401.

Breunlin, D., Schwartz, R., & Karrer, B. (1992). *Meta-frameworks: Transcending the models of family therapy.* San Francisco: Jossey-Bass.

Buehlman, K. T., Gottman, J. M., & Katz, L. F. (1992). How a couple views their past predicts their future: Predicting divorce from an oral history interview. *Journal of Family Psychology, 5,* 295–318.

Burman, B., Margolin, G., & John, R. S. (1993). America's angriest home videos: Behavioral contingencies observed in home reenactments of marital conflict. *Journal of Consulting and Clinical Psychology, 61,* 28–39.

Carter, B., & McGoldrick, M. (1988). *The changing family life cycle: A framework for family therapy* (2nd ed.). Boston: Allyn & Bacon.

Doherty, W. J. (1997). Proceedings of the Inaugural American Association for Marriage and Family Therapy Research Conference, Santa Fe, New Mexico, July 31, 1997, pp. 5–13.

Duncan, B. (2001). The future of psychotherapy: Beware the siren call of integrated care. *Psychotherapy Networker,* July/August, 24–33, 52, 53.

Fish, L. S., & Busby, D. (1996). The Delphi method. In D. H. Sprenkle & S. M. Moon (Eds.), *Research methods in family therapy* (pp. 469–484). New York: Guilford.

Fox, R. E. (1976). Family therapy. In I. B. Weiner (Ed.), *Clinical methods in psychology.* New York: Wiley.

Goldenberg, I., & Goldenberg, H. (2000). *Family therapy: An overview* (5th ed.). Pacific Grove, CA: Brooks/Cole.

Gottman, J. M. (1991). Predicting the longitudinal course of marriages. *Journal of Marital & Family Therapy, 17,* 3–7.

Gottman, J. M. (1992). The roles of conflict, engagement, escalation, and avoidance in marital interaction: A longitudinal view of five types of couples. *Journal of Consulting and Clinical Psychology, 61,* 6–15.

Gottman, J. M. (1993). A theory of marital dissolution and stability. *Journal of Family Psychology, 7,* 57–75.

Gottman, J. M., & Krokoff, L. (1989). Marital interaction and marital satisfaction: A longitudinal view. *Journal of Consulting and Clinical Psychology, 57,* 47–52.

Gurman, A. S., & Kniskern, D. P. (1981). Family therapy outcome research: Knowns and unknowns. In A. S. Gurman & D. P. Kniskern (Eds.) *Handbook of family therapy.* New York: Brunner/Mazel.

Gurman, A. S., Kniskern, D. P., & Pinsof, W. M. (1986). Research on the process and outcome of marital and family therapy. In S. Garfield & A. Bergin (Eds.), *Handbook of psychotherapy and behavior change* (3rd ed.). New York: Brunner/Mazel.

Hubble, M. A., Duncan, B. L., & Miller, S. D. (1999). Introduction. In M. A. Hubble, B. L. Duncan, & S. D. Miller (Eds.). *The heart and soul of change: What works in therapy* (pp. 1–32). Washington, DC: American Psychological Association.

Jacobson, N. S., Dobson, K., Fruzzetti, A., Schmaling, K. B., & Salusky, S. (1991). Marital therapy as a treatment for depression. *Journal of Consulting and Clinical Psychology, 59*, 547–557.

Jacobson, N. S., Schmaling, K. B., & Holtzworth-Munroe, A. (1987). Component analysis of behavioral marital therapy: Two-year follow up and prediction of relapse. *Journal of Marital and Family Therapy, 13*, 187–195.

Keeney, B. P., & Sprenkle, D. H. (1982). Ecosystem epistemology: Critical implications for the aesthetics and pragmatics of family therapy. *Family Process, 21*, 1–19.

Lambert, M. J. (1992). Psychotherapy outcome research: Implications for integrative and elective therapists. In J. C. Norcross & M. R. Goldfried (Eds.), *Handbook of psychotherapy integration* (pp. 94–129). New York: Basic Books.

Lambert, M. J., & Bergin, A. E. (1994). The effectiveness of psychotherapy. In A. E. Bergin & S. L. Garfield (Eds.), *Handbook of psychotherapy and behavior change* (4th ed., pp. 143–189). New York: Wiley.

Lebow, J. L. (1984). On the value of integrating approaches to family therapy. *Journal of Marital and Family Therapy, 10*, 127–138.

Lebow, J. L. (1987). Developing a personal integration in family therapy: Principles for model construction and practice. *Journal of Marital and Family Therapy, 13*, 1–14.

Lebow, J. L. (1995). Research assessing couple and family therapy. *Annual Review Psychology, 46*, 27–57.

Lebow, J. L. (1996). Do-it-yourself research: The practical advantages of studying your own practice. *Family Therapy Networker 20* (6) Nov./Dec., 61–63.

Lebow, J. L., & Gurman, A. S. (1995). Research assessing couple & family therapy. *Annual Review: Psychology 46*, 27–57.

Linstone, H., & Turoff, M. (1975). *The Delphi method: Techniques and applications.* Reading, MA: Wesley.

Miller, S. D., Duncan, B. L., & Hubble, M. A. (1997). *Escape from Babel: Toward a unifying language for psychotherapy practice.* New York: Norton.

Moon, S. M., Dillon, D. R., & Sprenkle, D. H. (1990). Family therapy and qualitative research. *Journal of Marital and Family Therapy, 16*, 357–373.

Murphy, C. M., & O'Leary, K. D. (1989). Psychological aggression predicts physical aggression in early marriage. *Journal of Consulting and Clinical Psychology, 57*, 579–582.

Paul, G. L. (1967). Outcome research in psychotherapy. *Journal of Consulting Psychology, 31,* 109–188.

Piercy, F. P., & Sprenkle, D. H. (1990). Marriage and family therapy: A decade review. *Journal of Marriage and the Family, 52*, 1116–1126.

Pinsof, W. M., & Wynne, L. C. (1995). The effectiveness and efficacy of marital and family therapy: Introduction to the special issue. *Journal of Marital and Family Therapy, 21*, 341–343.

Shadish, W. R., Montgomery, L. M., Wilson, P., Wilson, M. R., Bright, I., & Okwumabua, T. (1993). Effects of family and marital psychotherapies: A meta-analysis. *Journal of Consulting and Clinical Psychology, 61*, 992–1002.

Shadish, W. R., Ragsdale, K., Glaser, R. R., & Montgomery, L. M. (1995). The efficacy and effectiveness of marital and family therapy: A perspective from meta-analysis. *Journal of Marital and Family Therapy, 21,* 345–360.

Smith, M. L., Glass, G. V., & Miller, T. I. (1980). *The benefits of psychotherapy.* Baltimore, MD: Johns Hopkins University Press.

Snyder, D. K., & Wills, R. M. (1989). Behavioral versus insight-oriented marital therapy: Effects on individual and interspousal functioning. *Journal of Consulting and Clinical Psychology, 57,* 39–46.

Sprenkle, D. H. (1994). Editorial: The role of qualitative research and a few suggestions for aspiring authors. *Journal of Marital and Family Therapy, 20,* 227–229.

Sprenkle, D. H., Blow, A. J., & Dickey, M. H. (1999). Common factors and other non-technique variables in marriage and family therapy. In M. A. Hubble, B. L. Duncan, & S. D. Miller (Eds.), *The heart and soul of change: What works in therapy* (pp. 3–24). New York: Guilford.

Tomm, K. M. (1983). The old hat doesn't fit. *Family Therapy Networker, 7* (4), 39–41.

Walsh, F. (Ed.). (1993). *Normal Family Processes* (2nd ed.). New York: Guilford.

Wynne, L. C. (Ed.). (1988). *The state of the art in family therapy research: Controversies and recommendations.* New York: Family Process Press.

EPILOGUE

CHAPTER 14

Theories—How Similar or Different Are They?
Resources
Note from the Author

Family therapy is an exciting, challenging, and emotionally rewarding profession. New branches of family therapy continue to evolve. Mutations of older theories and practices, and exciting new ideas integrate with, and give birth to, ever expanding processes. How the therapist thinks about what he or she is doing within the therapy session, along with the therapist's ability to be flexible, while maintaining his or her ethical stance, is in continuous interaction with the client's worldview and behaviors. Most family therapists recognize there is no single theory exclusively correct for all people or situations. It is appropriate for the therapist to work from a framework most suitable for him or her, *and also* to remain open and responsive to the client's needs and behaviors. The therapist is then able to offer new perspectives and integrate a mix of interventions he or she believes will most effectively meet the specific needs of specific clients and their specific situations.

All theories may be stories. They reflect the context of the theorist's worldview. These stories provide therapists with useful ways of thinking that, when integrated into their own worldview, help them to focus on the *process* going on between clients and themselves, and between the clients and their *context*.

Family therapists need to be well-grounded in systemic thinking and have an understanding of the theories underlying the process of therapy. They need to have respect for the families they serve, and for their perceived place in society. They need to be flexible enough to adapt to the variety of people who come to them for help. And they need to care, for themselves, as well as for their clients. They need to be able to care about their clients and then to let go—not carry the client's problems home with them. Family therapists need to take themselves lightly, take their client's dilemmas seriously, and be able to share some laughter with their clients about the human condition.

A professional family therapist has the opportunity to grow from every therapeutic encounter with his or her clients.

THEORIES—HOW SIMILAR OR DIFFERENT ARE THEY?

Flexibility, and an openness to alternate ways of thinking and doing, are common to all the theories. Family therapists work toward expanding their clients' options. They approach their work in the same way—being open to new ideas and expanding their own therapeutic options. Common to all the theories is the understanding that repetitive, circular patterns of interactions tend to maintain symptoms. Even though each theorist offers his or her own vocabulary (terms to know) there are many terms with similar meanings. It is helpful to key into the similarities between theories, as well as the differences.

Most family therapy is purposefully brief, offering change in the here-and-now interactions and focus on symptom reduction. Symptom reduction is generally accomplished by an active, directive therapist who reframes the presenting problems in relational terms, and works toward changing the way family members interact. Even the postmodern therapists are active, with more subtlety, using questions and collaborative language to accomplish their goals.

Strategic and structural therapists focus on reorganizing family structure and establishing appropriate boundaries between the generations. Strategic therapists make a special point of establishing appropriate hierarchies. Bowenian family therapists may work with one family member and coach that person to make changes. When those changes are made, they believe that person's changes impact other family members and the relationships between family members. Behavioral family therapists tend to work with a parent/child dyad, or one couple, and develop measurable behavioral tasks and goals. Most of the other family therapists tend to work with as many family members as possible and think of triangular interactions as the basis for both problems and solutions. Postmodern therapists enter into collaborative conversations and listen to client stories and ask questions intended to extract clients' strengths and develop more successful life stories.

Intergenerational family therapists explore family history, looking at patterns of interaction over three generations and suggest how those patterns reflect on the client's symptoms in the present. Contextual family therapists work with as many family members as possible to "balance the ledger" of injustice that may have been hampering the growth and rapport between the generations. Contextual family therapy and feminist family therapy introduced value systems the other theorists had not addressed. Contextual family therapy seeks to change relational patterns over the generations in a way that generates more fairness and accountability that they hope will pass on to the next generation. Feminist family therapy focuses on the unequal balance of power between the genders and works toward educating men and women about how that imbalance of power victimizes both sexes. Their goal is to create more equality in relationships.

As a student learns about each theory and therapy, it is interesting to sort out and compare similarities and differences among the various theories. And as they learn, they realize the importance of establishing a respectful and trustworthy relationship with clients, as well as being open, flexible, and adaptable to the various needs of their client population.

RESOURCES

Anyone entering the field of family therapy owes it to themselves and to their clients to seek resources from both academic and community sources. Belonging to a professional organization keeps therapists and students up-to-date on the issues and treatments related to their work with families. Workshops, seminars, and supervision meetings are ongoing, essential for therapists in taking care of their own needs, expanding their worldview, and enhancing their professional skills. Supervision, which is required by most states and each profession's association, should also be an ongoing process. Beyond the required time for supervision, it should be continued in small groups, case conferences, and for specific issues, consultations with supervisors and other therapists. This ongoing supervision process not only helps the therapist bring the best treatment possible to the client, it also helps the therapist maintain his or her emotional stability, avoid getting sucked into client's dilemmas, maintain ethical behaviors, and reduce the possibility of burnout. Practicing therapists have found workshops and seminars also help to confirm their ideas and practices as well as introduce new possibilities. There are vast resources available, on the Internet and through professional organizations and conferences. Professional associations and the Internet offer video and audiotapes that demonstrate specific therapeutic practices. Movies, theater performances, novels, history books, biographies, and short stories can broaden a student's understanding of the context in which their clients live. Students may ask instructors for suggestions, or go on the Internet and look up family therapy resources, and the AAMFT or NASW web pages. Belonging to a professional organization keeps both student and therapist up to date on the latest thinking in the field.

NOTE FROM THE AUTHOR

My goal has been to introduce you to dynamic new ways of thinking about people. I hope you have been intrigued about the possibilities available for helping individuals and families, which may also have a positive effect on the way our society operates. Anecdotal evidence continues to support the importance of relationships to mental health. It has been recognized that intrapsychic conditions are involved the way individuals respond to inter-psychic influences. Family theorists and therapists are experienced in adapting new ideas and integrating them into their thinking and practice. The soil is fertile for the evolution of new branches, and for integrating new ideas, new ways of helping families and individuals in their search for solutions for their emotional dilemmas. Family therapy is an evolving profession that offers the opportunity for personal growth for both clients and therapists. Explore!

NAME INDEX

SUBJECT INDEX

TO THE OWNER OF THIS BOOK:

We hope that you have found *Introduction to Family Theory and Therapy* useful. So that this book can be improved in a future edition, would you take the time to complete this sheet and return it? Thank you.

School and address: _____

Department: _____

Instructor's name: _____

1. What I like most about this book is: _____

_____

_____

2. What I like least about this book is: _____

_____

_____

3. My general reaction to this book is: _____

_____

4. The name of the course in which I used this book is: _____

_____

5. Were all of the chapters of the book assigned for you to read? _____

   If not, which ones weren't? _____

6. In the space below, or on a separate sheet of paper, please write specific suggestions for improving this book and anything else you'd care to share about your experience in using the book.

_____

_____

_____

_____

Optional:

Your name: _____ Date: _____

May Brooks/Cole quote you, either in promotion for *Introduction to Family Theory and Therapy* or in future publishing ventures?

Yes: _____ No: _____

Sincerely,

June Blumenthal Green

IN-BOOK SURVEY

At Brooks/Cole, we are excited about creating new types of learning materials that are interactive, three-dimensional, and fun to use. To guide us in our publishing/development process, we hope that you'll take just a few moments to fill out the survey below. Your answers can help us make decisions that will allow us to produce a wide variety of videos, CD-ROMs, and Internet-based learning systems to complement standard textbooks. If you're interested in working with us as a student Beta-tester, be sure to fill in your name, telephone number, and address. We look forward to hearing from you!

In addition to books, which of the following learning tools do you currently use in your counseling/human services/social work courses?

_____ **Video** _____ in class _____ school library _____ own VCR

_____ **CD-ROM** _____ in class _____ in lab _____ own computer

_____ **Macintosh disks** _____ in class _____ in lab _____ own computer

_____ **Windows disks** _____ in class _____ in lab _____ own computer

_____ **Internet** _____ in class _____ in lab _____ own computer

How often do you access the Internet? _____ _____

My own home computer is a:

_____

The computer I use in class for counseling/human services/social work courses is a:

_____

If you are NOT currently using multimedia materials in your counseling/human services/social work courses, but can see ways that video, CD-ROM, Internet, or other technologies could enhance your learning, please comment below:

_____

_____

_____

Other comments (optional): _____

_____

Name _____ Telephone _____

Address _____

School _____

Professor/Course_____

You can fax this form to us at (650) 592-9081 or detach, fold, secure, and mail.

NO POSTAGE
NECESSARY
IF MAILED
IN THE
UNITED STATES

BUSINESS REPLY MAIL
FIRST CLASS   PERMIT NO. 358   PACIFIC GROVE, CA

POSTAGE WILL BE PAID BY ADDRESSEE

ATT: *Marketing*

**The Wadsworth Group
10 Davis Drive
Belmont, CA 94002**

Attention Professors:

Brooks/Cole is dedicated to publishing quality publications for education in the social work, counseling, and human services fields. If you are interested in learning more about our publications, please fill in your name and address and request our latest catalogue, using this prepaid mailer. Please choose one of the following:

☐ social work   ☐ counseling   ☐ human services

Name: _____

Street Address: _____

City, State, and Zip: _____

DATE DUE